The International Hospitality Industry

University
Of D

6 JON

The International Hospitality Industry

Organizational and Operational Issues

Edited by

Peter Jones

and

Abraham Pizam

Longman Group Limited
Longman House, Burnt Mill, Harlow
Essex CM20 2JE, England
and Associated Companies throughout the world

First published 1993
Reprinted 1993, 1994
Reprinted by Longman Group Limited 1995

British Library Cataloguing in Publication Data
A catalogue entry for this title is available from the British Library

ISBN 0-582-294113-4

Produced through Longman Malaysia, PA

Contents

Contributors

Editors

Peter Jones is Head of the Department of Service Sector Management at the University of Brighton Business School. He has worked in the hospitality industry in the UK and Belgium, both for large multinational chains, and as the owner-operator of his own Brussels-based restaurant. He is the author or co-author of four hospitality-related textbooks, editor of *Management in Service Industries* published by Pitman, and author of numerous journal articles. He has also presented conference papers in the UK, the USA and Canada, reflecting his research interest in effective operational performance in the hospitality industry. He holds an MBA from the London Business School and is a Fellow of the HCIMA. In 1991 he was elected the first President of EuroCHRIE.

Abraham Pizam is the Charles Forte Professor of Hotel Management in the Department of Management Studies for Tourism and Hotel Industries, University of Surrey. Prior to taking up this chair he was Chair of the Department of Hospitality Management and Director of the Dick Pope Snr Institute for Tourism Studies at the University of Central Florida, Orlando, and Director of Graduate Programs in the Hotel, Restaurant and Travel Administration Department, University of Massachusetts, Amherst. Professor Pizam has lectured and conducted seminars in more than 25 countries and held academic positions in the US, the UK, France, Austria, New Zealand, Israel and Switzerland. He is the author of more than 75 scientific publications and is on the editorial board of seven academic journals. He holds a Masters degree from New York University and a Ph.D. from Cornell University.

Contributors

Peter Barge had eight years' management experience in the hospitality industry and several years' experience of lecturing in the subject, before setting up his own tourism consulting firm in Sydney, Australia, in 1979. Following a merger, he was Managing Director of Horwath & Horwath Services Pty, which became Australia's largest hospitality and tourism consulting firm. He then became a principal of Transact Hotel & Tourism Property Pty Limited, an international hotel brokerage group, during which time he was President of the company's North American operations, based in New York. In 1991 this company merged with the hotel division of Jones Lang Wootton to form JLW TransAct, of which Peter is Managing Director. He specializes in the Australian and Asian hotel property market and has negotiated a large number of hotel acquisitions and operating agreements.

Andrew Byrne is Chief Executive of Small Luxury Hotels of the World and former Managing Director of Prestige Hotels. Prior to this he was the European Operations Director of Leading Hotels of the World. He has nearly ten years' management experience of hotel consortia and has travelled throughout the world in relation to this role. He is a graduate of Middlesex Polytechnic and a former chairperson of the Chartered Institute of Marketing's hotel section.

Chris Cooper is Senior Lecturer in Tourism Management at the University of Surrey. He received his Ph.D. from the University of London.

Simon Crawford-Welch was awarded his Ph.D. from Virginia Polytechnic Institute and State University in hospitality management with an emphasis in strategic management and marketing. He has held the positions of Assistant Professor of Hospitality Marketing and Research at the University of Nevada, Las Vegas, and Director of Marketing and Research for a major international resort development firm. He is currently President of SERVICE Associates, Inc., an international hospitality development, management and business consulting firm based in Las Vegas, USA. He is also Editor of the *Journal of Restaurant and Foodservice Marketing*.

Steven Goss-Turner is Senior Lecturer at the University of Brighton Business School. He has nearly twenty years of industry experience in operations and human resource management, largely with one multinational hotel company. He has recently authored the book *Managing People in the Hotel and Catering Industry*.

Michael Haywood is Associate Professor at the School of Hotel and Food Administration, University of Guelph, Canada. His teaching, research and consulting activities focus on strategic management, marketing and tourism. He recently received the John Wiley and Sons award for his lifetime contribution to research in the fields of hospitality and tourism from the Council on Hotel, Restaurant and Institutional Management.

Mahmood Khan is Head of the Department of Hotel, Restaurant and Institutional Management at Virginia Polytechnic Institute and State University, USA. Dr Khan is the author of two books: *Concepts of Foodservice Operations and Management* (1991) and *Restaurant Franchising* (1992), published by Van Nostrand Reinhold. Dr Khan has travelled extensively and lectured internationally as a visiting scholar in countries that include Australia, China, Malaysia, Thailand, Korea, Switzerland, the UK and Egypt. He is Editor of three journals: the *Electronic Journal of the International Academy of Hospitality Research*, *Journal of College and University Foodservice*, and *Journal of Nutrition* *in Recipe and Menu Development*. He has worked as a consultant across the hospitality industry for national and international corporations as well as government agencies, and also served as an expert witness in several legal cases.

Lee Kreul is currently Head of the Department of Restaurant, Hotel, Institutional and Tourism Management at Purdue University, USA, and holds the rank of Professor. Among his many publications are four volumes of *The Digest of Current Lodging Industry Market Research Studies* for the American Hotel and Motel Association and *Management Accounting for Hotels and Restaurants*, of which he is co-author. His international experience includes visiting professorships in the UK and Malaysia, and presentations and seminars for hospitality industry professionals in Canada, the UK, Sweden, Taiwan, Malaysia, India, China and France. He is Resident-Director of the University of Strasbourg–Purdue University summer study abroad program and serves on the advisory boards of the Beijing Institute of Tourism and the Shanghai Institute of Tourism.

David Littlejohn holds a senior position in the Department of Hospitality and Tourism Management, Napier University, Edinburgh, UK. He is Associate Editor of the *International Journal of Contemporary Hospitality Management*. He has written extensively in the tourism and hospitality management fields, specializing in the development of international organizations and international marketplaces, market analysis and commentaries on UK hospitality sectors.

Andrew Lockwood is Lecturer in the Department of Management Studies for Tourism and Hotel Industries, University of Surrey, UK. His main research interest is in quality management in the industry, and he has undertaken consultancy and run numerous courses on this subject both in the UK and elsewhere.

Katherine M. Merna is a Ph.D. candidate in the Department of Hotel, Restaurant and Institutional Management at Virginia Polytechnic Institute and State University, USA. She earned her MBA at Virginia Tech's Pamplin School of Business. In her current position as Research Associate for the Center for Hospitality Research and Service, she has been actively involved in scanning and researching the hospitality environment for the Center's Trends Database. She has published several articles in hospitality trade publications on trends in the industry.

Michael Olsen is a Professor at the Department of Hotel, Restaurant and Institutional Management at Virginia Polytechnic Institute and State University, USA, where he received his Ph.D. His international experience includes service as Visiting Professor in Australia, China, Finland, France, Hong Kong, Switzerland, the Netherlands and the UK. He is the

Founding President of the International Academy of Hospitality Research and Associate Editor of the *International Journal of Hospitality Management*.

Ray Pine has been Principal Lecturer in the Department of Hospitality Management at Hong Kong Polytechnic since 1987. He is also Honorary Lecturer in the University of Hong Kong Business School and Honorary Visiting Research Fellow of the Asia Pacific Business and Development Research Unit based at the University of Bradford in England. His research in the area of catering technology led to the award of an M.Phil. by CNAA in 1985. In 1991 he received a Ph.D. from the University of Bradford for his research entitled 'Technology transfer in the hotel industry'. His research work continues to look at management issues in the hotel industry in South-East Asia, with a particular emphasis on localization of hotel management staff in Hong Kong and the cultural problems affecting hotel management in mainland China.

Leo M. Renaghan is Associate Professor of Services Marketing in the School of Hotel Administration at Cornell University. He specializes in the translation of consumer decision-making into effective strategy for service businesses. He holds an MBA from the University of Massachusetts and a Ph.D. in Marketing from Penn State University. Professor Renaghan is a frequent lecturer and consultant to national associations and companies on marketing planning and strategy development. His clients include Inter-Continental Hotels, Hilton International Hotels, SAS International Hotels, where he is a member of the Board of Directors, and Mandarin Oriental Hotel Group, where he is a member of the corporate marketing strategy group. His awards include a Statler Hotel Foundation Doctoral Fellowship, and in 1984 the Tressler Award as Research Scholar of the Year, awarded by the Council on Hotel, Restaurant and Institutional Education.

Silvia Sussmann is Lecturer in Management Computing in the Department of Management Studies for Tourism and Hotel Industries at the University of Surrey. Her main current research interests are intelligent user interfaces and automation in the hospitality industry. She has direct knowledge of and personal links with the Latin American environment.

Brian Wise is Dean of the Faculty of Business, Victoria University of Technology, Australia. He received his B.Comm. and B.Ed. from the University of Melbourne and his M.Sc. in Tourism from the University of Strathclyde, UK. He is fellow of the Australian Society of Travel and Tourism, and of the British Tourism Society among others, and has special interest links with the People's Republic of China and many other Asia-Pacific institutions.

Preface

There is no doubt that hospitality is a global industry. The international expansion of some chains makes headlines, as when McDonald's opened their first restaurant in Moscow. Hotel chains now operate units on every continent except Antarctica. The Accor group has 770 hotels in the twelve countries of the European Community and almost as many again throughout the world. The Holiday Inn brand spans the globe with over 1,600 hotels, and many other international chains are expanding rapidly through acquisition and takeover. Brands that were until recently based in their home country are now mushrooming elsewhere. Newcomers from the USA to Europe include Domino's, TGI Fridays and Taco Bell, and you will find Pizza Hut and Burger King competing for customers alongside the pavement cafés of Paris.

This book attempts to answer a very simple question – what happens when hospitality firms become international? Although an easy question to ask, it is a very difficult one to answer. There are many reasons for this. Firms do not all follow the same pattern when they 'go international'. Even their reasons for doing so appear to depend on opportunity rather than planning. Why they do it and how they do it depends on the industry sector they operate in, where they are coming from and going to, management style and corporate culture, degree of marketing orientation, level of maturity of the firm and its markets, and a whole host of other factors. It is clear that there remains much to be learnt about the internationalisation of hospitality firms.

The editors of this book, therefore, asked some of the most eminent teachers, practitioners, researchers and authors in the field to think about and write about this international phenomenon in their own specialist area. In order to understand the international hospitality industry, one has to understand the world in which it operates. Although satellite communication has established the image of us living in a 'global village', the reality is that there are significant differences between one country and another, from one continent to the next. We begin therefore with five chapters each exploring in depth these characteristics.

International expansion has come about in a number of very different ways. One of the most significant decisions a firm makes is with regard to its business format. Ownership of the operating property and management of the business can be separated, either through franchising or management contracting. Likewise, individual hotels can band together independently to behave like international chains. Part 2 of this text looks at each of these alternative business formats from an international perspective.

Once international, managers in the various functions – operations, human resources, marketing, finance – are faced with new challenges. There is a

significant increase in the complexity of the environment and hence significant decisions have to be made about how best to manage that environment.
It would seem that international hospitality firms have adopted a very wide
range of responses to these challenges.

Finally, there are themes which run throughout the text that are explored
in depth in the last three chapters. These are the international hospitality consumer, cultural diversity, and technology transfer. Each of these is very
important, and both managers and researchers are only just starting to understand these issues in the hospitality context. Each of these chapters makes a
significant contribution to this understanding.

The book is aimed at undergraduate and postgraduate students of management and hospitality management, as well as hospitality practitioners. It is
designed to be used as an independent text or as a companion volume to
International Hospitality Management, also published by Pitman in the UK and
John Wiley & Sons in the USA. It provides the context in which international corporate strategy is practised. All of the chapter authors have extensive
international experience themselves – some are industry practitioners, some
are researchers, some are teachers – most are all three. They reflect the theme
of the text, living and working as they do in Australia, Canada, the USA,
Hong Kong, and the UK.

Many people have contributed to this text, some directly – such as the
authors, editors, proof-readers, and so on – and others indirectly, through
their encouragement and support. To be the editors of this text has been
exciting. To achieve its production within twelve months has been a miracle.
To work with colleagues such as these from around the world has been a
privilege. We thank you all sincerely. You have been enthusiastic, conscien-
tious, insightful, and cooperative. This book is a tribute to you all.

Peter Jones and Abraham Pizam
February 1993

Part I

The international hospitality industry

This section looks in detail at the magnitude and nature of the hospitality industry in the five major regions of the world: Western Europe; Eastern Europe; North America; the Far East and Pacific Rim; Latin America and Africa.

Within each region, the authors identify the main environmental factors and key conditions that affect the hospitality industry. The discussion normally begins with an overview of the demographic and economic structure of each region and then shifts to the tourism industry. Following a qualitative and quantitative description of the tourism industry in each major country within the region, the authors define the nature and composition of the hospitality industry and list its main characteristics. Finally, each author identifies the principal problems and challenges occurring in the hospitality and tourism industries within each region or country, examines their implications, and anticipates future prospects.

A close examination of the results presented in this section reveals that, although the largest tourism and hospitality industries exist in Western Europe and North America, the prospect for real growth and future development of these industries is in the Far East and Pacific Rim. With few exceptions, while Eastern Europe, Latin America and Africa have significant potential for further development of tourism and hospitality, this potential is currently constrained by a string of political, social and economic problems.

As the reader will note, because individual countries do not use the same definitions in their tourism and hospitality industries, some of the statistics presented in these chapters are not compatible with each other, a fact that makes any international comparison very difficult.

1

Western Europe

David Litteljohn

Overall, Western Europe provides a post-industrial setting for the analysis of the hospitality industry. It presents an economic profile of an affluent society whose industry is moving into services and has been identified as constituting, along with North America and Japan, one of the three main world trading blocs. As well as being characterized by economic affluence, these mature and developed economies are invariably populated by ageing populations. However, it is a mistake to consider the area as homogeneous. Not all parts are affluent. In addition there is a high degree of cultural diversity, with strong national and regional identities. This diversity, coupled with local regulatory frameworks and business conditions, means that there exist many barriers to the establishment of a single European marketplace. This chapter will examine economic and demographic characteristics, and go on to evaluate the nature of the tourism and hospitality industries in the area, through an investigation of demand and supply sectors. Later, some current trends in the business and regulatory environment are highlighted, so that a fuller appreciation of industry dynamics and future trends may be obtained.

It may be simplistic to conclude that the hospitality industry in Western Europe is mature, and one which will be subject to rationalization and shake-out. However, it would not be an exaggeration to say that a key need among European hospitality managers over the next decade will be the need to adapt and change in line with market demands for quality and value for money, and increased organizational attention will have to be given to profitability and professionalism.

For the purposes of this chapter, Western Europe refers to the countries of the European Community (EC) together with five members of the European Free Trade Association (EFTA): Austria, Finland, Norway, Sweden and Switzerland. Omitted from this analysis, for reasons of geography and size, are Iceland and Liechtenstein. Similarly, the Duchy of Luxembourg, an EC member, is not included in the statistics given below, for a population of just 370,000 means that its exclusion makes relatively little impact on the overall characteristics of the region. It must be stated that, due to the relatively recent reunion of East and West Germany, statistics covering both are often unavailable and only those judged reliable have been included.

Economic overview

Overall the European trend since 1948 has been one of fast, but not equally distributed, economic growth. For example, the UK, decolonizing and deindustrializing in parallel, has shown much slower growth than, for example, West Germany. In addition, many countries have severe problems in stimulating growth in what are considered economically depressed regions. Most countries too have seen changes in the structure of their economies with a transition away from primary economic activities to ones with a more service base. In addition, it has been a feature of most European economies that they have more diversified international links. This has come about through the general increase in world trade; by extending their own and hosting foreign multinational companies; and by exporting and importing capital to and from other countries. Again this has not occurred at a standard rate, but most countries exhibit at least some of these features.

Overarching the performance of individual countries has been the creation of supranational bodies, which now operate for a mix of economic and social reasons. These are the European Community, conceived by the Treaty of Rome in 1957, and the more limited, economically driven European Free Trade Association set up in 1960. The general purpose of these organizations has been to encourage greater harmonization among their European members in their commerce, industry and trade, and to help in specific areas of economic and social policy. Thus, Article 2 of the Treaty of Rome states that the Community shall establish a common market and that it will 'promote ... a harmonious development of economic activities, a continuous and balanced expansion, an increase in stability, an accelerated standard of living and closer relations between the states belonging to it'.

As indicated above, this aim is not necessarily an easy one to attain, given the patchwork of different social and economic conditions that make up the area. The pressure for further integration has most recently been seen by developments both within and outside the European Community. Within the Community the Single European Act (1987), coming into force in 1993, and more recently the terms of the Maastricht Treaty deepen the relationship between member states. From outside the Community there are pressures for enlargement advanced from some of the existing EFTA members, and some of the former communist Eastern European states. The extent to which all these pressures may be accommodated within the existing structure of the European Community is a matter of debate and an important one to which we will return later in the chapter. For now, though, it is necessary to conclude this overview by establishing an idea of the size and nature of the countries in this grouping, before turning attention to their economic characteristics.

As can be seen from Table 1.1 the total population of the countries is 377 million persons. The population is essentially an urban one, with ten of the countries having 70 percent or more of their population urban, and only Portugal having a majority of its population living outside its towns and

Table 1.1 Population in Western Europe, 1991

Country	Population (m)	Population (% urban)
Austria	7.7	56
Belgium	10.0	96
Denmark	5.1	86
Finland	5.0	64
France	57.6	73
Germany	79.0	84
Greece	10.1	60
Ireland	3.5	57
Italy	58.0	67
Netherlands	14.9	88
Norway	4.2	73
Portugal	10.4	31
Spain	39.2	76
Sweden	8.5	83
Switzerland	6.7	58
UK	57.4	92
Total	377.3	–

Source: *European Marketing Data and Statistics*, Euromonitor, June 1992.

cities. The top five in terms of size, which are Germany, Italy, France, the UK and Spain, have a combined population of 291 million – 70 percent of the total for the group.

The structure of Western European economies

The past period of economic growth has seen most economies transform themselves from ones which have had strong manufacturing and agricultural bases, where services played a relatively minimal role (with exceptions such as London, which has been a world financial center for a long time), to societies where services employ a major part of the workforce. This has come about not because consumption of manufactured goods has decreased: in fact increasing levels of affluence have had the opposite effect. Increasingly, manufactured goods are imported, while European manufacturers have become more productive through a mix of strategies which invariably have led to decreasing levels of employment as modernized fabrication and assembly methods have lower labour requirements.

Table 1.2 shows the distribution of workforce employment by sector: manufacturing; services, which include wholesale, retail and hotel catering and recreation, transport communication and storage, finance and business services, and community social and personal services; and primary sectors. It can be seen from this table that most economies have moved substantially into the service sectors, with an overall average for the sector of just over 58 per cent of all employment coming from these sources. On the other hand, on average, manufacturing accounts for 22 percent and the primary

Table 1.2 Employment structure of Western European economies, 1991

Country	Manufacturing (%)	Services (%)	Agriculture, mining, quarrying, (%)	Not adequately defined (%)	Total
Austria	27.6	53.5	17.8	–	98.9
Belgium	21.0	69.2	9.8	–	100.0
Denmark	19.9	67.4	12.7	–	100.0
Finland	21.2	60.8	18.0	–	100.0
France	21.1	64.0	15.8	–	100.9
Germany					
West	31.6	55.4	12.9	–	99.9
East	–	–	–	–	–
Greece	18.8	43.7	32.3	5.1	99.9
Ireland	15.8	47.5	19.8	17.1	100.2
Italy	22.4	58.7	18.8	–	99.9
Netherlands	17.2	63.2	11.1	7.0	98.5
Norway	15.3	69.2	15.4	–	99.9
Portugal	25.0	45.8	26.2	3.0	100.0
Spain	22.3	41.6	24.8	11.6	100.3
Sweden	21.6	66.0	10.9	1.5	100.0
Switzerland	24.8	58.6	16.6	–	100.0
UK	23.8	69.6	7.6	–	101.0
Average	21.8	58.4	16.9	3.0	–

Source: *Market Research Europe*, Euromonitor, June 1992.

industries of agriculture, mining and quarrying employ around 17 percent of the workforce.

The economy most advanced towards the provision of services is that of the UK with a share of 70 percent of employees in this sector. Also very high are Belgium and Norway (69 percent), Denmark (67 percent) and Sweden (66 percent), with Finland, France and the Netherlands all over 60 percent. On the other hand, the economies of Greece, Ireland, Portugal and Spain all show relatively immature service sectors, capable of significant growth.

Of course this analysis can only be taken together with core economic data to provide a more precise picture of the direction of economies. To this end, Table 1.3 relates to the power of the economies as generated by their gross domestic product and trends in their growth and stability. The total wealth created by the economies in 1991 was US$7050 billion. The five largest, accounted for by those with the highest populations, between them generated a GDP of US$5352.8 billion, or 76 per cent of the total. This emphasizes their powerful influence on the economic patterns within the region as a whole. Per capita wealth does not, however, follow the lead set by the largest population and economies. In fact, judged on the basis of GDP per capita, it is the smaller EFTA countries which score most highly, with Switzerland, Finland, Sweden and Norway all coming before the top EC member, Germany, which takes sixth place. The other 'top five' are spread quite widely at seventh (France), tenth (Italy), twelfth (UK) and thirteenth (Spain).

The highest growth rate during 1990 to 1991, in what has become recognized as the beginning of a prolonged period of economic recession in the

Table 1.3   Economic characteristics of Western Europe, 1991

Country	GDP ($ billion)	GDP ($ per capita)	Real GDP growth 1990/91	Inflation rate 1990/91 (%)	Unemployment rate 1990/91 (%)
Austria	161.9	20 971	4.2	4.1	5.0
Belgium	199.1	19 753	1.3	4.7	8.6
Denmark	131.2	25 475	1.8	2.8	9.6
Finland	150.0	30 120	1.0	6.0	7.6
France	1195.2	21 120	1.3	4.4	9.6
Germany					
West	1451.0	23 085	0.2	4.8	6.3
East	–	–	– 20.0	50.0	35.0
Greece	68.8	6 822	0.7	20.3	9.3
Ireland	44.2	12 462	1.3	5.0	19.1
Italy	1137.0	19 630	1.1	8.0	9.5
Netherlands	287.3	19 153	2.3	5.2	2.0
Norway	107.5	25 235	1.8	4.4	7.7
Portugal	69.1	6 576	2.0	12.6	5.8
Spain	526.9	13 470	2.5	6.5	15.5
Sweden	236.5	27 408	0.9	12.7	2.7
Switzerland	241.2	35 892	2.5	6.0	1.3
UK	1042.7	18 140	– 1.8	5.9	9.0
Tot/average	7049.6	20 332	0.2	9.6	9.6

Note: GDP average excludes E. Germany.
Source: *Market Research Europe*, Euromonitor, June 1992.

area, was achieved by Austria at 4.2 percent, with the Netherlands, Portugal, Spain and Switzerland all scoring above 2 percent. The overall average for the countries, distorted by the downturn in East Germany, was 0.2 percent; excluding East Germany the average rate of growth rises to 1.4 percent. The most stable economies in terms of low inflation and unemployment during the period were Austria, the Netherlands and Switzerland. The reunification of Germany in 1991 and the consequential economic destabilization that this caused to its economy, affected other European countries like the UK through, for example, their joint membership of the European Monetary System.

Analysis of the more current economic factors will take place later, but meanwhile it can be concluded that Western Europe, while showing the characteristics of a developed and mature, indeed post-industrial economy, possesses countries with considerable variations around the norm in terms of size, wealth per capita and stability. The top five countries account for the vast majority of wealth creation and consumption, but even between themselves they show different patterns of employment and stages of development.

Demographic and social issues

The EC 1990 population (345 million) together with the other countries of Western Europe give a total population of 377 million, which compares to 261 million for the USA and 124 million for Japan. Over the next 30 years the West European population is set to rise by a modest 0.75 percent to a figure approaching 376 million. Trends in population change, by country, are shown in Table 1.4.

In the major five countries, Eurostat estimates that populations will decline by a relatively small proportion, 0.6 percent (Litteljohn and Slattery, 1991). This reversal to normal trends in population growth will place strains on labor markets, and it will create further changes in demand patterns as it will be accompanied by a change in the age distribution of the population, giving a greater importance to the older age groups. In 1995 the over-65 sector in the top five countries alone will number around 43 million, ensuring a large demand for services (Litteljohn and Slattery, 1991). Among the requirements of this market there is sure to be an increase in demand for out-of-season holidays (older age groups will have the time available), and probably a need for more diverse holiday types as most existing recuperative/relaxation and activity packages may not have the same appeal to a leisured sector, in contrast to the provision of summer holidays aimed at a working population. This will have to be provided at excellent perceived value, for while grey markets have resources of time, they are still likely to be relatively constrained in budgetary terms.

Within Europe there are very different attitudes towards leisure and work, reflecting different value systems, different legal requirements for holidays, different work systems and different levels of economic development, including ownership of key possessions such as motor cars. The effects of education systems, for example, influence the timing of family holidays, as will attitudes towards women, particularly mothers, in the workplace and the

Table 1.4 Demographic trends in Western Europe, 1990–2020

Country	% change over period
Austria	−4.26
Belgium	−1.60
Denmark	7.20
Finland	3.48
France	7.22
Germany	−7.00
Greece	0.92
Ireland	29.25
Italy	−2.68
Netherlands	3.21
Norway	−1.61
Portugal	6.10
Spain	7.71
Sweden	−4.20
Switzerland	−0.72
UK	1.20

Source: European Marketing Data and Statistics, Euromonitor, 1992.

requirement for partners to have time off together for holidays away from home. Similarly, legislation on minimum length of paid holidays, or workforce practice and customs, will have an important impact on patterns of holiday taking among the population. However, it should be remembered that, just as Europe was the home of the industrial revolution, so it has been the cradle of modern tourism, generating substantial international flows since the development of inclusive package tours by Thomas Cook in Victorian times. This has led to consumers having not only a high interest in taking holidays, but also high expectations of the standard of provision.

Tourism demand

It is accepted that tourism is now the single largest economic activity in the European Community, with potential for further growth. It currently accounts for 5 percent of the Community's gross domestic product, and 5 percent of all foreign trade; in employment terms it provides 8 million jobs directly, and when indirect effects are taken into account the total rises to 16 million. While tourism in the more northern members of EFTA may not encompass the pleasure markets attracted to southern Europe, the northern countries are nevertheless significant as they will attract business and local markets, as well as international holiday tourists interested in things other than sea, sand and sun. Tourism here is examined in terms of both holiday/leisure tourism and business/conference-related tourism, as both of these types of stay-away from home affect suppliers in tourism and hospitality.

Holiday tourism

In the 1980s EC citizens spent some 7 percent of their household budgets on holidays (Commission of the European Community, 1985b). In developed economies where holiday-taking patterns are already high – with around 60 percent of the population taking trips – the market becomes more complex. More people take annual holidays, and increasing proportions take several holidays a year. Motivations for travel are also varied, and more people undertake long-haul travel, making destinations more diffuse. Thus the increasingly sophisticated customer makes the market less homogeneous.

Figure 1.1 shows the relationships that exist between levels of holiday taking and age and income groups within the EC.

Business tourism

The structural theory of business demand (Slattery and Johnson, 1991) holds that levels of business travel rise particularly quickly as economies become service intensive and as constituent industries become more concentrated. The approach rests on the inference that large organizations, particularly many of those in the service industries, by their very nature create substantial

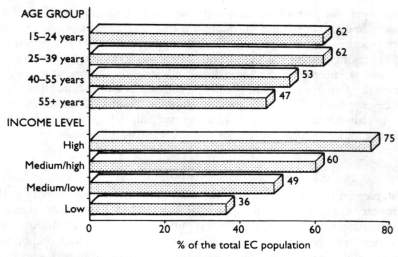

Figure 1.1 Holiday taking in the European Community, 1985
Source: Commission of the European Community (1985a).

amounts of business travel. This effect may be combined with the view that the process of concentration will engender considerable volumes of travel for training, sales, control and co-ordination purposes. Short-term factors such as growth rates and inflation will exert influences on the volume of travel, but will be less powerful than the structural factors underlying industrial organization.

Domestic and international tourism

Tourism may be generated from domestic or international markets. Within Western Europe the greatest proportion of travel occurs among local populations, and from neighbouring countries. Table 1.5 shows the trends in international tourism within Europe as a whole over the period 1960 to 1990.

Table 1.5 Trends in international tourism arrivals, 1960–90

	1960	1970	1983	1986	1988	1990
Numbers by region (000s)						
World	69 296	159 690	284 173	330 907	382 132	443 866
Europe	50 117	112 008	189 924	212 361	234 792	275 060
Receipts by region (US$m)						
World	6 867	17 900	98 395	140 023	197 712	254 816
Europe	3 884	11 023	53 607	74 345	102 628	134 017

Source: *Yearbook of Tourism Statistics*, WTO, vol. 1, 1992, pp. 2–24.

Between 1970 and 1980 international arrivals increased by a factor of nearly 100 percent, although their share of the total decreased from 75 to 64 percent; on the other hand, the European share of total receipts generated remained at around 60 percent.

Table 1.6 gives a more detailed breakdown of international tourist arrivals and receipts on a country-by-country basis. Table 1.7, on the other hand, gives an indication of the nature of international tourism flows within the region. The figures do not present the full picture of international tourism flows, for they show only the top three generating countries for each Western European recipient country. However, even in these figures it will be noticed that a major feature of international tourism is its intra-regional nature: for nine countries in the group, the Western European generating countries shown account, between them, for over half of that country's total international arrivals.

One of the main changes to manifest itself in the near future is the emergence of a post-*détente* Europe, characterized by disengagement of the closed communist regimes in the east. This could lead to substantial changes in patterns of travel: for example, Eastern Europeans, previously restricted to travel within the Eastern Bloc, may consider (cheap) holiday destinations on the Mediterranean coast; other markets, like the Americans travelling to West Germany, who did so in great part for business and military reasons associated with the cold war, may diminish substantially.

Table 1.6 International tourism in Western Europe, 1990

Country	International arrivals (m)	Tourist receipts ($ billion)	Share of accommodation market by foreigners	Share of accommodation market by nationals
Austria	19.0	13.02	76.8	23.2
Belgium	7.5	3.58	35.0	65.0
Denmark	8.7	3.32	41.2	58.8
Finland	1.9*	1.17	21.6	78.4
France	51.5	20.19	31.9	68.1
Germany				
West	17.0	8.66	14.3	85.7
East	–	–	–	–
Greece	9.3	2.57	78.8	11.2
Ireland	3.7	1.45	66.4	33.6
Italy	60.3	19.74	–	–
Netherlands	5.8	3.62	29.5	70.5
Norway	2.0	1.51	33.5	66.5
Portugal	18.4	3.56	59.4	40.6
Spain	52.0	18.59	51.5	48.5
Sweden	6.1	2.90	19.5	80.5
Switzerland	13.2	6.84	48.5	51.4
UK	18.0	15.00	33.0	67.0
Tot/average	292.5	125.72	42.7	56.6

* 1988 figure.
Source: World Tourist Organization/*European Marketing Data and Statistics*, Euromonitor, 1992.

Table 1.7 Main international tourism flows, 1988

Receiving country	No. 1 country	%	No. 2 country	%	No. 3 country	%	Total top 3 from W. Europe %
				Generating countries			
Austria	W. Germany	53.4	Netherlands	8.0	Italy	5.2	66.6
Belgium	Netherlands	38.5	W. Germany	16.0	France	9.2	63.7
Denmark	W. Germany	35.2	Sweden	20.7	Norway	12.3	68.2
Finland	Sweden	24.3	W. Germany	14.0	USSR	19.3	38.3
France	W. Germany	23.8	UK	17.4	Netherlands	10.6	51.8
Germany West	USA	14.3	Netherlands	14.3	UK	9.0	23.3
East	Czechoslovakia	11.7	USSR	10.8	Poland	4.7	0
Greece	UK	23.0	W. Germany	17.8	Italy	7.0	47.8
Ireland	UK	69.5	Canada	12.8	W. Germany	3.8	73.3
Italy	Switzerland	21.1	W. Germany	18.8	France	16.1	56.0
Netherlands	W. Germany	20.0	UK	18.2	USA	11.5	38.2
Norway	Denmark	19.2	Sweden	17.2	W. Germany	16.1	52.5
Portugal	Spain	45.1	UK	16.1	France	8.5	69.7
Spain	France	20.8	Portugal	17.4	UK	13.2	51.4
Sweden	Norway	32.1	W. Germany	19.4	Denmark	9.1	60.6
Switzerland	W. Germany	33.4	USA	10.7	France	7.7	41.1
UK	USA	16.6	France	12.5	W. Germany	11.6	24.1

Source: World Tourism Organization/European Marketing Data and Statistics, Euromonitor, 1991.

Tourism motivations

It must be remembered that, for most countries, the most important component of hospitality demand springs from domestic markets. Classifications of tourism travel used above can only be considered very general. This is particularly the case in a mature market where travel motivations will embrace a variety of factors. Sun, sea and sand may play an important part in attracting visitors to the Mediterranean, but there will be other important combinations of reasons for travel, whether visits are for holiday or business purposes. While Continental spas and hydropaths may still hold some of their original appeal, cold-water sea resorts in more northern locations, developed in the late 1800s or early 1900s, may now have to find new markets in summer and to bolster seasonality problems. Other locations may offer cultural attractions and/or activities such as winter sports, golf, sea angling, ornithology, scuba diving, riding, pony trekking, music and drama festivals, archaeological digs, industrial heritage and so on. There are purpose-built conference and exhibition centers for business markets.

Thus the tourism infrastructure of Western European countries often focuses on intangibles such as culture and scenery as well as the more tangible elements of hotels, airports, historic buildings and so on. The nature of the more tangible elements, often centuries old, can make the 'package' that individual tourists consume one which is very varied. Bearing in mind the waves of emigration that practically all countries of Western Europe have seen, there also exists, on an international basis, a large potential ethnic market which includes those visitors who are returning to the country of their birth and childhood, and others, whose ancestors may have left centuries ago, who want to sample the heritage and society of their forebears. All these reasons point to the diverse and sophisticated nature of the market, and the need for careful planning and targeting policies by suppliers.

The tourism industry

This section establishes a view as to the structure of the European tourism and hospitality industry. It does this by taking key areas and discussing their development.

Transportation infrastructure

More than 50 percent of the Community's international passenger movements are by road, about 30 percent are by air and the balance is shared almost equally between rail and ferry (Jefferson, 1992). The EC is preparing plans for land-based transport networks so that all regions can be linked; this promises to have an impact on tourist mobility, and is especially important for the more peripheral regions of the Community. In particular, it should be easier to travel by road and rail. However, while rail may increase its share somewhat, and certain member states are seeing something of a renaissance in rail travel, car-borne transport will retain its pre-eminent position. The opening of the Channel Tunnel will ensure that the UK has easier access to mainland Europe. Developments in air transportation are examined below.

Air travel

Travel Industry Monitor (1991) reports that the growth in air travel in the 1980s slowed down with the advent of the Gulf War, in combination with the less sudden but serious consequences of the sluggish economic recession. Decreases in air traffic growth were first felt in 1989, though this was due more to congestion in the airports and on air routes than to political and economic factors. Nevertheless, major European airports performed better than most in 1989. Among the top ten European airports by passenger numbers, Frankfurt, Rome (Fiumicino), Madrid and Düsseldorf recorded increases in annual passenger volumes of over 10 percent – only the UK's Gatwick and Stansted recorded decreases in passenger volume, while Heathrow, the busiest airport in Europe, registered an increase of nearly 8 percent.

The future will see major changes in the manner in which airlines are operated within Europe. Until recently the industry has, on the whole, been one which has had a high degree of national protection and encouragement, made possible through state ownership and governmental control of landing rights. This has resulted in a large number of airlines with fairly modest European networks and has also affected the routes they can fly and the places where they can take on and offload passengers. Sometimes the airports allocated may also be a point of issue.

Sector characteristics are changing due to a number of factors, including the need to obtain economies of scale (for example, to finance the development of sophisticated computer reservation systems), and the associated marketing requirement to provide an integrated airline system, rather than one which relies on supervising bodies like the International Air Travel Association. This has created a push for airlines to develop a critical mass through a series of mergers and strategic alliances with European and other partners which will weaken their 'flag carrying' status, as their ownership and market appeal will have to cross borders. Another factor which is driving the changes in the industry is the avowed aim of the Commission of the European Community to increase levels of competition on all air routes within the area, rather than relying on reciprocal arrangements between member states, such as the rather more liberal agreements that exist between the UK and the Netherlands. While the Commission's original plans have been somewhat weakened, some limited measures on liberalization have already been announced (1992). By January 1993 airlines will be free to fly anywhere within the Community at whatever fares they wish to charge. Meanwhile, harmonization of VAT rates and the removal of duty-free sales for travel within the EC could push up operating costs substantially, and make it necessary for carriers to increase fares accordingly.

Thus the combined impact of these measures on costs to passengers is uncertain. It can be argued (Doganis, 1992) that the establishment of the large airline companies and alliances will act against competition, as four or five airlines might control some 75–80 percent of the Community's scheduled air traffic. By mid-1992, for example, Air France had taken a major holding in UTA, France's largest independent carrier. This also gave it control of the leading domestic operator, Air Inter. The French airline has also forged a marketing alliance with Lufthansa (Germany), as has Iberia (Spain) with Alitalia, and British Midland with SAS.

Just as it was stated, at the start of this section, that congestion at airports was an important factor limiting growth, it should also be pointed out that congestion of air traffic routes, exacerbated by the lack of an overall air traffic management system, could also threaten growth rates in passenger volumes. This, essentially, is a problem for governments and civil aviation authorities to tackle.

Tour operators

The high tourism growth rates of the past, Europe's position as both a generator and a recipient of holiday and business travel and a trend towards the provision of packaged travel to customers provided the conditions for the development of a large and highly differentiated tour operating industry. The overall trend in the 1990s has been one of coping with recession and making structural adjustments to the conditions of a mature market, where changes are being forced on providers, on the one hand by more sophisticated customers with greater knowledge, and on the other hand by the information revolution and the new computerized central reservation systems (CRSs) operated by airlines, travel operators and retailers. The current supremacy of the large international CRSs indicates that there will be significant pressure on the smaller operators which cannot afford access to larger technologically developed systems and which will increasingly meet marketing and operating problems. The overcapacity which was apparent even as the recession began was most spectacularly illustrated by the collapse of the tour operator International Leisure Group, which had also become embroiled in scheduled airline operations (through its ownership of Air Europe) in early 1991. This overcapacity has encouraged rationalization in the industry through a series of amalgamations and takeovers. It is likely that these will, over the next five years, lead to the establishment of pan-European companies which will deal with a high percentage of tour operator business.

The European Community in its directive 90/314/EEC on package travel, package holidays and package tours intends to protect consumers from misleading statements and this means that operators and travel agents will have to take on the legal responsibility for the services they offer. In normal circumstances, organizers will be liable even if the tour was run by another company. They will have to pay compensation if the actual holiday did not match the claims made for the package sold. Meeting the conditions of this directive will obviously affect many operators in the industry and will tend to favour those operators with significant resources.

Discussing future trends in the UK sector Goulding (1990) states that concentration will increase further, as profit margins from the competitive short-haul, charter-inclusive tour operations remain low. It seems likely, from the above analysis of consumer and market trends, that these comments are equally applicable to the wider European environment.

Theme parks and attractions

More attention is now being paid to the provision of a high-quality visitor experience through the development of tourist attractions. An indication of their significance may be drawn from the fact that in 1989, for the UK, visitors to theme parks and other attractions totaled 330 million (English Tourist Board, 1991). Bearing in mind the fragmented nature of the European tourism industry – and attractions will vary from theme parks run commercially to museums and parks owned by the nation to large and small trusts sometimes operated on a voluntary basis – provision is often done on the basis of destination marketing groups (for example, by government-sponsored tourist industry bureaux at national and regional levels). However, there is also a trend towards the development of large dedicated centers, realized most recently near Paris with the Euro Disney theme park.

Undoubtedly well-themed attractions can do much to add to the quality of a visitor's stay. Yet, optimism about their future is sometimes misplaced and it has been observed that 'any particular development will have to be appraised carefully for viability' (Goulding and Litteljohn, 1992). To be successful, large attractions require very substantial operating and marketing skills. Three particular conditions appear essential to develop a successful enterprise:

- The right financial package to fund the project: increasingly the technology required to provide high-standard visitor attractions is becoming sophisticated and expensive.
- An appealing theme which may draw customers throughout the year.
- A large enough population catchment area to ensure high attendances. While the catchment area may refer not only to the population within close driving proximity of the attraction, it would appear that relying on seasonal visitors from further afield will not ensure sufficient numbers.

The hospitality industry

Currently Europe offers one of the most secure places for corporate hotel expansion. Not only does it already account for a sizable proportion of world tourism demand but, as indicated above, it provides much of this from internal sources. In this respect demand is fairly stable in that it is unlikely to be seriously affected by political events. From a supply point of view

Europe is a favorable location for further corporate expansion. This is due to the fact that, to date, there has been relatively little corporate expansion within the region. Figure 1.2 shows levels of corporate penetration (that is, affiliation of hotel rooms to companies which are quoted on public stock exchanges) within the EC. The average of total European hotel stock under corporate flags is 10 percent. As can be seen from the figure, only the Netherlands at 20 percent and France at 18 percent come close to the UK level of corporate penetration (23.5 percent). Particularly low are Greece, Italy, Denmark and Spain. There undoubtedly exists significant potential for further company expansion and takeovers within the industry.

Table 1.8 gives an indication of some of the major players in the field, though it concentrates on those with holdings in more than one country. It also excludes government-owned chains like the Pousadas of Portugal and the Paradores of Spain, along with the Meridien chain of hotels owned by the state-owned Air France.

However, the information contained in Table 1.8 points clearly to the concentration of internationally owned hotel capacity in the top five countries of the region, for their share of the total 2,320 hotels and 242,386 rooms controlled by the companies listed is over 90 percent of both properties and room capacity. It is likely, therefore, that the development of pan-European chains will at first be concentrated within these major markets; indeed,

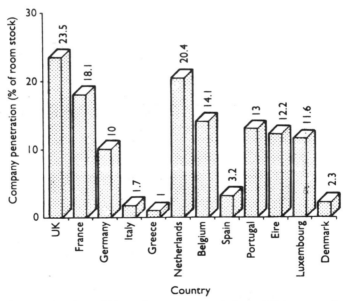

Figure 1.2 Penetration of European room stock by publicly quoted companies, 1990
Source: Slattery and Johnson (1991).

Table 1.8 International hotel companies in the European Community

	UK hotels	UK rooms	CEC hotels	CEC rooms	Total EC hotels	Total EC rooms	ECS hotels	ECS rooms
UK Companies								
BAA Hotels	3	1 123	1	188	4	1 311	3	1 123
Bass	65	4 897	34	6 978	99	11 875	89	9 864
Brent Walker	4	425	2	100	6	525	6	525
Bridgend Group	1	17	1	108	2	125	1	17
Buckingham Internat'l	6	304	9	994	15	1 298	6	304
Control Securities	10	938	13	3 888	23	4 826	23	4 826
Forte	328	29 212	23	4 350	351	33 562	343	32 591
Friendly Hotels	16	1 634	1	90	17	1 724	17	1 724
Ladbroke	35	7 206	16	5 781	51	12 987	54	13 974
Principal Hotels	12	861	4	634	16	1 495	12	861
Queens Moat Houses	102	9 954	72	9 718	174	19 672	143	16 579
Rank	72	7 726	1	100	73	7 826	72	7 726
Savoy	5	724	1	58	6	782	6	782
Sea Containers	2	208	4	353	6	561	5	411
Stakis	29	3 543	1	200	30	3 743	30	3 743
UK total	**690**	**68 772**	**183**	**33 540**	**873**	**102 312**	**810**	**95 050**
France								
Groupe Accor	22	3 277	751	71 332	773	74 609	731	69 462
Wagons-Lits	4	530	207	24 066	211	24 596	190	21 627
Société du Louvre	11	633	248	17 228	259	17 861	248	17 254
French total	**37**	**4 440**	**1206**	**112 626**	**1 243**	**117 066**	**1 166**	**108 343**
Spain (Cofir)	**0**	**0**	**37**	**3 859**	**37**	**3 859**	**37**	**3 859**

Italy								
Ciga	0	0	31	4 390	31	4 390	30	4 106
Jolly Hotels	0	0	35	5 757	35	5 757	33	5 359
Italian total	**0**	**0**	**66**	**10 147**	**66**	**10 147**	**63**	**9 465**
Germany (K'ski)	**0**	**0**	**4**	**1 350**	**4**	**1 350**	**4**	**1 350**
Ireland								
Jurys Hotel	1	137	4	800	5	937	1	137
Ryan	0	0	10	1 103	10	1 103	0	0
Irish total	**1**	**137**	**14**	**1 903**	**15**	**2 040**	**1**	**137**
USA								
Hilton Hotel Corp	1	160	1	203	2	363	1	160
ITT (Sheraton)	6	1 587	15	5 886	21	7 473	20	6 675
Marriott	1	223	7	2 328	8	2 551	6	1 880
USA total	**8**	**1 970**	**23**	**8 417**	**31**	**10 387**	**27**	**8 715**
Others								
New World (Hong Kong)	4	1 136	18	3 855	22	4 991	21	4 843
Seibu Saison (Japan)	6	2 482	23	8 182	29	10 664	28	10 624
Other total	**10**	**3 618**	**41**	**12 037**	**51**	**15 655**	**49**	**15 467**
Overall total	746	78 937	1 574	183 879	2 320	262 816	2 160	242 386

Note: CEC = Continental European Community; EC = European Community; EC5 = France, Germany, Italy, Spain, UK.
Source: Slattery and Johnson, 1991.

companies with major representation across borders in Europe are already located in these countries, although they will also target locations such as major industrial, commercial and communications centers: that is, they will place greater emphasis on the local setting than on overall national conditions.

One of the major decisions that chains will need to make is the extent to which they can develop single brand concepts for the whole of the European marketplace, or whether they should differentiate by location, and thus possibly more accurately meet local customer expectations (Olfermann and Robbins, 1987). This is not a straightforward decision because hotel services, provided to an international clientele, present a different standardization challenge from the branding strategies adopted for fast-moving consumer goods from confectionery to soft drinks and hamburgers. Current experience shows that many companies expanding within Europe are doing so with main brands (e.g. Holiday Inn Garden Court; Forte Travelodge; Accor with Novotel, Ibis and Formule 1), but that they will make some concessions to local marketplaces. Queens Moat House Hotels, on the other hand, have adopted a more country-specific brand strategy, with for example Queens Moat House in the UK, Queens in Germany, Bilderberg in Holland and Austrotel in Austria.

Tourism policy and regulatory frameworks

Governments have treated their tourism industries in a number of different ways in regard to regulatory, marketing, fiscal and development factors. In any event they have not been entirely consistent in their approach to the industry – at times highlighting possible contributions to the balance of payments, while at others promoting aspects such as income/employment generation, diversification of the economic base, regional development and even, less frequently through the imposition of tourism taxes, the revenue-earning capacity of the industry. Government influences are often of an indirect rather than a direct nature, through measures that affect the business environment, rather than by direct control of tourism resources. This is not to say that there are not examples of government-owned organizations which can have an impact on tourism. Pousadas (Portugal) and Paradores (Spain) have been mentioned in relation to government-owned hotel accommodation; to the state ownership in airlines also referred to above there might be added other publicly owned and operated transport services such as the railways.

Yet most of the tourism industry is under private ownership and will feel government policy through planning measures (for instance, land zoning and regulations affecting building standards). At various times governments have been keen to develop tourism through the medium of grants and loans for tourism projects, particularly for the development of accommodation. However, on a day-to-day basis, most businesses will relate to tourism issues through the consultative and coordinating organizations which governments have established. In fact, the resources and the duties given to national tourist organizations differ from country to country, so it is difficult to generalize on their functions.

Tourism policy has often suffered from a lack of resources and a misunderstanding of the important role it may play in an economy if developed sensitively. Furthermore, it is not specifically an issue which appears to have been high on the agenda within the European Community. Table 1.9 outlines the EC's policy framework for tourism.

According to Lickorish (1991) the adoption of any measures in EC tourism owes much to the interest of the European Parliament, as there was no explicit mention of tourism in the treaties which established the EC's direction and objectives. This interest bore further fruit in the organization of the European Year of Tourism (1990). The objectives of this event are related to the promotion of the single European market, and tourism's role in this; the integration of Europe's peoples through tourism; better distribution of tourism over time and location; and the development of EC tourism particularly by encouraging travel from outside the Community.

However, it must be pointed out that the Commission's attitude towards tourism does not accord it high priority, and it must be considered still an area of only peripheral interest. The Community spends around 50 times as much on agriculture as it does on tourism, and spreads the work over a large number of its directorates: for example, at least ten EC directorates have some responsibility for travel. Not that this treatment of tourism is unique to the EC: Jefferson (1992) reports that the governments of Sweden and Switzerland have made large cuts in the funds available to their national tourist organizations. Thus, at least until a better system of representation and coordination is obtained, Community measures and ones in other countries are more likely to have indirect effects on hospitality and tourism businesses,

Table 1.9 The European Community policy framework for tourism

(a) *Freedom of movement and the protection of EC tourists*
easing of customs checks; reduction of police checks at frontiers; social security provisions for tourists; assistance for tourists and regulation of car insurance; protection of tourists' interests (e.g. in complaints about the shortcomings of tourist services)

(b) *Working conditions for those engaged in tourism*
right of establishment and freedom to provide tourist services; vocational training grants and mutual recognition of qualifications; aid from the European Social Fund; promotion of staggered holidays; harmonization of taxation; promotion of energy efficiency

(c) *Common transport policy*

(d) *Safeguarding of the European heritage*
environmental protection; arts heritage

(e) *Regional development*
through funding (e.g. the Social Development Fund)

Source: Based on Williams (1987), p. 239.

rather than to be advocated purely for their effects on tourism. Prime among these measures are the current developments in the structural evolution of the Community.

Changes in the European Community

Two types of change currently affect the nature of the relationships between member states in the Community. There are those measures which are deepening, by creating more common areas, the relationship between member states. These are discussed below, though attention will first be given to the pressures which form the second change to the EC – demands to increase the Community's size.

Of those Western European countries that are not EC members (1992), Austria, Finland and Sweden have initiated the process to apply for entry, and at the time of writing it is expected that Norway will also make an application. These countries have advanced economies and would put little strain on the EC's budget: in fact, they would be net contributors to Community coffers. Indeed, the relationship between the EC and EFTA will be getting closer with the proposed implementation of the European Economic Area, which is intended to operate from January 1993. Under this measure the flow of goods, services, labor and capital between EC and EFTA states should be freer. However, other pressures for membership – though not yet as advanced – have come from some Eastern European countries. If their applications were granted in the near future, this would effect a change in the nature of the Community, which would be unlikely to have the resources, or the willingness to make the large commitment, required to fund large schemes to modernize their economies.

In relation to the strengthening of the ties among EC members, the measures enacted under the aegis of the Single European Act, which came into force in 1987 and was implemented in 1993, will undoubtedly help stimulate the flow of goods across borders. The creation of the European Economic Area mentioned above will also strengthen the links within subscribing states. The tourist industry, however, is likely to be less immediately affected than others. One specific measure aimed to abolish intra-Community frontier controls. The UK government, however, was determined that some element of control was kept to minimize criminal activities and illegal immigration. This objection has not prevented most other countries from achieving easier crossings, for what is known as the Schengen group (all EC members with the exception of Denmark, Ireland and the UK) started from January 1993, to allow movement across their borders without passports. In addition, the phasing-in of a single visa for entering the EC will make movement within the Community easier for non-member nationals. Thus, while most travel within the Community will be considerably freer, there will no overarching policy.

Other issues which have been particularly brought to the forefront by the Maastricht Treaty relate to the social protocol. Essentially this looks to make employers responsible, in line with national systems, for non-wage social costs. The speed and extent to which agreement will be established among all member states is uncertain, and the UK has negotiated special conditions which will allow it some divergence from the measures adopted by other members. However, it is unlikely that, on its own, this arrangement will greatly affect the operation of industry, and therefore its impact on tourism enterprises, even if they are multinational, will not be substantial. Directives giving more priority to vocational qualifications within the EC and encouraging greater mobility among the labor force may well lead to different management opportunities and career paths.

The Community has also recommended that hotel grading schemes be harmonized; the terms of the recommendation, however, have little legislative force and it currently seems that the will to promote a uniform standard is lacking. In food hygiene matters, on the other hand, it does seem that there is a desire to enforce similar standards on a Community-wide basis.

The introduction of a single European currency would undoubtedly be a convenience to international tourists, reducing the need for them to exchange currency as borders are crossed. It might also help tourism businesses, as it could reduce the need for them to use different currencies for some of their international transactions. However, the debate about how, when and the extent to which common monetary systems should be established is continuing: there are still dissenting voices, and the whole issue of monetary integration is very much undecided.

The EC aim to increase the quality of the environment will undoubtedly ensure that aspects like conservation and heritage will obtain a higher profile, which should help most forms of tourism. However, equally, measures to protect the environment will have to be paid for and this may increase the development and operating costs of some tourism and hospitality projects. Mediterranean resort areas often have a poor environmental record, and some will welcome these initiatives since, although costly in the short term, they may provide the framework for future survival.

Conclusion

Western Europe will provide a key world market for tourism and hospitality in the twenty-first century. Trends towards the harmonization of economic conditions within the countries of the EC and EFTA are likely to enhance the demand for pan-European organizations, as well as lowering the barriers to their growth.

However, the conditions of the marketplace are characterized not so much by growth as by maturity. The development of large hospitality and tourism organizations will be achieved 'at the expense' of the smaller suppliers. If this results in better customer services, more profitable operations and greater professionalism, significant improvements may be apparent in the competitiveness of the industry. If, conversely, the main outcome of increasing levels of concentration is higher customer prices, the industry will be creating problems for itself, allowing destinations outside the area to become more attractive and creating entry opportunities for firms from outside Europe.

Thus, within an international marketplace, the industry must gear up to compete with long-haul destinations. This requires both that standards at Europe's destinations are world class and that they are promoted to appropriate markets. This, in turn, calls for the cultivation of bodies which can coordinate and synthesize promotional policies within Europe, and globally. In addition, there are some problems – such as the development of integrated travel systems and the introduction of pan-European industry standards – which can only be resolved by governments and with inter-country collaboration. This requires the creation of a political will to recognize the role and needs of tourism and hospitality operators, and to ensure that governments and their organizations provide adequate networks and funding to meet these requirements.

All these developments are taking place within economic, social and regulatory frameworks which are in a state of flux. Taken together, the conditions point to a business environment for hospitality and tourism characterized by change and turbulence; conditions placing managers in an area of significant challenges and, hopefully, significant rewards.

References

Commission of the European Community (1985a), *Europeans and Their Holidays*, Brussels: Commission of the EC.

Commission of the European Community (1985b) *Tourism in the Community*, Brussels: Commission of the EC, European File, 11/85.

Doganis, R. (1992) 'No freedom in the skies', *Financial Times*, 24 April.

English Tourist Board (1991) *Sightseeing in the UK*, London: English Tourist Board.

European Marketing Data and Statistics (1992), London: Euromonitor.

Goulding, P. (1990) *Britain's Tour and Travel Industry*, Bristol: Jordan's Business Sector Publications.

Goulding, P., and Litteljohn, D. (1992) *Britain's Commercial Leisure Industry*, Bristol: Jordan's Business Sector Publications.

Jefferson, A. (1992) 'European dimension', *Horizons*, British Tourist Authority, no. 11 (August), pp. 24–5.

Lickorish, L. J. (1991) 'Developing a single European tourism policy', *Tourism Management*, September, pp. 178–84.

Litteljohn, D., and Slattery P. (1991) 'The structure of Europe's economies and demand for hotel accommodation', *Travel and Tourism Analyst*, vol. 3, no. 4, pp. 20–37.

Market Research Europe (1992), Euromonitor, June.

Olfermann, J., and Robbins, K. L. (1987) 'Standardisation versus differentiation', *European Management Journal*, vol. 5, no. 4, pp. 250–6.

Slattery P., and Johnson, S. (1991) *Quoted Hotel Companies: The world markets*, London: Kleinwort Benson Securities.

Travel Industry Monitor (1991) 'Airports', *Travel Industry Monitor*, no. 14 (May), pp. 14–15.

Williams, A. (1987) *The Western European Economy*, London: Hutchinson Education.

2

Eastern Europe and the former Soviet states

Andrew Lockwood

When looking at the picture of international tourism arrivals, expenditures and receipts worldwide, Europe as a region stands out as playing a highly significant role in world tourism. In 1990 Europe welcomed 275 million out of a world total of 443.8 million tourists, or 61.96 percent. Regarding receipts, Europe collected just under 52.6 percent (US$134 017 million) of the world's total of US$254 816 million. In terms of expenditure, Europe spent US$127 009 million on tourism, almost 2.7 times its nearest regional rival, North America.

These summary statistics hide significant differences within the region. Northern, Southern and Western Europe account for the vast majority of the totals quoted above, leaving Eastern Europe with a much smaller role to play, particularly regarding receipts and expenditures. Cut off by political and economic circumstances from the development of world tourism over the past decades, Eastern Europe stands poised, occupying the same land mass as the 'powerhouse' of world tourism and with all barriers dissolved, to capitalize on the mystery that exclusion has generated.

This chapter looks at the existing patterns of tourism and hospitality within the region and considers the factors that will encourage and hinder the development of the industry in the future.

The region under consideration includes Bulgaria, Czechoslovakia (now two states), Hungary, Poland, Romania and the former USSR. The collection of reliable statistics for this region is notoriously difficult and does not necessarily conform to standard definitions (Buckley and Witt, 1990; Hall, 1991). However, the figures provided should be indicative of the likely current and future situations.

This study does not include Albania since up-to-date and reliable statistics and other information are not yet available. The report also excludes the German Democratic Republic following its reunification with West Germany, although most of the main issues will still apply. Yugoslavia is not included as it would more naturally fall within the Southern Europe classification of other Mediterranean destinations. In addition, the ongoing war in the area means that, when peace returns, the tourism industry will need to be completely rebuilt alongside the rest of the country. All those states that previously formed the USSR as yet have no individual statistics, so they are discussed collectively as the USSR.

Economic structure

Table 2.1 provides some basic structural data for the countries that make up the region. Within the countries of the region the USSR obviously occupies the largest land mass, with Hungary occupying the smallest area. In terms of population density, although the USSR has by far the largest population, because of its size it has a very low population density. Hungary, on the other hand, has quite a high population density, but Czechoslovakia and Poland have the highest in the region. The GNP figures for the USSR are not quoted as there is no reliable source for these data, with estimates ranging from $1780 to $9230. Inside the region, Czechoslovakia shows the highest GNP per capita at $3140 and Romania the lowest at $1640.

Some comparisons with other countries will help to clarify the region's relative size and economic development. In terms of area the EC countries occupy some 2261 square kilometres, one tenth of the size of the USSR and about three times the area of the other countries. The Netherlands has a population of just under 15 million, which equates to that of Czechoslovakia. However, the Netherlands had an overall GNP in 1990 of $258 million or $17 330 per capita compared to Czechoslovakia's $49 million and $3140 per capita. Spain at 39 million has roughly the same population as Poland but GNP figures of $429 million, nearly seven times Poland's GNP, and $10 920 per capita, over six times Poland's GNP per capita. Portugal has around the same population as Hungary with GNP figures of 51 million and $4890 per capita, both nearly twice as high as Hungary. Countries with similar GNP per capita figures to the countries of Eastern Europe include Thailand ($1420), Turkey ($1630), South Africa ($2520) and Brazil ($2680).

In the early 1960s the countries of Eastern Europe showed a high proportion of the workforce in the agricultural sector, ranging from 65 percent in

Table 2.1 Basic structural indicators

Country	Area (000km²)	Population			GNP		GNP per capita	
		1990 (000s)	Density (per km²)	Growth 1980–90 (%)	1990 (US$000s)	Growth 1980–90 (%)	1990 (US$)	Growth 1980–90 (%)
Bulgaria	110.9	8 991	81.07	0.2	19 875	2.5	2210	2.3
Czechoslovakia	127.9	15 680	122.60	0.3	49 225	1.5	3140	1.3
Hungary	93.4	10 554	113.00	−0.2	30 047	1.4	2780	1.5
Poland	312.7	37 966	121.41	0.7	64 480	1.8	1700	1.2
Romania	237.5	23 249	97.89	0.4	38 025	1.5	1640	1.1
USSR	22 402.2	288 734	12.89	0.9	n/a	n/a	n/a	n/a

Source: *World Bank Atlas*, 1991.

Romania to 25 percent in Czechoslovakia. From that time, central planning has moved employment out of the agricultural sector and into the industrial and service sectors (Caselli and Pastrello, 1992). While, during high periods of growth, industrial and service investment have been of equal standing, from 1975 planners tried to save the growth of material production by cutting service investment. This has left the service sector small in comparison to Western economies, such as the UK, Germany and the Netherlands. At the same time, the moves toward a market-based economy have shown that productivity in the region is between 30 and 50 percent lower than in the West. Making these industries economic has resulted in high levels of unemployment. It is expected that the service sectors, such as financial services, tourism and hospitality will expand and take up some of the excess labor. How far tourism and the hospitality industry can respond to this challenge will depend, to a large degree, on how current tourism patterns can be expanded and extended.

The structure of tourism

The development of tourism to Eastern Europe may be an attractive proposition for several reasons.

Curiosity. The former unavailability of this region will make it attractive to those tourists who are looking for something a little different and who wish to be part of 'history in the making'.

Natural and historical attractions. The size of the area means that nearly every type of holiday destination is available: the sun, sea and sand of the Black Sea; the mountains and lakes of Poland, Romania and Bulgaria; the vast unspoiled reaches of Siberia and Lake Baikal; the castles and historic towns across the whole region; and the particular attractions of cities such as Prague, Budapest, Moscow and St Petersburg.

Visiting friends and relatives. Many thousands of individuals have emigrated or escaped from Eastern Europe over the past decades and the new political climate should make it possible for these individuals to return to their home towns and visit the friends and relations they have been forbidden to see for so long.

Health cures and spas. The region is well supplied with natural springs and already has a well-established network of spas suitable for the development of balnearic tourism.

Prices. The general level of prices across the region is low in comparison to the West, except that these prices may not be offered to Western visitors. In addition, exchange rates are not as yet in free market conditions, also resulting in prices available for tourists not comparing with true domestic prices (Buckley and Witt, 1987). This management of the exchange rates can have dramatic effects on the costs of tourism.

Proximity. One of the prime attractions of this region is its proximity to the major tourism-generating countries of Western Europe and its accessibility by road and rail transport.

Safety. The level of crime in Eastern Europe is substantially lower than in the West both in the country areas and in the city centres. There must remain, however, some question about political instability and unrest in some regions.

Tourism policy

The background to the current movements of tourists in Eastern Europe can be traced for the USSR to 1917 and for the other countries to 1945–8. Since then political dogma has virtually cut these countries off from the rest of the world. In attempting to support the ideological internal view that the communist system was superior to the capitalist system, it was necessary to restrict any exchange between the two areas. Tourism flows to the West were in practice banned and tourists from the West were only allowed in small numbers, as part of organized groups, if at all. These groups were strictly supervised and directed, to avoid as much contact with the local population as possible. For example, in some countries regulations about compulsory currency exchange at artificially high exchange rates were introduced; tourists were expected to register with the police on arrival and possibly before departure as well; and foreigners were restricted to specific areas. These measures, together with severe restrictions on the granting of visas, were enough to keep all but the most courageous and persistent out of the area.

At the same time, the governments did not see tourism between the countries of Eastern Europe as a high priority in economic terms. Any priority governments gave to domestic recreational tourism relied on the provisions of the state-owned transport and accommodation sectors. In particular, this led to the practice of pricing accommodation services for citizens of Eastern bloc countries at about 10 percent of those charged to Western tourists. The trade unions subsidized these services as a benefit or reward for their members. In some cases, however, restrictions extended even to movement between like-minded countries.

These restrictions have resulted in the severe lack of a basic tourism infrastructure with transport, accommodation, restaurant, heritage and attractions sectors that are ill equipped to cope with the demands of the modern tourist.

Relaxations in the restrictions, particularly to Western tourists, were slow and faltering before the early 1990s. Yugoslavia was the first to respond to the expanding market demands of the package holiday business of the 1960s and 1970s by dropping most labor and tourism barriers. This led to a thriving Western market that brought in much needed revenues in hard currency. It is all the more devastating then that the removal of communist domination in the region as a whole in the early 1990s has resulted in the strife that has torn Yugoslavia apart, destroyed it as a tourist destination and killed or displaced many thousands of innocent citizens.

Current tourism patterns

A report by the Economist Intelligence Unit (Kerpel, 1990b) discusses the structure of tourism flows across the region for 1988. It highlights the importance of visitors from Eastern bloc countries. For instance, 90 percent of Romania's and nearly 80 percent of Poland's tourists came from other Eastern bloc countries. It should be noted that most Western visitors tend to stay only in major cities, and in particular the capitals such as Budapest, Prague, Warsaw and Moscow. It is also the case that much of this activity derives from business rather than leisure travelers. Table 2.2 is based on World Tourism Organization statistics, and compares 1989 with 1990. A striking feature is the growth in arrivals, even over this short period, particularly to Poland and Hungary.

Bulgaria has seen a steady growth in foreign visitor arrivals over the 1980s to reach a total of 10.3 million visitors in 1990. This figure is, however, rather misleading. Of those visitors over half are in transit, mainly from Turkey, which also inflates the figure for visitors from market economies. The figure for Western tourists has reached around 1 million in 1988 following some relaxation of restrictions through the 1980s. Bulgaria now appears in several summer and winter holiday brochures offered by the major tour operators and has appeared in the TV travel programs as a 'new' destination.

Czechoslovakia shows a very high total of 30 million visitors by 1989 but again this is inflated by transit and day visitors, who in this case account for over 71 percent of arrivals. Most of these visitors came from East Germany, Poland and Hungary, with only 6.9 percent of visitors coming from outside the East European countries. Czechoslovakia occupies an ideal place in the centre of Europe and has many natural and architectural attractions. This accounts for the strong growth in tourism since 1985 and its continuing appeal, especially for weekend and short break holidays in Prague and the surrounding area.

Hungary began moves toward economic reforms in 1968 and managed to avoid the political backlash experienced by Czechoslovakia and Poland by

Table 2.2 International tourist arrivals and receipts: WTO statistics

Country	Arrivals 1989 (million)	Arrivals 1990 (million)	Receipts 1989 (US$M)	Receipts 1990 (US$M)
Bulgaria	8.22	10.32	362	394
Czechoslovakia	29.68	n/a	581	470
Hungary	24.92	37.63	798	1000
Poland	8.23	18.21	202	266
Romania	4.85	6.53	167	106
USSR	7.75	7.20	250	270

Source: *Yearbook of Tourism Statistics*, vols 1 and 2, WTO, 1992.

making only very gradual changes to the system. These changes occurred during a period of political stability and Western tourists responded to these changes favorably. Hungary offered a safe and welcoming environment similar to that found in the West and was able to offer the substantial attractions of Budapest and Lake Balaton, the largest lake in Europe. By 1990, out of the total of 37 million foreign visitors to Hungary, more than two-thirds were from the West. This considerable success is tempered by the fact that Hungary earns disproportionately less from tourism than other non-socialist countries with a similar number of tourists (Kerpel, 1990a). The low prices in Hungary compared to the West partly explain this, but in addition there are, outside the main centres, limited shopping, entertainment or restaurant facilities on which tourists can spend additional money.

Before the early 1980s *Poland* attracted over 10 million foreign visitors a year. The upheaval of those years, martial law, strikes, police suppression and the eventual rise of 'Solidarity' reduced tourism to just over one million visitors and it has taken considerable effort to encourage the return of 8.2 million visitors by 1989. Following the revolution, these figures increased dramatically to 18.21 million in 1990 and 36.84 million in 1991. More importantly, the percentage of tourists from non-Eastern European countries has increased from 22.3 percent in 1989 to 55.6 percent in 1991.

Reliable statistics for *Romania* are very hard to find, but it is estimated that around 6.5 million foreigners visited the country in 1990. Less than 10 per cent of those were from outside the socialist countries. The new government of Romania would like to encourage tourism, but the paucity of the facilities remaining after the harshness of the Ceausescu regime will make this difficult. Some small-scale development has already taken place and some UK tour operators are now offering winter sports holidays in Romania in their 1993 brochures.

Tourism in the *Soviet Union* has never achieved high priority and has been treated as one of the non-productive industries. Consequently, investment in tourism facilities and infrastructure for foreign visitors has been very low, although the government has been reasonably supportive of facilities for domestic tourism as part of general social policy. The level of foreign visitors to the USSR is consequently low, for such a large and potentially attractive destination, at 7.2 million in 1990. Even this figure is rather questionable as the Soviet Union does not use the standard WTO categories. For example, the figure quoted in the table for visitors in 'transit' or excursionists is actually the figure for 'personnel of the means of transportation'. The size of this figure suggests that this must be made up in large part by the drivers of commercial vehicles. This causes some interesting anomalies. The largest number of visitors in 1988 came from Poland, amounting to just over 1.8 million – one-third of all visitors. Of these, 741 000 are transport personnel and 544 000 are visiting friends or relations. With 254 000 visiting on business, this leaves 316 000 leisure visitors. In contrast, the largest number of non-socialist visitors come from Finland – around 700 000 in total. Of these well over half a million are leisure visitors and only 90 000 are transport personnel.

Overall visitors from non-socialist countries make up about one-third of all visitors. Estimates indicate that around 80 percent of foreign visitors still come on some form of organized package. Although visa and bureaucratic restrictions are now slowly disappearing, making it easier for the independent traveler, the lack of a basic tourism infrastructure still makes independent travel very difficult to achieve in practice.

In summary, across the region, the pattern of tourism appears remarkably similar. Eastern European countries previously paid limited attention to tourism development, and tourism was mainly restricted to domestic tourism within the country or to a limited extent between the socialist countries. Gradually there has been a realization across the region that international tourism has potential for economic growth and restrictions on foreign visitors have been lifted. Unfortunately, as previous investment in tourism has been low, the existing facilities and infrastructure are ill prepared to meet a rapid expansion in numbers of 'discerning' Western tourists.

The structure of the hospitality industry

Obtaining an accurate picture of the size and structure of the hospitality industry in Eastern Europe is extremely difficult. The official figures as quoted in Kerpel (1990b) seem authoritative but are rather patchy. Other data – for example, Kleinwort Benson Securities (1991), summarized in Table 2.4 – differ widely from the 'official' figures and are calculated on a definitional base relating to quoted hotel companies. Other figures – such as Salomon Brothers (Krutik, 1991) summarized in Table 2.5 – are different again. These figures do, however, provide some insights into the structure and nature of the hotel industry and, as implied by Carper (1990) and Baum (1990), the picture is in such a state of change that no statistics can be truly reliable.

If figures for the accommodation sector are difficult to find and of questionable reliability then details of other sectors of the hospitality industry are practically non-existent. Some of the author's personal experiences of a recent visit to the region should illustrate some of the problems these sectors face.

The hotel industry

The hotel industry in the region has been dominated by the large state-owned hotel companies such as Balkantourist in Bulgaria, Intourist in the USSR, and Hungar, Danubius and Panonia in Hungary. There has been no room until very recently for privately owned hotels, so there is no established tradition of small family-run establishments of the sort to be found across the rest of Europe. Some moves to rent out rooms in private houses have been made particularly in Hungary. The hotel stock consists of three main types: old traditional hotels that were built in a different era, but which have been left to run down and have lost most of their former splendor; concrete and glass dormitories built postwar to house visitors from other East European countries, with few of the facilities expected by Western tourists; and the new hotels

Table 2.3 Number of rooms: hotels and similar establishments – WTO statistics

Country	No. of rooms 1989	No. of rooms 1990
Bulgaria	62 121	60 137
Czechoslovakia	70 294	70 300
Hungary	23 264	24 432
Poland	284 892*	273 857*
Romania	87 500	87 500
USSR	32 000	32 000

* According to a communication received from the Warsaw Institute of Tourism, this figure represents the all-year number of beds from both commercial and non-commercial (i.e. factory and institutional recreation houses) enterprises. The appropriate figure for 1991 was 216 930.

Source: Yearbook of Tourism Statistics, vols 1 and 2, WTO, 1992.

built or upgraded to international standards through the involvement of international companies. Hotel grading across the region is not reliable and does not conform to international standards. The majority of the hotel stock shown in Table 2.3 would probably not be considered wholly acceptable to a Western tourist.

Table 2.4 highlights a growing dichotomy for the region's hotels. The major chains have, not surprisingly, shown interest in taking over or developing hotels in the capital cities of Eastern Europe, creating large and prestigious four- and five-star hotels. However, in very few cases are these companies engaging in joint ventures or equity participation. Their involvement is essentially on the basis of franchise agreements or equity-free management contracts. Slattery (1992) only cites two examples of joint ventures, both in Warsaw, by Marriott Corporation and Forte Hotels.

Business demand in these cities, in particular, is currently running so high that there is a shortage of accommodation, and occupancies and profits are good. This should provide further incentives for companies to develop more upmarket properties in these cities. A recent review of the tourism potential of the former Soviet states (Lennon, 1992) identified thirteen proposed hotel developments in Moscow alone since 1990, with chains ranging from

Table 2.4 Hotel affiliation, 1991

Country	Room stock	Affiliated to publicly quoted companies worldwide				
		Number	Concentration (%)	Rooms in capital city	% of country total	Capital
Bulgaria	55 000	1301	2.4	982	75.5	Sofia
Czechoslovakia	40 000	1155	2.9	925	80.1	Prague
Hungary	26 000	1550	6.0	1550	100	Budapest
Poland	26 000	3459	13.3	2164	62.6	Warsaw
Romania	15 000	423	2.8	423	100	Bucharest
USSR	75 000	158	0.3	158	100	Moscow

Source: Kleinwort Benson Securities. (1991).

Sheraton and Holiday Inn to Kempinski and Oberoi. Again, Slattery (1992) believes all of these to be based on local capital investment.

The chains, however, represent only a very small percentage of the total room stock of the countries – ranging from 0.3 percent in the USSR to 13.3 percent in Poland. In some cases 100 percent of these rooms are in the capital cities. This leaves the vast majority of the hotel stock, probably still owned by the state, although increasingly being moved into private hands, located in secondary towns or resort areas. These hotels need investment to upgrade their facilities, but they are unlikely to attract much outside backing. Internal funding is in very short supply.

Table 2.5 shows the dominance of the state-owned hotel chains in owner- ship of the hotel stock. The majority of these chains are reported to be up for privatization, but finding buyers is proving to be difficult. Even the state- owned Interhotel chain in East Germany was purchased not by a Western hotel chain, but by a property developer. Subsequently, this developer has managed to sell only one of the hotels in the East to a Western chain. More recently, it has been suggested that these chains may be listed themselves on an exchange in order to raise equity capital. So far this has not happened.

In summary, the development of the hospitality industry in Eastern Europe will initially be driven by the attraction of high-spending foreign business travelers to key centers. These will be concentrated in capital or major cities. There will also be small pockets of development in resort areas – summer or

Table 2.5 Top twenty companies in Eastern Europe, 1991

Company	Number of hotels	Number of rooms	Main country of operation
Balkantourist	386	58 250	Bulgaria
Intourist	112	27 500	USSR
Cedok	212	14 775	Czechoslovakia
Balnea	330	12 603	Czechoslovakia
Orbis	57	12 000	Poland
Plava Laguna	35	10 117	Yugoslavia
Interhotel	33	9 195	East Germany
Hungarhotel	50	7 381	Hungary
Seibu Saison plc	12	4 596	Major cities
Pannonia	39	4 111	Hungary
Accor	10	2 635	Poland, Bulgaria, USSR, Hungary
Top Portoroz	21	2 267	
Danubis Hotels	16	2 214	Hungary
Bass	4	1 085	
Reso	2	515	
Sol Group	1	492	USSR
Penta	1	394	USSR
Ladbroke	1	323	
ITT/Sheraton	1	187	
New World/Ramada	1	163	Hungary

Source: Krutik (1991).

winter. Overall the development of the industry will be slow due to the lack of domestic demand and of money available for investment.

Current issues

Wherever these hospitality developments are, they will have to overcome a number of serious problems if they are to reach their full potential.

Instability. Any period of rapid social, political and economic change must create or release tensions and instability within a society. The example of Yugoslavia and unrest among many of the former Soviet states provides graphic evidence of this problem. Within other areas the instability may not be so obvious, but the potential for disruption may still exist. Czechoslovakia seemed perfectly settled until the elections signaled a splitting of the Czech and Slovak states. This possibility of unrest, either actual or feared, must cause some doubts in the minds of potential tourists and potential outside investors.

Economic change. Similarly, during a period of economic restructuring and moves toward a more market-based economy, there is bound to be instability in exchange rates, high levels of unemployment and high inflation. These are obviously not the ideal conditions for secure business performance or for a tourist's peace of mind.

Foreign involvement/investment. Franck (1990) suggests that it is beyond the capabilities of Eastern Europe simultaneously to implement the far-reaching economic reforms mentioned above and to finance the necessary investment needed to produce stability and improve the general living standards. Massive inputs of capital will be needed to improve the neglected infrastructure and to begin new developments. Western hotel companies, soon after the Berlin Wall came down, initially expressed a great deal of interest in such developments. However, they are extremely reluctant to invest in this way for two main reasons. First, it is not at all clear who owns what, and hence Western companies cannot be sure what legally they would be getting for their money. Second, socialist accounting principles and standards are so different from those in the West that no meaningful analysis of operational performance or feasibility study is possible.

Currently the emphasis is on franchises and management contracts, which are a very indirect intervention in the economic structure. This approach also means that the host country still retains involvement in what is going on while the foreign partner gains access to the new market. Examples in the tourism and hospitality field include the Taj hotels partnership with Intourist to develop hotels in Moscow, Tashkent, Samarkand and Bukhara. Typically, the state may own the land, the privatized state hotel company or agency would own the property, and the outside hotel company would invest money in the renovation of the property in return for profits. The international chains still face problems with regard to franchises and management contracts. In the case of the former the hotel stock is so poor that it rarely meets the brand specifications. In the case of contracts, details of these agreements take time to complete, especially in countries where obstructive administrative bureaucracy has a long history.

Supply of materials and equipment. Businesses in the West have begun to realize the importance of their suppliers in the chain of operations that deliver quality to the customer. Unfortunately, it is still difficult to guarantee the quality and continuity of local supplies of raw materials, construction materials or equipment. This means that a large part of a business's supplies, particularly during renovation, must be brought in from outside. This obviously increases the costs and the time taken in obtaining import licenses and arranging shipment.

General infrastructure. Forty years of regarding the infrastructure as of low priority in allocating budgets has left the transport and telecommunications networks in a serious state of neglect. Although there are variations from country to country, the roads are in general need of updating. They are acceptable in Czechoslovakia and Hungary, at least on the main routes, worse in Bulgaria and Poland, and very difficult in Romania and the USSR. The railway system outside Czechoslovakia and Hungary is unreliable, slow and not very clean; in some cases, as recent accidents in the USSR have shown, it is downright unsafe, due to neglect of track and signals. The telecommunications network is chaotic. In Hungary a business may have to wait years for a new telephone line. In Poland it is a similar picture. Moscow does not even have a telephone directory for the city. This lack of infrastructure extends to tourist needs as well. Outside the main cities, there are very few banks, few retail outlets and practically no tourist information offices. The museums are well stocked but not really geared to the needs and expectations of the foreign visitor.

Labor. Hotel operations in Eastern Europe demonstrate an extreme paradox – a high degree of overmanning but a huge skill shortage. The socialist philosophy of ensuring full employment has meant that hotels are staffed with many more employees than would be the case in the West. However, these workers are poorly trained and achieve low standards of performance. The low priority of tourism on the political and economic agenda has left Eastern Europe with few schools and colleges offering courses in hotel and catering skills. Those schools that there are have turned out some very good people, but the current expansion of the industry leaves the labor pool woefully short of skilled labor. At the same time the hotel companies moving into the area have found that many staff who have previously worked in hotels and restaurants do not have the right approach to the customer. This has meant a heavy emphasis on training. In some cases, hotels have preferred to recruit staff with no previous experience of the industry so that they can be developed from scratch to meet that company's standards and service philosophy (Trollope, 1992). Bringing employees up to the productivity standards of their Western counterparts is also going to be a major challenge.

Ownership. An issue facing those companies wanting to purchase sites in the area is the difficulty of identifying clear title on the land. Land which was previously confiscated under Nazi or Russian occupation is now being reclaimed. As these 'owners' may now be many thousands of miles away, tracing absolute title will be very difficult (Scott and Renaghan, 1991).

Future trends

There can be no doubt that Eastern Europe and the former Soviet states offer a tremendous variety of exciting destinations for holiday tourism. The region has historical cities, fine beaches and magnificent mountains. There are currently shortages of hospitality services in the capital cities and existing resorts, and international companies are making efforts to take advantage of the opportunities this offers.

The hospitality services available outside these centers are much less developed and are likely to remain so. Small rural and highly seasonal developments are much less attractive to outside investors, and internal funding is limited. Holiday visitors are most likely to visit the area as part of some package, as a 'city break', a beach-based holiday center or a ski resort. Independent travelers will find that although access is relatively easy, the lack of expected facilities and services will make the holiday more of an adventure than some visitors will be prepared to accept. The potential for business tourism is also enormous. According to the Kleinwort Benson (1991) structural theory of hotel business demand, Eastern Europe and the Soviet states fall into Phase I. In this phase, economies that are dominated by extractive and manufacturing industries and single-site firms are seen to have a low level of domestic business demand. The only business travelers are sales, marketing and distribution executives. As the service sector grows and the number of national service multiples increases, so the economy enters Phase II and business travel expands to service these new businesses. In Phase III, when the corporate structures of such service multiples become settled, business travel remains at a high level but does not show the growth achieved in Phase II. The UK moved into Phase II in the mid-1970s and is just moving into Phase III. Continental Europe is seen to be on the edge of moving into Phase II. It will take quite some time for Eastern Europe to catch up.

This explains why Kleinwort Benson are skeptical about the international hotel groups' espoused interest in developing in Eastern Europe. They see it as the fashionable thing to do rather than indicative of any real commitment. They suggest that 'Eastern Europe will not provide a substantial part of international hotel company portfolios for many decades to come ... we see no hope whatsoever of any real domestic market developing until well into the next century'. In particular, there is a 'capital famine' in the West that is increasingly making participation in East European economies less likely. First, the only country in Europe with a high level of corporate financing expertise is the UK. Financiers in the UK are currently reluctant to invest outside of the UK due to its economic troubles, and are focusing on investing in their own country as a means of helping to solve these problems. They see the East as a very high-risk investment.

This rather pessimistic view is in contrast to the buoyant reports of development activity in the trade journals. It seems likely that such reports are rhetoric rather than reality. Although a number of high-profile deals have been signed and many more are reported to be under negotiation, the full revival of the tourism and hospitality industry of Eastern Europe and the Soviet states will be a long-term process.

References

Baum, C. (1990) 'Here come the hotel chains', *Hotels*, October, pp. 71–4.

Buckley, P. J., and Witt, S. F. (1987) 'The tourism market in Eastern Europe', *Service Industries Journal*, vol. 7, no. 1, pp. 91–104.

Buckley, P. J., and Witt, S. F. (1990) 'Tourism in the centrally-planned economies of Europe', *Annals of Tourism Research*, vol. 17, no. 1, pp. 7–18.

Carper, S. (1990) 'The east is open', *Hotels*, October, pp. 66–9.

Caselli, G. P., and Pastrello, G. (1992) 'The service sector in planned economies of Eastern Europe: past experiences and future perspectives', *Service Industries Journal*, vol. 12, no. 2, pp. 220–37.

Franck, C. (1990) 'Tourism investment in central and eastern Europe', *Tourism Management*, December, pp. 333–8.

Hall, D. R. (ed.) (1991) *Tourism and Economic Development in Eastern Europe and the Soviet Union*, London: Bellhaven Press.

Kerpel, E. (1990a) 'Tourism potential in Eastern Europe', *Travel and Tourism Analyst*, vol. 1, pp. 68–86, London: Economist Intelligence Unit.

Kerpel, E. (1990b) *Tourism in Eastern Europe and the Soviet Union: Special report no. 2042*, London: Economist Intelligence Unit.

Kleinwort Benson Securities (1991) *Quoted Hotel Companies: The world markets*, 5th annual review, London: Kleinwort Benson Securities.

Krutik, J. S. (1991) *The European Hotel Industry: The race is on*, New York: Salomon Brothers.

Lennon, J. (1992) 'Opening the box: unlocking the tourism potential of the former Soviet States', International Association of Hotel Management Schools Conference, Manchester Polytechnic, UK, 7–9 May.

Scott, J. F., and Renaghan, L. M. (1991) 'Hotel development in eastern Germany: opportunities and obstacles', *Cornell Hotel and Restaurant Quarterly*, October, pp. 44–51.

Slattery, P. (1992) *Quoted Hotel Companies: The European Markets*, London: Kleinwort Benson Securities.

Trollope, K. (1992) 'In Moscow business begins with basic training', *Hotels*, May, pp. 63–4.

The World Bank (1991) *World Bank Atlas*, Washington: World Bank.

World Tourism Organization (1992) *Compendium of Tourism Statistics*, Madrid: WTO.

World Travel and Tourism Review (1992).

3

North America

Michael Haywood

The United States of America and Canada, the focus of this chapter, are two of the largest and wealthiest nations in the world. In 1991 the gross domestic product for the USA amounted to $5672.6 billion or, on a per capita basis, $22 456 (all $ amounts cited for the USA are in US dollars). Canada's gross domestic product was $679 billion or $23 717 per capita (all $ amounts for Canada are in Canadian dollars). It is estimated that tourism contributed $329 billion dollars to the US economy and $25 billion to the Canadian economy. The industry sectors benefiting from tourism include transportation, lodging, travel facilitation, foodservice, entertainment and recreation. Related consumer expenditures are also made in a vast array of retail businesses for the purchase of such items as travel/recreation equipment, supplies and gasoline. Tourism businesses also purchase numerous goods and services to operate and to serve their clientele, so the economic spin-offs are significant.

The hospitality industry, comprised of lodging and foodservice, depends to a great extent on tourism and travel activity. However, hospitality cannot be subsumed totally under the tourism umbrella. Restaurants and hotels not only cater to the leisure requirements of people in communities, but provide vital business services to organizations which want to feed and entertain their customers, clients or employees. Hospitality is a huge industry in its own right. Its economic contribution in 1991 amounted to $330 billion in the USA and $33 billion in Canada. Of this only 15–20 percent of foodservice revenue is attributed to tourism.

To appreciate the complex, contextual issues of the hospitality and tourism industries within North America, this chapter starts with a socioeconomic overview, with information pertaining to consumer markets, consumption patterns and a broader view of the economic climate within each country. The hospitality industry and tourism activity are then examined. The chapter concludes with a brief discussion of current and future trends affecting the growth and development of hospitality tourism.

Socioeconomic profile: United States

In 1990, 250 million people resided in the USA. By the year 2010, the population is expected to grow to 283 million, an average annual growth rate of 0.6 percent. The most significant aspect of population growth, however, is the age group shift. As Table 3.1 suggests, the 'baby-boomer bubble', a large group of people born between 1945 and 1955, represents a vital market for hospitality and tourism. In 1989, for example, the baby boomers were the highest per week spenders on food away from home: $45.79 (US Department of Labor, Bureau of Labor Statistics, 1988–9). The 45–54-year-old age group is forecast to grow from 25 million in 1989, to 37 million in the year 2000, and 43 million in 2010, or 15 percent of the population.

The acceleration of the 65-and-over population is also notable because of the assumptions about increased buying power (Dychtwald, 1990). By the year 2010 this market will represent 14 percent of the population, up from 12.9 percent in 1989. In anticipation of growing and changing demand for services, some hospitality firms in the USA are expanding into 'life care' products. However, there is serious concern for the ever-increasing costs associated with the entitlements that retirees consider their rightful due. If benefits to the elderly are trimmed and pension funds deemed inadequate, this market is unlikely to provide the financial windfall that the hospitality/tourism industry now expects.

Important geographic population shifts are also occurring. In 1960, 24.9 percent of the population lived in the north-east. In 1990 this figure was down to 20.4 percent and it is expected to fall to 19.6 percent in the year 2000. The US Bureau of the Census expects a similar decline in the Midwest. The beneficiaries are the south, which will increase its share of the population from 30.7 percent in 1960 to 35.7 percent in 2000, and the west, where growth will be from 15.6 to 22.1 percent during the same time period.

Interestingly, consumer expenditures also vary by region. For example, the US Department of Labor (1991) indicates that average foodservice expenditures were highest, at $1971 per year, in the north-east, and lowest, at $1619, in the south. Such variations may be due to many factors – opportunity, need and financial wherewithal.

Hospitality and tourism expenditures do correlate with disposable personal income. As incomes rise, so do expenditures on travel and eating out. With the number of people in the $50 000+ family income bracket increasing from

Table 3.1 US Population by age group, 1989–2010

Year	1–17	18–24	25–34	35–44	45–54	55–64	65+	Total
1989	64 082	26 564	44 048	36 584	24 905	21 593	30 984	248 762
1995	65 173	24 281	40 962	42 336	31 297	22 325	33 764	271 135
2000	65 713	25 231	37 149	43 911	37 223	24 158	34 882	268 266
2005	64 082	26 918	35 997	40 951	41 619	29 761	36 274	275 604
2010	62 646	27 155	37 572	37 202	43 207	35 430	39 362	282 575

Source: US Bureau of the Census, *Current Population Report*, Series P–25, nos. 519, 917, 1045, 1057 and 1018.

15 percent in 1970 to 24.6 percent in 1990, it is not surprising to find that the hospitality/tourism industry has undergone tremendous expansion, particularly in the 1980s, to meet the needs of this growing leisure-oriented market.

Consumer spending patterns are also linked to the amount of time people spend working, the type of job and their overall level of employment. Despite unemployment rates ranging from highs of 9.5 percent in 1982 and 1983 to a low of 5.2 percent in 1989, employment levels grew throughout the 1980s. In 1990 the labor force was comprised of 124.8 million people, representing 66.4 per cent of the civilian population 16 years of age and over. By the year 2000, it is forecasted that 141.1 million people will be in the labor force, or 69 percent of the population 16 years old and older. In 1989 the actual number of people employed was 117.3 million; the number of unemployed was 6.6 million. Of those employed, 53 million were women. Their participation in the workforce has increased, on average, by 3.1 percent per year since 1970. With the increase in two-wage-earner families has come an increased demand for convenience, the need for child care and the overall requirement for more services.

The macro context of the US economy also has profound effects on the hospitality/tourism sectors and their performance. Table 3.2 summarizes some of the key economic indicators. While the country is in the midst of recovering from a deep recession, it appears as if the economic rebound will be sluggish. For example, at the time of writing, the Conference Board's Consumer Confidence Index remains low. All questions concern jobs. In the 1980s the movement to global trade hurt many factory workers whose companies competed with foreign rivals. As these people were laid off or suffered wage cuts, a glut of job candidates helped keep wage rates down. Affected across a wide spectrum of industries were 64 million workers who never went beyond high school. The college-educated fared better. The 54 million people in the USA blessed with high skills were fortified by the fact that new

Table 3.2 USA: Major economic factors

	1990	1991
Gross domestic product (US$bn)	5 514	5 673
Gross domestic product (constant 1987 US$bn)	4 885	4 849
Net exports (US$bn)	−74.4	−30.7
Net exports (constant 1987 US$bn)	−51.4	−20.8
Disposable personal income (US$bn)	4 059	4 218
Savings rate (%)	5.09	5.21
Population (000s)	249 811	252 585
Labor force (000s)	124 801	125 316
Employment (000s)	117 917	116 870
Unemployment rate (%)	5.52	6.74
Consumer Price Index (1980 = 100)	158.6	165.4

Source: US Department of Commerce (1992).

technologies increased demand for the work they did. But even they were not insulated from foreign competition, new technology, the recessionary period and the massive restructuring of companies throughout the country.

Many economists are convinced that the newly signed North American Free Trade Agreement (NAFTA) between the USA, Mexico and Canada, and any new GATT deal will add to world GDP growth, lift manufacturing output and create tens of thousands of new US jobs. There is concern, however, that the agreements will leave labor-intensive industries even more vulnerable to foreign rivals. As a result, economic growth may slow, the poverty rate stay up, and the tab for welfare and unemployment mount, inflating taxes. A worst-case scenario suggests that resentment of the wealthy could lead to class warfare and riots like those in Los Angeles in 1992.

Prospects for future US economic growth are predicated not only on job creation but on productivity growth. As measured by GNP per person employed, productivity growth was only 1.0 percent during the 1970–90 period. This has been attributed to a marked slowdown in capital formation, a drop in per worker constant dollar expenditure on infrastructure, and declines in the quality and quantity of education (to name a few factors). However, it is expected that reductions in US national defense outlays, increases in the computerization of capital goods (i.e. a shift to 'smart machines' and 'smart buildings'), improvements in education, and a slowdown in the growth of the labor force could result in productivity growth of 1.1 percent in the 1990s, and higher in the following decades (Terlekyj, 1991).

Besides jobs, economic recovery is also signaled by sales figures and debt load. As of mid-1992, retail sales had yet to rebound, though car sales were increasing slightly. Residential real estate was in the doldrums and commercial real estate was in a dismal state. Of the 170 US hotels sold in 1990, for example, the average selling price per room fell from $21 539 in 1990 to $18 400 in 1991 (Jusko, 1992). More problematic has been the inability to manage the explosion of debt. It went from 140 percent of GNP in 1980 to 190 percent in 1990, and is conservatively estimated to amount to $11 trillion. Of this amount, $4 trillion is private (household sector) debt, $3.6 trillion non-financial corporation debt, and $3.4 trillion government debt. The latter continues to increase – partly due to the savings and loan industry crisis. As a result, there is an urgent need for action.

Finally, it is worth noting the impact of politics on the country's economic future. As an election year, 1992 fuelled protectionist sentiment, particularly among those people whose jobs have disappeared. US domestic policies continue to demand attention, but the country, while remaining the only super-power left, operates in a new political world – a world comprised of umbrella-type organizations (now dictated by trade zones, the United Nations, the World Bank and the International Monetary Fund), and enduring tribalism brought about by smaller nationalistic states breaking away from and destroying larger nation states, such as the Soviet Union, Yugoslavia and Czechoslovakia. This new reality requires cooperation and coordination as politicians struggle to act globally while protecting the interests of their home constituencies.

Socioeconomic framework: Canada

According to Statistics Canada, Canada's population in 1990 was 26.6 million, representing an annual increase of 0.97 percent since 1981. About 36.5 percent of the population reside in the province of Ontario and 25.5 percent in Quebec. There has been a population shift to the west, particularly to the provinces of Alberta and British Columbia, which have 9.3 and 11.6 percent of the population respectively. About 8.8 percent of the population live in the Atlantic provinces, 7.9 percent in the prairie provinces, and 0.3 percent in Yukon and the Northwest Territories. Similar to the USA, Canada's urban population has increased dramatically, to 76 percent. The population age group shifts are also similar to those in the USA. The 1986 census revealed a median age of 31.6 years, up from 29.6 in 1981. The number of Canadians aged 65 and over rose 14.3 percent to 2.7 million; and the 35–44 age group increased by 22.7 percent to 3.6 million.

In 1986 the number of households in Canada increased by 8.6 percent from 1981 to approximately 9 million, with an average of 2.8 people per household. About 84 percent of Canadians lived in families, a total of 6.7 million with an average family size of 3.2 members. It is expected that family size will continue to decline, though by 1996 eight million families are forecast. In 1990 Canada's total labor force amounted to 13.68 million people, of which 12.57 million were employed and 1.109 million unemployed. The unemployment rate was 8.1 percent, but it increased in 1991 to 10.3 percent due to the economic recession. The latter also caused real disposable incomes to fall, reducing consumer spending in 1991 and leaving consumers with very low savings at year end. As of 1991, personal disposable income was $468 395 million, up 3.2 percent over 1990, and the personal savings rate was 10.05 percent down 0.8 percent.

In 1991 retail sales fell 2.3 percent from 1990, to $179 130 million. Restaurant receipts amounted to $17 821.9 million, virtually the same as in 1990. On a per capita basis, restaurant expenditures amounted to $670 (or 4.1 percent of personal disposable income). These figures amount to 27 percent of total food expenditures (Statistics Canada, 1991). According to a poll taken by Market Facts (1992), and commissioned by the Canadian Restaurant and Foodservice Association, budget-minded customers had cut back most often on clothing (44 percent), groceries (32 percent) and dining out (32 percent). It would appear that eating out has become part of Canadians' everyday lifestyle; 'luxury' occasions may be eliminated rather than the 'necessary' ones.

As in the USA, expenditures on eating out vary considerably by income group, geographic region and other consumer demographics. For example, people in the lowest income group spend only 13 percent of their total food dollars on this activity, as compared to 33 percent in the top income category

($60 000+). Average spending by a family in St John's, Newfoundland, was only $936 in 1986, as compared to $1727 for a typical family in Toronto, Ontario. Single, unattached individuals spent 40 percent of their food budget in restaurants, whereas families of five or more persons spent 20 percent (Statistics Canada, 1986a). In 1990 Canadians spent a total of $22 001 million in restaurants and hotels combined. These expenditures fell to $18 770 million in 1991.

A summary of economic indicators for Canada is contained in Table 3.3. Overall, Canada's economy barely grew between 1990 and 1991. In fact, real gross domestic product dropped 3.6 percent from peak to trough. A fundamental reason for Canada's slow emergence from recession has been that the cyclical downturn coincided with the need for massive industrial restructuring to restore the country's competitiveness. The restructuring process has involved the closing of some manufacturing plants and retail distribution outlets. Due to the free trade agreements, some production has moved and will continue to move to the United States or Mexico.

As of mid-1992, the Canadian retail sector had not rebounded. Spending was held down by high unemployment, slow growth in incomes, low levels of consumer confidence and high household debt burdens. As comparisons between the consumer price indexes in Canada and the USA indicate, Canadians have found it considerably cheaper to shop in the USA. Cross-border shopping has been a major drain on Canada's retail trade, and demonstrates that competitive restructuring, now taking place, is much needed. While the number of same-day trips by Canadians to the United States, an indicator of the problem, may have peaked, it appears that Canadians have a low regard for the goods and services tax (GST) introduced on 1 January 1991. It has increased prices beyond what many people consider to be reasonable.

With interest rates expected to decline throughout 1992–3, the momentum of Canada's economic recovery could be strong. If employment growth is rapid, personal incomes rise and inflation is controlled, consumer

Table 3.3 Canada: Major economic factors

	1990	1991
Gross domestic product (Can $m)	667 843	647 388
Gross domestic product (constant 1986 Can $m)	563 060	553 457
Net exports (Can $m)	9 920	5 780
Net exports (constant 1986 Can $m)	3 232	1 331
Disposable personal income (Can $m)	453 630	467 151
Savings rate (%)	10.1	10.3
Population (000s)	26 610	27 296
Labor force (000s)	13 681	13 757
Employment (000s)	12 572	12 340
Unemployment rate (%)	8.1	10.3
Consumer Price Index (1980 = 100)	177.8	187.8

Source: Statistics Canada, *Canadian Economic Observer*, 6/92; National Institute, *Economic Review*, 2/92, no. 140. Reproduced with the permission of the Canadian Minister of Industry, Science and Technology, 1993.

spending, which accounts for 60 percent of Canadian economic activity, will intensify. Growing domestic demand and lower interest rates will provide firms with an opportunity to increase capital spending, though this is not expected to be as strong as in 1986–8. During 1992–3, the Canadian dollar is expected to fall to around the 82 US cent mark, as Canada–United States short-term interest rate spreads narrow appreciably. The effect of this depreciation of the Canadian dollar should create a period of strong growth in Canada's merchandise exports and a steady improvement in the current account deficit.

Risks to this forecast are the intensity of structural changes brought about by the free trade agreements, the ability of the US economy to recover from the recession, the strength of the US dollar, and the ability of both federal and provincial governments to implement deficit-reducing fiscal policies. For example, the Canadian government has projected that the $34.4 billion deficit in 1991–2 will fall to $5.5 billion in 1996–7, though growing fiscal deficits at the provincial levels could offset this trend and maintain upward pressure on interest rates. A political factor of some consequence is Quebec's future role in the Canadian Confederation. A Canada-wide referendum held in the fall of 1992, aimed at resolving this issue, led to the rejection of the constitutional amendment and continued uncertainty.

Tourism

In North America, tourism may be the least understood and respected of industries. It lacks the cachet of being high-tech; it is not highly visible or tangible; and the jobs are perceived as low-paying and servile. Yet its economic impact is substantial. As Table 3.4 reveals, domestic and international receipts in 1990 amounted to $329 billion in the United States (6 percent of GNP), and $25 billion in Canada. International tourism ranked as Canada's third most important earner of foreign exchange, behind motor vehicles and autoparts. The US Travel Data Center (1991) stated that in 1990 travel and tourism directly supported 5.9 million jobs, more than 5 percent of total non-agricultural payroll, thus making it a leading private employer, second only to health services. Since 1972 tourism jobs have more than doubled, while total US payroll employment increased by less than one-half. It is estimated that tourism in Canada provides approximately 614 000 direct jobs.

Domestic tourism has been the major contributor: for example, in 1990 it accounted for 88 percent of tourism expenditures in the USA and in Canada. However, its potential for growth may be limited. Approximately 22.4 million Canadians aged 15 and over made an overnight non-business trip in Canada in 1990. However, with population growth taken into account, domestic travel participation did not increase between 1986 and 1988, and was lower in 1990 than in 1984. Domestic tourism growth in the USA may not be as threatened as in Canada due to the large number of sun destinations, but people are tending towards taking shorter trips (in 1990,

Table 3.4(a)   Canada: Tourism receipts and payments, 1989–91 (Can $m)

	1989	1990	1991
Receipts			
Domestic tourism	17 900	18 400	16 800
United States of America	4 277	4 407	4 519
Other countries	1 955	3 341	3 283
Payments			
United States of America	6 602	9 289	10 804
Other countries	3 106	5 218	4 561
Balance			
United States of America	− 2 325	− 4 882	− 6 285
Other countries	− 1 151	− 1 877	− 1 278

Table 3.4(b)   USA: Tourism receipts and payments, 1989–90 (US $m)

	1989	1990
Receipts		
Domestic tourism	294 000	288 000
Other countries	28 571	31 290
Payments		
Canada	n/a	n/a
Other countries	30 271	34 264
Balance		
Canada	n/a	n/a
Other countries	− 1 700	− 2 974

Source: Statistics Canada, *International Travel*, 66–001; US Travel Data Center, *Economic Review of Travel in America 1990–91*. Reproduced with the permission of the Canadian Minister of Industry, Science and Technology, 1993.

62 percent of all trips lasted three nights or less), and in recent years travel prices have risen faster than the Consumer Price Index.

Travel abroad has tremendous appeal. For example, the number of Canadians traveling to the USA has increased dramatically. About 19 percent of the Canadian population took at least one non-business trip in 1984; the travel rate increased to 23 percent in 1988 and 28 percent in 1990, and should be considerably higher in both 1991 and 1992. Influencing factors for the trend have been a favorable exchange rate, harsh weather in Canada, the imposition of the goods and services tax (GST) and perceived shopping and travel bargains. Overseas destinations also claimed an increasing market share during the 1980s, though in 1991 there was a drop of 10 percent from the previous year. The recession, higher air fares and perceived security concerns seem to have restricted growth, though for the first part of 1992 there has been a resurgence in travel to both the USA and Europe.

Expenditures by Canadians traveling outside their country amounted to

$15.4 billion in 1991. Since foreign visitors only spent $7.8 billion, Canada's deficit in its international travel account shot up to $7.5 billion. For 1992 it is expected to be an astounding $8.5 billion. In contrast, the USA enjoyed a surplus of $1.9 billion in 1990 in its travel account, particularly due to the contribution of Canadians and a pent-up demand from Europeans and the Japanese who, because of favourable exchange rates, view travel to the USA as a bargain. Indeed, foreign visitor expenditures have risen by 129 percent since the US dollar peaked in value in 1985.

According to Tourism Canada, tourism revenues in Canada are distributed to various segments in the following percentage amounts: transportation 41 percent, food and beverage 25 percent, accommodation 16 percent, recreation and entertainment 8 percent, and miscellaneous 12 percent. Of these sectors, transportation, particularly air transportation, deserves special comment because the future state of the industry will have a significant impact on who will be traveling where and at what cost. Since deregulation in 1978, numerous US airlines have gone out of business or have been absorbed by a few dominant carriers. The marketplace has ruled that bigger is better, and barriers to entry are very high. As a result, a 'natural monopoly' seems to be occurring because the bigger companies enjoy lower average costs and huge cost savings that result from marketing advantages associated with scale, i.e. market power from an integrated hub-and-spoke system; the ability to price selectively using yield management systems so as to maximize airline revenues and undercut low-fare carriers; frequent-flyer programs that act as a barrier to entry; hidden bonus commissions, 'overrides', to travel agencies to steer bookings to a specific airline; and abuse of airline computer reservation systems.

While deregulation has led to vastly increased service, the problem is that broader services and lower fares are unlikely to endure in both the United States and Canada. The cost of air travel will increase significantly, particularly in single-carrier markets. The big questions are: will concentration of the industry remain unabated; will there be calls for re-regulation; and are there competitive strategies to realize the promise of deregulation?

The hospitality industry

The hospitality industry is composed of lodging and foodservice./Lodging includes room, food, beverage and miscellaneous revenues generated from hotels, motels, trailer parks and camps/Foodservice refers to sales of food and beverages sold in a wide variety of commercial outlets (restaurants, fast-food outlets, cafeterias, bars, department and convenience stores, recreation venues) and institutional settings (hospitals and other health or extended care facilities, schools, businesses, transportation, military). Hospitality in North America is a $350 billion + industry that employs an estimated 9 million in the United States and 650 000 in Canada.

The National Restaurant Association estimates that there are 537 000 commercial food service units, 172 000 institutional units and 1000 military units operating within the United States. For 1988, in Canada, best estimates suggest 36 900 commercial outlets; 15 000 accommodation businesses (most of which have one or more food and beverage outlets); 28 000 leisure-oriented and residential care facilities; 16 000 schools, colleges and universities; 210 National Defense units; and 183 prisons. Not included in these counts are other food service outlets in gas stations, pharmacies, supermarkets, factories and offices (Haywood and Bauer, 1990).

Foodservice

In the United States, foodservice has shown continuous growth over the past 20 years with the exception of 1974 and 1980. According to the International Foodservice Manufacturers' Association, average annual real growth has been 2.3 percent with the restaurant segment achieving an average annual real growth of 4–5 percent. In 1992, as shown in Table 3.5, industry sales amounted to approximately $255 billion, with commercial restaurant sales at

Table 3.5 The hospitality industry estimated revenues: USA (1992) and Canada, 1991

	USA (U$m)	Canada (Can $m)
Foodservice		
Eating and drinking places	190 855	17 852
Department stores	10 607	238
Other retail establishments		199 *
Lodging	15 170	3 800 *
Recreation	8 100	1 100 *
Total commercial	224 732	23 189
Hospitals	10 643	1 500
Residential care	4 845	370 *
Education	12 904	560 *
Business and industry	7 255	295 *
Vending	5 777	388
Transportation	3 097	610 *
Military	1 163	225 *
(Adjustment for catered service)	– 15 494	– 1 500 *
*Total non commercial**	30 190	2 448
Total foodservice	254 922	25 637
Lodging room sales	36 000	7 800 *
Total hospitality industry	290 922	33 437

* Estimates
Sources: International Foodservice Manufacturers' Assoc., *Foodservice Encyclopedia*, 1992; National Restaurant Association; Canadian Foodservice and Restaurant Association InfoStats; Statistics Canada, 63–011, 63–204, 63–233, 63–002, 62–213, 51–206.
Note: US and Canadian data are not totally comparable due to differences in definitions and categories. Reproduced with permission of the Canadian Minister of Industry, Science and Technology, 1993.

$225 billion and institutional at $30 billion. In Canada, since 1980, average annual growth has been in the 11 percent range. Revenues in 1991 are expected to reach $23 billion for the commercial operations and just over $2 billion for institutional, producing a total of 25.6 billion. The fastest growth in both the USA and Canada has come from fast-food and large chain/ franchise organizations. In the USA the number of units has doubled since 1972, while sales of $78 billion in 1991 represented an eightfold increase.

Major chain organizations dominate certain menu categories. In the quick-service restaurant sector and measured on the basis of market share, the regional chains in the USA controlled 92 percent of the hamburger category, 76 percent of the chicken category, 51 percent of pizza, 67 percent of ice cream, 79 percent of fish/seafood and 80 percent of Mexican, for a total of 63 percent of the quick-service restaurant market. In the midscale format (family/sit-down) chains had 27 percent of the market share, with predominance in the steak house category. The presence of chains in the upscale category is minimal; they held an 8 percent share of the market in 1991 (IFMA, 1992).

In the near term, many experts sense that the proliferation of foodservice outlets will slow down. Arguments regarding the 'maturity of the industry', 'saturation' and 'overcapacity' have been heard for years. Yet the development of niche markets associated with grocery and convenience store foodservice, child care, elderly care and recreational outlets continues. New locations, new concepts and different menus, all aimed at enhancing convenience, providing variety and meeting the changing lifestyles of consumers, will continue to emerge. While long-term growth rates for the industry will not be near the levels achieved during the 1980s, industry forecasts suggest that full-menu operators should average 1.0 percent real growth, while limited-menu restaurants are expected to post 2.0 percent annual real growth through 1996.

Non-commercial foodservice has also grown in importance. This segment represents 19 percent of total foodservice revenues in the USA (when catered service is factored in), and 19 percent in Canada. Changes in non-commercial food services are dictated by the requirements of the organizations that hire them. For example, in health care, many institutions are rethinking their foodservice strategies in light of reduced budgets and shorter patient stays. Health care foodservice directors are aiming to stretch their dollars, maintain or reduce labor costs and search out new sources of revenue beyond patient feeding. It is expected that, within the institutional segment, the contract portion will continue to grow at significantly faster rates than internal operations.

Lodging

In the USA there are 14 350 hotels, 16 000 motels and 4500 trailer parks and camps operating (US Department of Commerce, 1987). Smith Travel Research (1992) estimated that in 1990 there were 3 066 000 hotel rooms available for sale, a 2.4 percent increase from 1990. The Canadian lodging sector is comprised of 4922 hotels and motor hotels, 4150 motels, 1613 tourist courts and guest houses, 2399 camping grounds and trailer parks, and 1699 recreation and vacation camps – a 6.7 percent increase in the total number of locations from 1988. Total revenues for the Canadian lodging sector amounted to $8090 million, 44 percent being generated from rooms, 25 percent from alcoholic beverages, 22 percent from food and 9 percent miscellaneous (Statistics Canada, 1987–9).

Because the lodging industry is dependent on tourism, it is worth noting that travel activity fell appreciably during the recession. According to Coopers and Lybrand's *Forecast and Analysis for the Hospitality Industry* (1992), occupancy rates during the first quarter of 1991 hit their lowest levels in 20 years – 55.8 percent. Smith Travel Research (1992) reported a 60.9 percent average occupancy in the US hotel sector for 1991, and an average daily rate of $58.94 – a 0.4 percent increase from 1990. Falling occupancies and flat room rates are causing losses to escalate. Coopers and Lybrand report that an average $949 per available room was lost in 1989. Performance in 1990 appears to have deteriorated further; over 60 percent of hotels experienced a net loss that year.

While the decade of the 1980s was one of overbuilding and segmentation of hotels, particularly in three categories – all suites, luxury resorts and budget properties – the 1990s, it appears, will be one of conversion and reaffiliation. Some properties will convert to another brand or strike relationships with partners – especially foreign investors – with deep pockets. Well-positioned and well-managed companies may attempt to take advantage of the situation. For example, the Canadian Four Seasons Hotel chain continues to expand into international markets. By acquiring ownership of Regent International Hotels of Hong Kong for only $122 million in 1992, the company has expanded its empire to 43 locations with 14 400 rooms in 17 countries, turning Four Seasons into the world's largest luxury hotel chain. Other companies are forging partnerships around the world. Radisson, for example, is linked with chains such as Mövenpick (Switzerland), Edwardian (England) and Hotel des Gouverneurs (Canada). However, relative to UK, French and Japanese hotel chains, US and Canadian penetration of foreign markets is relatively poor. For instance, Hilton Hotels Corporation of America has fewer than ten hotels outside the US, and Marriott Corporation about thirty.

Current and future issues

As the preceding comments suggest, there are pressing issues facing the North American tourism and hospitality industries. Foodservice companies are having difficulty finding economically feasible sites in a saturated marketplace. Depending on the type of business and market served, the challenge will be to find non-traditional venues, such as multi-concept shared sites, and mobile carts, kiosks and down-scaled units in alternative locations such as schools, supermarkets and airports. Some firms are experiencing difficulty in finding and training capable managers and employees, and keeping labor costs down. Computerization, automation and/or centralization of food production may create savings, including shrinking the size of kitchens. Concern about health and food safety are challenging menu makers. Virtually every foodservice company wants a healthful image along with offering flavorful, convenient food at a moderate price.

Increases in minimum wages, payment of health benefits, government regulations and taxes continue to annoy the industry. A steep increase in the US federal excise tax (FET) on alcoholic beverages, the FICA tax on tips, and the Canadian GST are typical irritants that are increasing the cost of dining out. Fast-food restaurants are also feeling the pressure of environment groups to change their packaging and improve the management of solid waste.

Saturation in quick-service restaurant segments and rampant price cutting ('value pricing') signal an ongoing shake-out. The better-managed firms will continue to invest in new products and technology, expand operations (internationally or through purchase of other companies), track lifestyles and consumer trends, and keep customers satisfied while controlling costs.

Excessive building in the lodging industry, brought about by prevailing tax laws (liberal depreciation and tax write-off provisions), market segmentation and lenient lending practices, resulted in the late 1980s in supply growth well in excess of demand, which has fallen significantly. Massive financial restructuring is under way. During the 1990s the big issues will focus on what will happen within the segments. Will the economy properties replace the mid-price, full-service segment as the backbone of the industry? Has the all-suite segment peaked? An issue that needs to be debated is the separation of management and ownership in the industry: do management companies have a sufficient stake in how the property performs for the owner, and are cost structures too high to maintain a preferred image? Finally, while occupancies are expected to recover, management will have to increase revenues. While room rates have lagged behind inflation during the latter part of the 1980s and early 1990s, there is concern as to how quickly they can be raised. Hotel companies may turn to non-rooms revenues, especially from gaming activities, as an alternative.

In the global marketplace, improving competitiveness has become the hot topic. Unfortunately, as far as tourism is concerned, there is little understanding of how it is connected to other industrial sectors of the economy. Tourism plays an acknowledged role in the economies of the United States and Canada, and yet its impact on tourism-dependent communities, the growing concentration of ownership in key sectors, and moves to improve productivity are not well understood. If hospitality and tourism managers are the key factor in determining competitiveness, they will have to identify the kind of information they will require in order to cope with a dynamic and uncertain environment. Attention will also have to be concentrated on a number of key areas. [Market segments must be better understood and defined if viable niche strategies are to be developed.] The phenomenon of 'consumer schizophrenia', whereby the same consumer buys high-end for one product and low-end for another, suggests that thorough research needs to be undertaken on markets – demographically as well as psychographically.

The second challenge is to find ways of improving service. Hospitality and tourism are sales-driven, but managers often fail to take full advantage of their human resources. To break out of the cycle of failure (Heskett, 1986), the whole process of managing people has to be reassessed and changed. This will require a new mind-set toward employees, who need to be trusted, trained to take initiative, and better rewarded for achieving corporate goals.

The third challenge is to build business networks essential for survival. Tourism, by its very nature, involves firms from the same industry, or closely related industry sectors, suppliers, customers, competitors and the non-business infrastructure. The difficulty will be in aligning and harmonizing their competitive strategies for mutual advantage.

References

Canadian Restaurant and Foodservice Association (1992) 'Are consumers cutting back on restaurant spending?', *Eating Out*, vol. 5, no. 1, pp. 1–5.

Coopers and Lybrand (1992) *Hospitality Directions: Forecast and analysis for the hospitality industry*, New York, vol. 1, no. 1.

Dychtwald, Ken (1990) *Age Wave: The challenges and opportunities of an aging America*, New York: Bantam.

Haywood, K. Michael, and Bauer, J. A. (1990) *Foodservice and Hospitality Business Fact File* (8th edn), Toronto: Kotstuch Communications Ltd.

Heskett, James L. (1986) *Managing in the Service Economy*, Boston, Mass.: Harvard Business School Press.

International Foodservice Manufacturers Association (1992) *Foodservice Encyclopedia*, Chicago: IFMA.

Jusko, Jill (1992) 'Broker group launches study', *Hotel and Motel Management*, 27 July.

Market Facts (1992) *Eating Out*, vol. 5, no. 1, pp. 1–4.

Smith Travel Research (1992) *The Lodging Industry*.

Statistics Canada (1986a) *Family Food Expenditures in Canada*, (62–554).

Statistics Canada (1986b) *Census of Canada*.

Statistics Canada (1991) *Restaurant Caterer and Tavern Statistics*.

Statistics Canada (1992) *Current Survey of Business*.

Terleckyj, Nestor (1991) 'Prospects far US economic growth to 2020', *Looking Ahead – National Planning Association*, vol. 13, no. 3, pp. 1–8.

US Bureau of the Census, *Current Population Reports P–20, P–25*.

US Department of Commerce (1992) *Survey of Current Business*.

US Department of Labor, Bureau of Labor Statistics (1991) *Consumer US Expenditure Survey*, August.

US Travel Data Center (1991) *Outlook for Travel and Tourism*, Washington, DC.

4

The Far East
and Australasia

Brian Wise

The Far East and Australasia region encompasses more than one-third of the earth's surface, and comprises a collective of diverse countries and cultures. The common perception of the Asian region over the past decade is that of a region growing at a frantic pace with real GDP growth rates in the range of 7.5 to 10 percent. Such a perception, however, does not accurately reflect the diversity of the region in terms of wealth and growth in individual countries.

During the 1980s selected Asian economies have outperformed OECD countries in terms of economic growth. To better understand countries in the region, they can be divided for the purposes of this chapter into four subareas:

- South-East Asia, which includes the strong growth countries of Singapore, Thailand, Indonesia and Malaysia as well as more undeveloped countries such as Brunei and the Philippines. These countries are members of what is termed the ASEAN group.
- South Asia, or the area often referred to as the Indian subcontinent.
- North-East Asia, which includes Japan, South Korea, Taiwan and the People's Republic of China.
- The South-west Pacific area, including Australia and New Zealand, Hawaii and its nearby Pacific island neighbours.

The above classification includes within each subarea individual countries or groups of countries which play a vital role in the economic growth being experienced in the region as a whole. Such nations include Japan and the group of countries often referred to as the Asian Tigers or the newly industrializing Asian economies: namely, Hong Kong, South Korea, Singapore and Taiwan.

Asia-Pacific economies and growth

While the perception of the region may be that of rapid economic growth from a relatively low base, not all countries are sharing equally in such growth.

The high-profile countries referred to earlier, from which the main source of dynamism comes, are located in North-East Asia: namely, China, Hong Kong, Japan, Korea and Taiwan. This region is now the most important source of world savings. Greene and Isard (1991), after analyzing the relevance of financial structure and policies to economic growth in countries such as Hong Kong, South Korea, Singapore and Taiwan, concluded that differences in financial structures and policies outweighed similarities in those countries. Nevertheless, despite such differences they found two common characteristics stood out: the absence of pressure for monetary expansion to finance large and continuous fiscal deficits; and the fact that none of the four countries allowed its currency to appreciate in real terms solely as a result of inflationary monetary expansion.

Greene and Isard believe that the above countries have achieved remarkable economic transformations over the past three decades based on outward-oriented development strategies. In the view of McKinnon (1973) these transformations have not been without risk. In Korea, for example. in 1965 measures taken to liberalize exchange and trade restrictions resulted in a high inflow of short- and medium-term private capital. The Korean authorities avoided imposing restrictions on inflow and accepted a rapid accumulation of international reserves and external obligations along with substantial monetary expansion. This, in turn, led to higher inflation and a major devaluation of the won in June 1971.

The dynamic Asian economies referred to above, which have followed the lead of Japan, have grown at a real average rate of almost 9 percent during the 1980s – three times that for a typical mature industrialized country. In contrast, Australia's growth rate in the 1980s was 3.5 percent and New Zealand's 2.4 percent.

Chia (1991) calculates that, based on a continuation of the growth rates of the 1980s, Taiwan, South Korea and Singapore will have higher standards of living than Australia by the year 2000 or shortly after. Byrnes (1991) believes that, while most Asian economies will continue to grow through the 1990s, the strongest performers, Thailand, Malaysia, Singapore and South Korea, will experience marginal decreases from growth rates experienced in the 1980s. Allen (1991) also points to declining growth rates in Asian industrializing economies which are experiencing tight labor markets, rising wages and infrastructure bottlenecks.

The deficiencies of infrastructure existing alongside rapid industrial growth are forcing growth to slow down until the necessary infrastructure is in place. It has been estimated that Asia's gross domestic product, excluding Japan, will be around US$5 trillion by 2000, rivalling the EC and almost equal to the USA. At least US$500 billion has been earmarked for public works and capital improvement in Asia (excluding Japan). With the push to raise living standards it is possible that spending will reach US$1 trillion by 2000.

These rapidly industrializing countries of the ASEAN group and of

North-East Asia are one type of economy to be found in the Asia-Pacific region. However there is a wide disparity in income and economic activity between these and other countries, as illustrated in Table 4.1. By comparison with the figures in the table, in 1990 GNP per capita in $US for the United States was $21 800, Australia $17 300 and New Zealand $12 700.

The 1991 World Bank Report noted that, while the rapidly industrializing open economies of South Korea, Thailand, Malaysia and Indonesia were sustaining growth momentum based on sound economic management, structural reforms and long-term investing, this did not apply to all countries. While the proportion of the population living in poverty had fallen below 20 percent in these countries, this was not the case in countries such as Bangladesh, Burma, Laos, Nepal, Sri Lanka, Vietnam and the Philippines. In these countries, with a collective population of over 330 million, the future prospects were clouded. The World Bank noted that bad policies, natural disasters, political instability and war against insurgents combined to cause declining growth rates and uncertainty. The report noted that Vietnam remained one of the poorest countries in Asia, while two giants, China and India, faced serious macroeconomic imbalances that required stabilization and structural reform.

In countries such as those shown in the table, the 1980s was a decade of low or even declining growth rates. Each country shared problems of rapid

Table 4.1 Asia: 1989 population and per capita GNP of countries that borrowed from the World Bank during fiscal years 1989–91

Country	Population[1] (000)	Per capita GNP (US dollars)[2]
Bangladesh	110 700	180
China	1 113 900	350
Fiji	740	1650
India	832 500	340
Indonesia	178 200	500
Korea, Republic of	42 400	4400
Lao People's Democratic Republic	4 100	180
Malaysia	17 400	2160
Maldives	210	420
Nepal	18 400	180
Papua New Guinea	3 800	890
Philippines	60 000	710
Sri Lanka	16 800	430
Thailand	55 400	1220
Tonga	98	910
Vanuatu	152	860
Western Samoa	163	700

Note: The 1989 estimates of GNP per capita presented above are from the 'World Development Indicators' section of World Development Report, 1991.
[1] Estimates from mid-1989.
[2] World Bank Atlas methodology, 1987–9 base period.
Source: World Bank (1991).

population growth, ecological vulnerability, a large number of absolute poor and economic problems. In the Pacific island countries the World Bank Report indicated that performance is mixed. Fiji achieved a growth rate of 10 percent in 1990 in manufacturing and tourism, while the Solomon Islands and the Maldives also experienced strong growth. Such was not the experience in Tonga, Western Samoa and Kiribati, which suffered the effects of a cyclone and lower copra prices.

Australia and New Zealand, with their relatively small populations and traditional reliance on the production of raw materials and primary industries, account for only a very small share of East Asia's trade. Most of these exports still consist of unprocessed agricultural and mineral products, although sales of manufactured goods and services have been growing more rapidly.

The growth of tourism

Countries at the forefront of economic growth in the Asia-Pacific region have also been major contributors to the growth of tourism in the region. In this respect the importance of Japan to the region cannot be underestimated – particularly its role in the last decade as a source of both investment funds and outbound tourists. Its emergence as an economic power following the Second World War has been of great significance to all countries, including the United States (in particular Hawaii), Australia and New Zealand.

Between 1986 and 1989 Japanese corporations channeled some $170 billion into direct overseas investment. Figures from the Australia–Japan Economic Institute show that some $8.8 billion reached Australia, of which 40 percent or $3.4 billion went into tourism in those four years. By comparison Japan poured $85 billion into North America, including $22.5 billion into tourism (Chenoweth, 1991). In 1989 member countries of the Pacific Asia Travel Association welcomed 42 million visitor arrivals, an increase of approximately 8.9 percent over the previous year (Pacific Asia Travel Association, 1990). The growth rates in tourism paralleled the growth rates in GDP outlined earlier in the chapter, reflecting the unabated strength of outbound demand from residents of the newly industrialized economies of North-East Asia as well as the continued demand from Japan. The increasing importance of inter-regional travel is indicated by the projected figures (Ernst and Young, 1991) for Far East and Australasia tourism arrivals of 19.6 million in 1988 to 46 million by the year 2000. Visitor arrivals from outside the region are expected to increase from 9.7 million to 19.1 million for the same period. Forecasts of travel to the region during this period indicate an average of 7 percent of annual growth and an overall average of 50 percent increase in visitor arrivals. The expected length of stay is also expected to increase by 50 percent.

In 1989 South Korea's outbound travellers exceeded one million, an increase of 67.3 percent, outbound travel from Taiwan increased by 31.6 percent to 2.1 million, while Japan experienced an increase of 14.7 percent to 9.7 million. Given the Brynes and Allens forecast that economic growth rates will decline marginally, the estimate of 72 million arrivals by 2000 appears feasible.

Growth of this magnitude will continue to provide an expansionary context for every sector of the hospitality industry. Each destination in the region is confronted with supply issues ranging from infrastructure such as airports, roads, water and sewerage to superstructure such as hotels and other built facilities. The magnitude of such development required to service the needs of tourists is of increasing environmental concern. IATA forecasts that demand in the Asia-Pacific area will saturate existing and new airport facilities.

Taiwan has commenced a US$300 billion sixth national plan to support further development. In Thailand the government grapples with the problems of congestion in Bangkok, while new airports are under construction in Macau and Hong Kong, and in Malaysia development of the manufacturing and services sector continues. Private sector investment in Malaysia is projected to increase at a 14.8 percent annual growth rate, until the year 2000 (Outline Perspective Plan 1990–2000). The trend in South-East Asian countries has been toward government policies which deregulate economic activity, enlarge the role of the private sector through privatization and encourage 'build, operate, transfer' schemes.

To better examine the role of government with respect to infrastructure development, reference can be made to the considerable debate concerning which sector, public or private, should be responsible for the development, planning, financing, control and operation of the tourist industry. In Australia this has led to division of opinion on issues such as who should develop the major infrastructure, such as airports. While the answer clearly continues to be the Commonwealth government, the requirement that users of airports pay for the use of such facilities has become increasingly accepted. The Australian tourist industry constantly seeks government or taxpayers' support with respect to education and training, research, traveling, promotion and financial incentives while accepting a major role in the development of superstructure (hotels, resorts) and the conduct of management of tourism centers from hotels to travel agencies. Australian Commonwealth and state governments look to cooperation with the private sector, maintaining that government support is of necessity limited because tourism is essentially a private industry sector.

Virtually all countries of the Asia-Pacific region have mixed public and private involvement. In most countries surveyed, the airlines, railways and some hotel facilities are government owned and operated, but most of the tourist industry is in the private sector. In Australia the Commonwealth government is presently planning to privatize all or part of the national carrier, a move which follows upon deregulation of the airline industry.

The growth in the number of outbound intra-regional travelers also brings into sharper focus the future importance of domestic tourism to each country. Domestic tourism has its own distinct advantages – in Australia, for instance, domestic tourism demand represents 80–4 percent of total demand. The more residents who holiday 'at home', the less the leakage of spending in foreign destinations. Domestic tourism encourages greater awareness of one's own country and national pride in its features and attractions. It requires greater private investment, particularly in small businesses to cater for local needs. It can act as a buttress to the industry in general, particularly when there is a slump in overseas arrivals. With rising living standards, especially in South-East Asian countries, the quality of the facilities provided for domestic tourists and recreational facilities such as national parks will become increasingly popular with the budget-conscious international market, as well as with local residents.

Government policy and involvement through public sector operation sets the scene for the level of private operations. If government policies are unduly restrictive – for example, in terms of ownership, the length of time that foreign management can stay and the transfer of profits out of the country – then overseas investment may be difficult to attract. In examining the public role in a range of Asia-Pacific countries, it has been obvious that governments have had to decide whether tourism as an industry should be supported by the financial resources of the country in preference to other industries such as manufacturing and agriculture. The importance attached to tourism has tended to be related to special features of each particular country's development.

Given that particular governments, such as Vietnam, decide that tourism should be accorded priority in terms of development, the question of availability of resources represents the next barrier. The resources needed to develop the infrastructure – roads, sewerage, airports, drainage – and possibly some elements of superstructure, such as hotels and resorts, may be beyond the existing resources. While the returns from particular projects are seen as vital for the short- and medium-term development of a country, or an area within a country, the call on resources for education, hospitals, transport and public amenities may have a higher priority. Certain developments such as roads and transportation, vital to tourism, can be equally vital to the development of other industry sectors as well as public amenity.

In the view of Wise (1990) a certain level of government investment which entails national or private borrowing from overseas sources, including developmental organizations, may therefore be justified. The balance of resources needed given the level of financial support by the home country could then be provided by the private sector, either from within the nation or from international sources.

The hospitality industry

What are the implications for the hotel and accommodation sector in each country? The 1980s have witnessed a decade of unprecedented hotel and resort development in virtually all the new industrializing nations including the ASEAN growth countries of Thailand, Malaysia and Indonesia, as well as Australia and New Zealand.

The development of the hotel sector in the Asia-Pacific region has historically been dominated from a management and operational viewpoint by the
major US chains, although now many of these are not US owned and operated, such as the Hilton International, Holiday Inn and Accor Group. The
range of major international hotel groups operating in the region is set out
in Table 4.2. Oversupply of properties particularly in the five-star category has
not been uncommon, particularly in countries that have suffered major political, economic or natural disasters, such as the People's Republic of China,
Hong Kong and the Philippines.

While the figures in Table 4.2 represent total worldwide figures for the
major groups, the Asia Pacific Division of Holiday Inn World Wide (in turn
of Bass plc) claims a larger share of the business and leisure travelers in the
region than any other chain. Holiday Inn now offers 47 hotels with nearly
15 000 rooms in 12 countries and territories in the Asia-Pacific region
(Holiday Inn World Wide Asia Pacific, 1991). The other major groups listed
all have a strong presence in Asia-Pacific.

In view of the above it is not surprising to find that in Asia-Pacific management of the international hotels is dominated by European and American
expatriates (*PATA Travel News*, 1988). The report found that when international chains first arrived on Asian shores they brought their own managerial and skilled workforce, which unfortunately is the way it has stayed. The
report likened hotels in Asia to 'a double layer cake, white on top; brown
or yellow at the bottom'. In Australia criticism has been leveled against such
management citing agreements too heavily in favour of the operators. While
that criticism may be valid, without the services of these skilled operating
companies Australia may not have been able to develop any kind of tourism
industry; however, it is also the case that no major hotel has an Australian
as its general manager.

Table 4.2   Major worldwide hotel groups

	Total rooms 1990	Number of hotels
Holiday Inn World Wide	320 599	1606
Accor	159 877	1421
ITT Sheraton Corp	130 862	429
Hilton Hotels	94 232	263
Hyatt Hotels	76 794	161
Intercontinental Hotels	38 723	104
Western/Caesar Park	36 480	72
New World/Ramada	34 723	121
Tokyo Hotel Group	20 222	75
Prince Hotels	17 990	66
Omni Hotels	16 487	41
Fujitar Tourist Enterprises	14 470	65
Ana Enterprises	10 057	31
Southern Pacific Hotels	9 592	55

Source: *Hotels Magazine*, July 1991, vol. 25, no. 7.

In Australasia since the late 1960s the hotel industry has shifted from small owner hotels, motels, motor lodges and resorts to a greater focus on national and international chains. The new products include all-suite hotels, deluxe hotels and resorts such as the Sheraton Mirage. Although growth holds out the certainty of another major phase of infrastructure development for the Australian industry, there are very good reasons for anticipating that the emphasis will be on medium- and budget-priced accommodation. The lower-priced operators are in general terms achieving far higher yields than the glamour end of the market and on sites with huge potential for future redevelopment. Some of the recent investment in hotels and resorts in Australia has been appropriate to markets with more than 20 million inbound visitors a year rather than 2 million. This has jeopardized the pricing integrity of top-bracket properties in Australia, which have been retailed for less than five-star hotels in Paris, Hong Kong or New York, but nevertheless at prices higher than most visitors or Australian tourists would normally be prepared to pay. Australia differs from most developed countries in having its top-bracket properties priced beyond the pockets of the majority of its population, including a major proportion of its business travelers whose bills are paid for by companies and governments. Future success will be linked to marketing linkages, product development and chain affiliation: that is, the ability of hotel groups to compete, market their product and operate on a global and subregional basis.

The major chains listed in Table 4.2 are anticipated to continue to build their presence in the region. An example of this is the Pritzker family's ownership of Hyatt Hotels and part ownership of Southern Pacific Hotel Corporation, through which one company now manages the majority of international-class hotel rooms in the Pacific region. The implications of expanded chain hotel groups and CRSs for the regional tourism market as a whole are very positive. These groups have a vested interest in ensuring that a hotel or destination succeeds.

Through their international networks and marketing prowess these chains have the ability – along with the airlines and wholesalers – to create an environment conducive to tourism growth. Examples of recent hotel-driven demand growth include Bali, Phuket, Fiji and Sydney, where new hotel chains have stimulated both inbound and conference business.

Marketing in the hotel industry is in the process of rapid change. Democratic and social evolution is causing fundamental changes in available markets, customer profiles and source markets. Technological development, at a pace inconceivable to previous generations, is causing fundamental changes in the ways in which hotels reach their customers and in the ways in which potential customers choose their hotels. Use of CRSs and affiliations with major global hotel networks will have significant positive influences upon attracting visitors to new destinations. Holiday Inn World Wide offers a range of global marketing programs directed towards the travel trade and consumer. These include the frequent traveler program with an excess of 2 million members, the worldwide corporate account program and travel agents' centralized commission payment programs. Each regional office – for example, Hong Kong in the Asia-Pacific – is responsible for the implementation of the worldwide global marketing program.

The question of expatriate versus local management leads to the question of national versus international groups. National groups do exist: for instance, in Thailand the locally based Dusit Thani group continues to expand, with the Princess Park View Hotel of 240 rooms scheduled to open in 1992 and the 715-room Dusit Riverside in 1993. Other Thai groups such as the Siam Lodge and Imperial Family of Hotels also compete with the international groups in Thailand.

Current issues

Regional and international trade agreements

The General Agreement on Tariffs and Trade (GATT) sets out the basic rules of the game for international trade, limiting arbitrary interventions or interference to trade by individual countries. GATT stresses the importance of nondiscrimination in trading relationships. Countries which adhere to GATT use its rules as a basis for their trade policies. The fundamental advantage of a multilateral nondiscriminatory trade system is that it permits countries to tap the most competitive sources of supply for imports. The World Bank (1991) reported that negotiations to seek further trade liberalization in tariff and nontariff barriers, covering agriculture, textiles and clothing as well as services and intellectual property, are continuing and are of particular importance to developing countries. The report refers to several studies which conclude that annual costs in foregone income to developing countries amount to about twice the annual interest they pay on their external public debt, and are about twice the annual volume of assistance they receive from industrialized countries, although the benefits may differ substantially from country to country. Bilateral arrangements are becoming increasingly prevalent in the region notwithstanding that regional trade liberalization is the aim of APEC (Asia Pacific Economic Cooperation), which serves as a model of open regionalism that can compete rather than undermine the GATT free trade system (Lee Sang-Ock, 1991). The danger is the effect of trading blocs such as the EC upon the region.

In releasing the government outline perspective plan for Malaysia 1990–2000 the *Star* on 18 June 1991 called for increased intra-ASEAN cooperation in trade, communications and services. A decision has been taken by the ASEAN nations to establish their own free trade zone, which modifies a proposal that non-Asean nations – Japan, China, Taiwan and South Korea – be invited to join. While Indonesia, Thailand, the Philippines, Malaysia, Singapore and Brunei insist that the pact is not a trade bloc, it is an interesting development between economies better known for competitiveness.

Manpower planning

Warin Wonghanchao (1989), Director of the Institute of Social Research, Chulalongkorn University, believes that the future of tourism in Thailand will depend largely upon the capabilities of its employees – thus education and training are essential prerequisites for the successful development of tourism. What is required is a complete and well-formulated education and training system that includes upgrading of those already engaged in the field, as well as new entrants.

WTO surveys indicate that many countries, including developed ones, do not have a clear answer concerning such basic matters as number of jobs provided, distribution by occupation, sector skills, extent of formal training, opportunity to upgrade skills, and the extent to which expatriates are employed because of the lack of adequately trained local personnel.

Unfortunately, education and training often suffers from a lack of financial resources, inhouse training programs and manpower planning, together with a shortage of training institutions, programs and instructors capable and efficient enough to satisfy training needs. In developing countries in particular, governments often cannot afford to provide publicly funded training facilities of sufficient quality, or to compete for training and educational staff against the competition from major chains. This, in turn, leaves the international chains to import senior and middle management staff and to conduct their own training programs for skilled and semi-skilled positions.

Holiday Inn professes to believe in the development of self-reliance at a local level in essential management skills – particularly in Asia-Pacific. With respect to management training it cites China as a country where the training of local staff for management positions is proving highly successful. That this may be a stated requirement for operating in the People's Republic of China is not mentioned. In rapidly developing industrializing countries such as Hong Kong and South Korea, as well as Australia, tourism and hospitality courses are in high demand from students seeking a future career in what is now accepted as a major service industry. If students are only offered the least desirable occupations within the industry, then such interest will of necessity decline.

Foreign investment

The question of foreign funding of new development costs evokes different responses in different countries. In Australia in 1991 a survey by Dasett, Boma (1991) indicated that 44 percent of new development costs are funded by foreign countries, 83 percent of which funding is from Japan. Approximately 49 percent for all five-star establishments in Australia are owned by foreign interests. The other interesting finding was that the majority of foreign investment concentrates in the five-star sector, as illustrated in Table 4.3.

In Australia, New Zealand and the Pacific, because of the depressed nature of the economy, oversupply of accommodation and decreasing occupancies,

Table 4.3 Foreign investment in existing Australian hotel stock by star rating, December 1990

Star rating	% Foreign investment
Three	2.0
Three and a half	11.4
Four	8.5
Four and a half	16.1
Five	49.5
Unclassified	23.5
Total	15.5

Source: Dasett, Boma (1991). Reprinted with the permission of Arthur Andersen.

the demand for professional management companies is expected to increase. Hotel companies generally do not have any equity in the property or group of companies. In Asia, with more management companies entering the hotel scene, competition for good management contracts is intensifying and management fees are being forced down. Contracts which saw chains take 20–30 percent of gross operating profits are less common, with some contracts being based on the bottom line: namely, net profit. Because of this, some companies are taking up equity in hotel projects not only to help obtain the management contract but to provide returns on investment. By doing this chains are forging real partnerships with owners and sharing property gains and risks.

The discussion above relates to hotel and resort development in the rapidly developing or developed countries which have relative political stability and well-developed infrastructure. Poorer countries such as Nepal, Vietnam, Bangladesh and Sri Lanka, or the small Pacific communities referred to in the World Bank Report, are not in the position where they can afford the required infrastructure or superstructure investment. Financial support from aid agencies will be focused more on programs likely to benefit the poor. Tourism projects, therefore, compete with other development options.

In 1991 the World Bank wrote loans for various projects to the value of US$22 billion. Of this total, approximately US$6.5 billion was for loans to Asian countries. In the same period the Asian Development Bank wrote loans for various projects to the value of US$4 billion. Loans to the value of US$10.5 billion per annum will be provided by these institutions to governments of developing countries in Asia for infrastructure and social development. It is important to recognize that the allocation of funds to various industry sectors including tourism is determined by Development Bank policy, not by the borrower.

Jackson (1991) believes that, as the pace of infrastructure project development in Asia increases, the available sources of finance will ultimately become more broadly based. The financing technology to serve this rapidly emerging market is developing quickly. Jackson suggests that, as the world of the 1990s heads towards the twenty-first century, it is likely to become considerably more regionalized than has been the case to date. With the emergence of a unified Europe and the restructuring of the erstwhile communist bloc, available capital in the region is likely to be heavily contested by regional users. Developments in Europe and the Americas imply that the sources of capital for infrastructure development in Asia are likely to be increasingly Asian. The predominant source of financing in Asia remains Japan. Nonetheless, there are moves afoot to liberalize the Taiwanese banking system with its huge store of wealth, and both Hong Kong and Singapore remain sizable sources of capital. This means that in order to attract the investment required to develop a tourism industry, developing countries often need to provide incentives such as tax holidays to foreign investors.

Political issues

Politics also play a significant part. Vietnam, for instance, has battled against a trade and investment embargo by the United States which has nothing to do with economics. The result is that the Vietnamese government cannot import sufficient fertilizer to raise crops in agriculture while at the same time it urgently needs to rebuild its infrastructure. Nevertheless, Nguyen Van Uyen, Director of the Biotechnology Research Centre, Saigon, is reported by Hodgson (1991) as stating that 'our infrastructure is low, but our brain power is high'. Computer science, biotechnology and chemistry are all flourishing as Vietnam opens its markets and laboratories to the West. According to Do Hoang Phu, General Director of the Foreign Investment Department of the Ministry of Commerce, only a trickle of investors passed through his office in 1988, but by January 1991, 217 licenses had been granted to foreign investors for a total of $1.47 billion. Of these, five are joint ventures.

The investment laws promulgated in Vietnam in 1988 were intended to encourage investors. Tourism was seen to be a major part of the Vietnam–Cambodian drive to generate foreign exchange to finance their national development plans. It may be that, in Vietnam, science is providing the source of hard currency as local technologies begin to offer the quality that overseas customers require. Hanoi's Institute of Computer Science is taking full advantage of the new commercial climate and is developing software for domestic and foreign consumption, including a hotel reservation and accounting system. The Institute hopes to make ICS South-East Asia's regional software training center, and has already trained a number of students from mainland China. To attract more foreigners the Institute organizes an annual international conference on advanced informatics – UN agencies provide the funding.

In a reverse situation, Taiwan government policies encouraged an outbound surge, announcing a policy of encouraging Taiwanese to travel more overseas. This was an attempt to reduce the republic's large foreign exchange reserves ($70 billion) and to ease congestion of domestic airports. Although outward travel has boomed, Taiwan is now ranked as Asia's second most expensive destination after Tokyo. The business travel sector has shrunk in length of stay from 3.5 to 2 days.

Paxton (1991) believes that, before Taiwan's tourism industry can gain a higher profile internationally, it has to gain government priority. If government did give such recognition, it would then need to synergize all the relevant departments and ministries and get them working together for tourism development. Taiwan also represents an excellent illustration of the influence of politics upon tourism flows. The political stance of the Australian government in its lack of recognition of Taiwan as an independent nation has hampered business relations and constrained Taiwanese tourists to Australia. Taiwanese planning to visit Australia have to go to Hong Kong to get visas, and until 1991 there had been no direct flights between the two countries (*Australian Financial Review*, October 1990).

In Australia, the Foreign Investment Review Board (FIRB) plays a major part in directing overseas real estate investment and has been the major force behind the heavy involvement of foreign purchasers, particularly the Japanese, in the ownership of tourism plant. This has been achieved by virtually barring overseas interest in other forms of real estate investment. However, the long lead times in hotel/resort developments have also played a part; local investors have traditionally lacked a long-term perspective and required immediate returns on their investment, which means that they have tended to avoid hotel/resort developments, leaving them to overseas investors. Since October 1987, approval for purchases of undeveloped land has been conditional upon development in one to two years. Where development does not go ahead, the FIRB has the power to order divestiture and fines of $250 000 for a corporation and $50 000 and two years' jail for an individual (Howes, 1990).

In Singapore, the government is an important economic regulatory mechanism. It takes the initiative in almost every sector of the economy. In the hotel sector its influence is both direct and indirect. It has direct investments in two hotels, the most notable being the Raffles City. Being labor intensive, hotels have been closely monitored by the government in terms of labor requirement. Work permits for foreigners to work in hotels were restricted at one time. The 1988 Budget increased the foreign worker levy from $140 to $170 per worker for the hotel and manufacturing sectors. The objectives of the government have been both economic and political, requiring not only that the hotel industry does not siphon off much needed labor from the market but also that it does not increase the intake of foreign workers into the country.

Future trends

The theme of the 1991 PATA Conference held in Bali, Indonesia, focused on tourism and the environment. This conference reflects a growing acceptance of the need for regulations that require mandatory impact analysis. The costs of such regulations and their implementation were viewed as part of the project's investment costs. From a conservation point of view, tourism is seen as having a charter to improve the life of indigenous people by conserving the environment and providing employment opportunities for the locals, as well as offering opportunities for visitors to enjoy local culture and environment.

Indonesia, for example, is in the process of developing a national protected area system in which over 520 separate land and sea areas have been identified for protection. Burke (1991) believes that tourism can make a significant contribution in making it easier for people to access cultural and environmental diversity – which in turn fosters in host countries a desire to develop and strengthen their natural cultural identities. In Bali, Ardika (1991) advised that the Indonesian government has recently introduced legislation which set out guidelines to preserve culture and environment, to increase the use of national products, and to create employment.

If the principle of sensitivity to the local environment and culture is adhered to, it is likely that there will be greater emphasis upon less intrusive hotels and resorts; greater pressure for employment of indigenous people at all levels; and more concern with individual or small group travelers as opposed to mass tourism.

The importance of interregional investment and travel will also continue to increase. The importance of investment by regional investors, such as Japan, Taiwan, Singapore and Hong Kong, is already established. Tourism invested more than US$350 billion in facilities and equipment in 1980, more than 7 percent of the world's capital investment and growing more than 60 percent faster than capital investment at large. In Asia-Pacific the annual growth has been 52 percent over the last couple of years – about US$130 billion a year (PATA, 1991). Intra-country tourism will continue to increase. Japan with its 9.7 million outbound travelers has provided a major market segment to most other countries in the region. Indonesia, for example, is reliant upon its nearest neighbors for visits. In 1990 its visitors came from Singapore (579 460), Korea (43 521), Taiwan (117 198), Japan (259 634) and Australia (160 000).

Another likely trend is greater regional cooperation. The European Travel Commission plays an active role in increasing tourist arrivals to Europe and provides a forum for member NTOs to exchange ideas and experiences. In the Asian region the ASEAN nations have joined to promote Visit ASEAN Year in 1992, designed to attract 22 million visitors to the region. This promotion has received the full support of member governments and commitments from airlines and hotels to provide special fares and packages. Globalization of the airline industry puts pressure on the regulatory environment with regional aviation blocs beginning to emerge. Increasing regional cooperation will lead, in the view of New Zealand Tourism FX, to multi-country holidays and each country being encouraged to retain its cultural identity (Tourism FX, 1991).

Another trend will be the gradual substitution of expatriate with local staff. Because of the internationality of the industry a mix of nationalities will

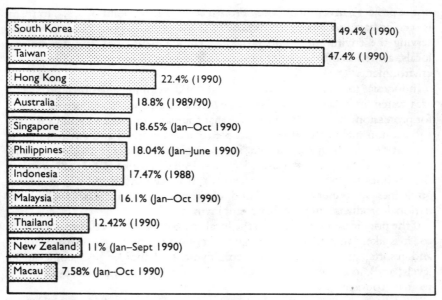

Figure 4.1 Importance of Japan to Asia-Pacific destinations (percent of Japanese in total arrivals)
Source: *PATA Travel News*, March 1991, p. 9.

gradually emerge to replace the complete dominance held by American and European managers, despite the current influence of the major international groups. Love (1989) believes that it is important for local Chinese hotel managers to be appointed in Hong Kong as 90 percent of the actual travel business is transacted through Chinese agents.

Asia-Pacific tourism and travel will continue to experience higher growth rates until at least the end of the century because of a continuation of fast-growing economies in the region. This is particularly true for travel between countries in the region.

The tourism and travel industry will be the beneficiary of continually increasing business travel, particularly through the prime gateways of Singapore, Hong Kong, Bangkok and Kuala Lumpur. Increased affluence in the form of a growing middle class will also stimulate both outbound and domestic tourists, who in turn will demand increasingly sophisticated facilities and standards of service.

The formation of the Growth Triangle economic alliance of Batam, Johore and Singapore, for example, has resulted in the development of marinas, golf courses and beach resorts in the nearby islands. Regional tourism is in line for a boost and Singapore has much to gain from the spillover. Although Europe and the USA are important, Asia and ASEAN account for 64 percent of total visitor arrivals.

In Malaysia, Badri Masri of the Tourism Development Corporation believes that the corporation needs to realign its marketing strategies to concentrate on the ASEAN and East Asia markets and to encourage domestic tourism. The pattern for the South-East Asia market has always been regional travel for first-time travelers followed by traveling further afield as they become more seasoned. Asman Harun, President of the Malaysian Association of Hotels, has stated that 'the consolation for Malaysia is, its biggest market is ASEAN and if certain countries were to become more liberal in travel regulations, then prospects will still be good'. The *Economic Report* released by Malaysia's Central Bank in March 1991 shows that strong growth is expected to continue in the manufacturing, construction and service sectors. The country's economy is now more resilient and diversified. In 1990, for the first time in fourteen years, Malaysia's economy registered a double-digit (i.e. greater than 9.9) gross domestic product and growth of 10 percent compared to 8.8 percent in 1989. Corporate bookings in hotels are up from the previous year.

References

Allen, Jamie (1991) 'Asian Tigers start to lose their roar', *Business Review Weekly*, 18 October.

Ardika, I. Gede (1991) 'Bali in reconciling two environments', PATA 40th Annual Conference, Bali, Indonesia, 10–13 April.

Burke, James (1991) 'The changing world', PATA 40th Annual Conference, Bali, Indonesia, 10–13 April 1991.

Byrnes, Michael (1991) 'Asia pauses for breath in sprint for economic growth', *Financial Review*, 19 September.

Chenoweth, Neil (1991) 'Hostage of Japan', *Australian Business*, 13 February.

Chia, Seow Yire (1991) cited in *Asia Pacific Insight Business Review Weekly*, 26 April.

Dasett, Boma (1991) *Tourism Investment Overview*, Arthur Andersen, July.

Ernst & Young (1991) *The Future for PATA: A discussion document*, PATA Advisory Council Meeting, Queenstown, New Zealand, 4–5 December, citing Anthony Edward's estimates, Economist Intelligence Unit, Special Report no. 2030.

Greene, Joshua E., and Isard, Peter (1991) *Currency Convertibility and the Transformation of Centrally Planned Economies*, Washington, DC: International Monetary Fund, June.

Hodgson, Gregor (1991) 'Vietnam on the tech trail', *New Scientist*, 6 July, pp. 39–42.

Holiday Inn World Wide Asia Pacific (1991), *Holiday Inn World Wide*, in-house magazine.

Howes, Stephen (1990) *Australian Accountant*, October.

Jackson, Allan (1991) 'Financing infrastructure projects in Asia', Australian Investment Conference.

Lee Sang-Ock (1991) Third Ministerial Meeting of Asia Pacific Economic Co-operation (APEC), South Korea, 12–14 November, cited in *Sun Herald* (Aust.), 13 November.

Love, David (1989) 'He came, he saw, he loved ... and left', *PATA Travel News*, June 1989.

McKinnon, Ronald I. (1973) *Money: Capital in economic development*, Washington, DC: The Brookings Institute.

Malaysia Central Bank (1991) *Economic Report*, March.

Pacific Asia Travel Association (1990), Annual Report 1989–90, p. 3.

PATA Travel News (1988) 'Hotel job market – Asians v. Expats', January.

PATA Travel News (1991), p. 9, March.

Paxton, Philip (1991) cited in 'War adds to Taiwan's woes', *PATA Travel News*, March.

Tourism FX (1991) *Quarterly Analysis of New Zealand Tourism*, January.

Wise, Brian (1990) 'Tourism development and finance', World Tourism Organization and Indian Institute of Tourism and Travel Management, Advanced Course in Tourism Education in Universities, New Delhi, India, 4–30 June.

Wonghanchao, Warin (1989) 'Tourism investment in Thailand', *Tourism Review No. 2*, 'Tourism management development', Report of a workshop organized by Economic and Social Commission for Asia and the Pacific (ESCAP) in Bangkok, 16–20 May, 1988, New York: United Nations.

World Bank (1991) *Annual Report*, Washington, DC: World Bank, 20433.

5
Latin America
and Africa

Silvia Sussmann and Chris Cooper

The geographic areas covered by this chapter span two very different continents that share some similar tourism characteristics. Latin America includes
all those countries of the American continent south of the border between
the USA and Mexico. It includes two distinct cultural entities, the Caribbean
islands, mostly English speaking, and Central and South America, colonized
from the sixteenth century onwards by Europeans from the Iberian peninsula
who imposed their languages, culture and religion on the native Indians
(Boniface and Cooper, 1987). As a result, this part of Latin America is composed of Spanish-speaking republics, with the exception of Portuguese-
speaking Brazil. Africa is also a large land mass with a colonial history, so that
a number of European languages such as English and French are spoken along
with indigenous languages such as Arabic and Swahili.

In development terms, these two continents can be regarded as part of the
Third World, but there are significant differences in level of development not
only between separate countries but also between the major cities – which
have a European feel, such as Buenos Aires or Cape Town, resemble US
capitals, such as Caracas or Mexico City, or remain unique to that country,
such as Casablanca and Cairo – and the more remote areas of countryside,
firmly placed in a pre-industrial era.

The two continents will be examined in accordance with the WTO classification. Latin America can be divided into three main areas. The Caribbean
includes some 26 island states, the majority of which are English speaking
with the exception of French-speaking Haiti, Martinique and Guadeloupe
and Spanish-speaking Cuba and Dominican Republic. Central America in this
classification includes Mexico, Belize, Costa Rica, El Salvador, Guatemala,
Honduras and Panama. Mexico is by far the most important country in this
group, in terms of its size, economic power and tourism development.
Finally, South America includes the northern republics of Venezuela,
Colombia, Guyana and Surinam, the Andean area of Peru, Ecuador and
Bolivia, and the southern republics of Chile, Paraguay, Argentina and Uru-
guay, with Brazil in a category of its own determined by size, language and

culture. Likewise, Africa can be divided into North Africa, with its largely Arabic influence; sub-Saharan Africa, including most of west, central and east Africa; and the Republic of South Africa, which like Brazil, has some substantial differences from its neighbors.

Economic background

Latin America

There are considerable economic disparities between the countries of the region, as can be seen comparing the figures for GNP per capita in 1990 from Table 5.1. This table also includes the real rates of growth – when inflation

Table 5.1 Latin American countries: economic indicators

Countries by area	GNP/capita 1990 (US$)	Real growth rate 1980–90 (%)
Caribbean		
Antigua and Barbuda	4 600	4.7
Bahamas	11 510	1.7
Barbados	6 540	1.4
Dominica	1 940	3.0
Grenada	2 120	5.1
Haiti	370	−2.3
Jamaica	1 510	−0.4
Puerto Rico	6 470	2.1
St Kitts-Nevis	3 300	6.0
St Vincent	1 610	5.7
Trinidad and Tobago	3 470	−6.0
US Virgin Islands	12 330	1.2
Central America		
Belize	1 970	2.5
Costa Rica	1 910	0.6
El Salvador	1 100	−0.6
Guatemala	900	−2.1
Honduras	590	−1.2
Mexico	2 490	−0.9
Panama	1 830	−2.0
South America		
Argentina	2 370	−1.8
Bolivia	620	−2.6
Brazil	2 680	0.6
Chile	1 940	1.1
Colombia	1 240	1.1
Ecuador	960	−0.8
Guyana	370	−3.2
Paraguay	1 110	−1.3
Peru	1 170	−2.0
Surinam	3 050	−5.0
Uruguay	2 560	−0.9
Venezuela	2 560	−2.0

Source: World Bank (1992).

is taken into account – for the period 1980–90, showing the devastating effect of chronic inflation, since even the strongest economies of the region, like Mexico, Venezuela, Brazil and Argentina show negative or insignificant growth during that period.

Another interesting fact emerging from Table 5.1 is the difference between regions, with some of the small islands of the Caribbean having the highest GNPs, comparable to some European countries. The influence of tourism receipts on this prosperity is exemplified in the Bahamas, where they accounted in 1988 for more of one-third of all exports and more than three-quarters of the nation's GDP (Harrison, 1992). On the other hand, those countries in the same region which have experienced difficulty in building their tourism industry due to a perception of political instability or violence (Richter, 1992) are among the 64 per cent of the world's population with GNPs less than US$1500 in 1990 (World Bank, 1992). Haiti, for instance, with one of the lowest GNPs in the world, was consistently quoted as one the 'losers' in tourist arrivals in the Caribbean region (EIU, 1989). The effect of political instability on tourism will be discussed in more detail later.

Africa

Most countries in sub-Saharan Africa are rural in character and have low per capita GNP with a burgeoning population (see Table 5.2). Unemployment rates are therefore high and economic activity rates correspondingly low. Many countries rely on exports of primary products and are vulnerable to international price variations in their commodities. The region as a whole is largely dependent upon aid from Western donor countries and has large foreign debts. The majority of Africa is therefore part of the world's economic

Table 5.2   Africa: social and economic indicators

Area (square kilometers)	30 208 000
Population (1991)	671 997 000
Population projection (2010)	1 138 606 000
Gross national product (1989) (US$m)	386 230
Gross national product (1989) (%)	
Agriculture	20
Industry	35
Services	45
Gross national product/capita (1989) (US$)	610
Gross national product growth 1980–9 (%)	1.7
Labor force (1990) (000s)	242 784

Source: *Britannica Book of the Year.* Encyclopedia Britannica, Chicago, 1992.

periphery and it is similarly peripheral in terms of its role in world tourism (Burton, 1991). Indeed, despite having 15 percent of the world's population, Africa only has a share of 3.2 percent of international tourist arrivals (WTO, 1991).

Tourism characteristics

Latin America

Latin America, says Schlüter (1991), 'has excited the European traveler imagination ever since it was discovered'. Since the Second World War, the region has tried to appeal to mass tourism, with the provision and marketing of attractions like the four Ss (sun, sand, sea and sex), an exotic culture and unspoilt nature. However, even though the international tourist flows increased thirtyfold between 1950 and 1988, the bulk of the international tourism to Latin America originates in neighboring countries (Schlüter, 1991). This explains the higher incidence of tourist receipts in the economy of those countries – the Caribbean, Mexico and some Central American destinations – where the neighboring countries are the USA and Canada. This is evident in Table 5.3, which shows the 1990 figures for tourism arrivals, receipts, expenditures and account balances. The consistent increases in tourist arrivals for the Caribbean area were predicted to end in 1991, with a forecasted annual decrease of 4.5 percent, due to the recession in North America. The 1991 forecast for Central and South America indicates an annual increase in tourism arrivals of 3.9 percent and an increase in tourism receipts of 15.2 percent (*World Travel and Tourism Review*, 1992).

Tourism in the Caribbean region is the major, and in some cases the only, hard currency earner for many island economies: for example, tourism expenditure accounted for 84.9 percent of GDP in Bermuda in 1988 (Hall, 1992). In the last year, concern has been voiced by the Caribbean Hotel Association (Bell, 1991) about a series of developments that threaten their position, such as the competition of new locations opened in Eastern Europe and especially in the Pacific, the exploitation of the area by the cruise industry, which erodes land-based tourism, the recession in North America and tourism investment in Cuba. Some of the solutions proposed include improved marketing penetration as provided by the launching of Charms, a computerized reservation system linking all hotels in the area with the international retail travel trade; better environmental protection and control over air access; and reduced operating costs, by controlling prices of public utilities and indirect taxation. Another suggestion is a single Caribbean tourist passport, which would enable visitors to enter the Caribbean only once.

On the other hand, *Cuba*'s attempt to regain its position as a tourism destination after the demise of the communist bloc is well documented in Hall (1992). In 1987 the country's leadership assigned top economic priority to tourism, and a sum of US$395 million was earmarked to develop and upgrade key resorts, such as Varadero and Cayo Largo. Hall (1992) maintains

Table 5.3 International tourism arrivals, receipts, expenditure and account balance

Region	Tourist arrivals		Tourism receipts		Tourism expenditure		Tourism account balance	
	1990 (m)	Change 1985–90 (%)	1990 (US$m)	Change 1985–90 (%)	1990 (US$m)	Change 1985–90 (%)	1990 (US$m)	Change 1985–90 (%)
World	438.6	6.3	256 761	17.2	n/a	n/a	n/a	n/a
Caribbean	11.51	7.9	8 723	11.9	1599	6.6	7124	n/a
Central America	8.39	8.7	6 137	12.7	5910	18.5	227	n/a
South America	9.03	6.0	4 661	3.5	4553	5.6	108	n/a

Note: n/a = not available.
Source: *Yearbook of Statistics*, WTO, 1991, as quoted in *World Travel and Tourism Review*, 1992.

that these developments are compromised by the leadership's dogmatic approach, which has alienated some of the main markets, such as Canada and Spain, and by the closed US market.

Though not strictly in Central America, *Mexico* is the most important country in terms of economic strength and tourism development (Fish and Gibbons, 1991). Statistics from WTO (1990) show that Mexico had by far the greatest share of the regional total of tourists from abroad in 1988, at 5.692 million visitors or 37.6 percent. The reason for this success, according to Chant (1992), is an extensive range of tourism resources, from beaches and volcanoes to archaeological sites. This is coupled with the best tourism accommodation facilities in Latin America, with 310 470 rooms in hotels and similar establishments in 1988, one-quarter of these in the four- to five-star range.

Costa Rica has centered its tourism industry around environmental resources, with 24 national parks situated in most of the country's major ecological zones. The lack of tourist infrastructure, argues Chant (1992) helps to enhance Costa Rica's role as a provider of 'green holidays' for environmentally friendly tourists. This type of holiday involves higher prices as a balance for restricted access. By 1988 the tourist industry in Costa Rica was worth US$165 million, a 100 percent increase on 1980 figures. The 'Mayan Route', incorporating Mexico, Guatemala, Belize and El Salvador is another interesting development, with both lodging facilities and roads being planned, all of low ecological impact, to join the different Mayan archaeological sites (Schlüter, 1991).

The northern republics of Venezuela, Colombia, Guyana and Surinam could potentially offer the same attractions to North American tourists as Mexico or the Caribbean. In reality, the lack of adequate infrastructure and standards of service prevents them from making any serious inroads into the market. In *Venezuela*, for instance, the contribution of tourism to the balance of payments was US$416 million in 1987, against total export earnings from goods of US$10.6 billion (Bywater, 1989b). Venezuela's main tourist attractions are beaches, the jungle and the Andes, and the facilities are only modest in most destinations. There has, however, been a considerable increase in the number of foreign tourists in the late 1980s, with total arrivals more than tripling between 1983 and 1987. The USA has always been and remains the main source of visitors. There has also been a considerable increase in Canadian visitors, especially to the beach resorts, which are seen as winter-break destinations. They also offer lower costs than comparable destinations, but with lower facilities. Lack of hotel rooms has been one of the major constraints. Another serious problem is airport congestion at Caracas at peak hours (Bywater, 1989b).

Brazil is the world's fifth largest country, with 48 percent of the total land area of South America and 50 percent of its population. It offers a wide range of natural and cultural attractions, from world-famous beaches like Copacabana to less well-known precious Portuguese baroque towns like Ouro Preto in Minas Geraes. It also offers great cultural and ethnic diversity, with enclaves from Germany, Italy, Japan and of course Portugal and Spain. There are 6 percent of Brazilians of African origin, and a Japanese colony of 1.5 million, 70 per cent of whom live in the state of São Paulo. This ethnic mixture has traditionally managed a remarkably harmonious existence. Brazil also offers enormous economic disparities, with some areas having per capita incomes comparable to California, and others where Ethiopia is a better basis for comparison (Rizzotto, 1992a). The unbalanced growth of the country is further exemplified by the fact that three states (São Paulo, Rio de Janeiro and Minas Geraes) employ about 70 percent of the workforce and generate 70 percent of federal taxes (Rabahy and Ruschmann, 1991). In terms of tourism potential, Brazil has 28 percent of the accommodation capacity of the whole of South America, and receives only 0.3 percent of international tourists. The international visitor arrivals increased steadily from 1970 to a peak of 1.929 million in 1987, but have declined to 1.078 million in 1990. The main factors in this decline have been economic instability and concerns over the state of public services and safety, in particular in Rio de Janeiro, which receives most of the visitors from Europe and North America (Ruschmann, 1992). Another factor distorting tourism receipts is that the majority of visitors have always come from neighboring countries, and their average expenditure is half of those coming from Europe or North America (Rabahy and Ruschmann, 1991; Schlüter, 1991). These tourists originate mostly from Argentina and Uruguay and are more likely to visit beach resorts and towns in the southern part of the country, like Porto Alegre or Florianópolis. The accommodation provision currently exceeds demand, with the Brazilian Hotel Convention reporting average occupancy rates below 40 percent (Rizzotto, 1992a). A more detailed description of the existing provision is given in the following section. Brazil is also currently evaluating 38 projects for the development of ecological tourism in Amazonia, some of which are supported by multinational companies which hope to provide new motivations for tourist travel (Ruschmann, 1992).

Argentina held the second position as a tourist destination in 1988, with 2.119 million arrivals, below Mexico on 5.692 million. This did not, however, reflect in receipts, because the main markets for Argentina are the bordering countries (79 percent), followed by Europeans at only 9 percent (Schlüter, 1991). The balance on the travel account has remained negative, in the South American country with the largest and most affluent middle class, and where nearly one and a half million people – out of a population of 28 million – travel abroad every year even if it is mainly to the neighboring countries of Brazil and Uruguay. Bywater (1987) also points out that the tourism industry in 1986 was estimated to employ 350 000 people, mostly supported by domestic tourism, with 22 percent of Argentines taking a holiday each year, an extremely high percentage for the region. In terms of international tourism, Argentina appears mostly as part of a package with Brazil, usually including Buenos Aires and the Iguazu Falls (in the border between Brazil and Argentina) with the stopover on the Brazilian side where the accommodation facilities are better. As a single destination, tourists to

Argentina combine Buenos Aires with either the Iguazu Falls and/or Bariloche, in the Andean Lake District. More recently, Patagonia, the Perito Moreno glacier and the skiing resorts of Cerro Catedral in Bariloche, Chapelco in Neuquén and Las Leñas in Mendoza have attracted some international tourists (Bywater, 1987; Schlüter, 1991). The potential of an area like the north-west (Catamarca, Tucumán, Salta y Jujuy), with subtropical forests, impressive subAndean scenery and unspoilt colonial cities such as Salta, is largely untapped except by domestic tourism, due to lack of coordination and total absence of the adequate infrastructure. Bywater (1987) points to the lack of national direction in tourism policy, as the federal system implies that the responsibility for tourism development and promotion is devolved to the provinces, threatening fundamental standards, such as the homogeneity of hotel classifications. The existence of a strong tradition of domestic tourism, bolstered by the development of 'social' tourism, including pensioners, schoolchildren and trade union members, and the fact that most international tourism originates 'next door' in Chile, Bolivia, Paraguay, Uruguay and Brazil, has somehow discouraged the tourist industry from adapting to the requirements of tourists from developed countries. The high cost of air fares has also constituted a disincentive to travelers from the northern hemisphere, but Bywater (1987) reports the development of new packages, boosted by the introduction of nonstop flights from the USA and Canada, and the opening of a Pacific link, particularly from Australia and New Zealand, helped by a weekly flight from Auckland to Buenos Aires.

Bywater (1989a) and Morgan (1987) provide comprehensive coverage of the tourism developments in the Andean countries of Chile and Bolivia respectively. In the case of *Chile*, the picture is remarkably similar to that of Argentina, with neighboring – mostly Argentine, which accounts for 50 percent – and domestic tourism being the mainstay of the industry. Chile's major tourism attraction for non-South American tourism is Easter Island, mostly for backpackers and adventure tourists, but it suffers from its remoteness, isolation and poor infrastructure. Other potential areas are the northern desert, the capital, Santiago de Chile, and the beach resort of Viña del Mar, which is popular with Argentine tourists. Tourist infrastructure is generally underdeveloped by international standards. There is also a new ski resort, Valle Nevado, 50 kilometers from Santiago, which is a joint venture with the company that built the Les Arcs resort in France. The elongated shape of the country means that it is possible to swim in the sea and ski on the same day. There are also ski resorts further south in the lake district, but this area is generally marketed together with the Argentine Lake District for European and US tourists visiting the southern cone of the hemisphere (Bywater, 1989a).

Bolivia, a landlocked country that boasts both the highest capital city – La Paz – and the highest lake – Lake Titicaca – in the world, is the poorest and least well-known of the Andean countries. It is however, together with Peru, one of the two South American countries where Europe is a more important market than the neighboring countries, due to a combination of adventure tourism and important pre-Hispanic and colonial sites (Morgan, 1987;

Schlüter, 1991). The majority of the visitors include Bolivia for three or four days in a package mainly centered in *Peru*, where the ruins of Machu-Pichu have long been an important tourist destination, seriously affected in the last few years by the violence of the guerrilla movement known as 'Sendero Luminoso' (Richter, 1992). Another well-known destination in the area is the Galapagos Islands (*Ecuador*), which can only be visited on cruises, popular in the USA and Europe, to watch the giant tortoises and land and sea iguanas (Machlis and Costa, 1991).

Africa

Africa is a very extensive land mass and its sheer size is at once an asset and a hindrance to the tourism industry. On the one hand, most of the continent is sparsely populated, offering wide open spaces and tribal cultures. However, apart from North Africa, which has taken advantage of proximity to European generating markets, Africa's tourist potential is largely undeveloped (Boniface and Cooper, 1987). In the past the lack of development has been due to poor transport infrastructure; a poorly organized public sector, particularly at the regional level; and the fact that many countries, especially in sub-Saharan Africa, have placed tourism low on the list of political priorities.

However, some countries do see tourism as a source of foreign exchange and an economic development tool, such as the Gambia, Kenya, South Africa, Tunisia and Morocco. More recently, concerns over the physical security of tourists and heightened awareness of health risks have frustrated Africa's ability to take advantage of the growing international long-haul market. At the same time, levels of economic development have denied any significant volume of domestic tourism. Indeed, out of more than 50 countries in the region, fewer than half have developed significant tourism industries (see Table 5.4). Tourism arrivals are extremely unevenly distributed across the continent. Four North African countries, Morocco, Tunisia, Algeria and Egypt, accounted for over 75 percent of total international tourist arrivals in 1990. These four countries can almost be seen as part of the European tourist system, as they receive around half of all their international tourists from across the Mediterranean. This is reinforced by their former status as French colonies, which makes them more welcoming to European visitors (Burton, 1991).

Statistics overall clearly demonstrate the small scale of international tourism activity in Africa. In 1990 the continent received 14 million international tourist arrivals and earned US$5 billion (a 2 percent share of world receipts). In total, Africa's international arrivals represent a significantly smaller number than tourist arrivals to the UK in 1990. Although Africa's share of international arrivals has more than doubled since 1970, predictions for the early 1990s suggest a decline in absolute volume and value, and thus market share, as other regions compete successfully for the world's international travelers.

Table 5.4 Structure of tourism in Africa, 1990

	International tourist arrivals (thousand)	International tourist receipts (US$ million)	Bedspaces in hotels and similar establishments
AFRICA	14 023	5 052	
Algeria	1 137	64	53 812
Benin	75	n/a	n/a
Botswana	844[2]	65	2 231[1]
Burkina Faso	46	8	421
Burundi	109	4	874[1]
Cameroon	100	21	11 143
Chad	29	12	378
Comoros	8	2	634
Congo	46	7	3 385[4]
Ivory Coast	196	48	12 402[3]
Egypt	2 411	1 994	101 469
Ethiopia	73	25	5 515
Gabon	108	4	n/a
Gambia	101	26	4 792
Ghana	146	72[2]	9 086
Kenya	695	443	47 000
Lesotho	171	17	1 534[1]
Madagascar	53	43	7 814[3]
Malawi	117[2,3]	6[5]	561[3]
Mali	44	37	1 731
Mauritius	292	94	9 572
Morocco	4 024	1 259	111 321
Niger	21	13[3]	3 004
Nigeria	190	25	45 000[6]
Reunion	200	169[5]	1 675[3]
Senegal	246	152	12 230
South Africa	1 029	1 029	88 356[1]
Sudan	33	5	6 694
Swaziland	270[3]	31	2 200[3]
Sierra Leone	98	19	2 210[1]
Tanzania	153[2]	65	9 649
Togo	103	23	4 010
Tunisia	3 204	953	116 534
Uganda	50	10	4 128[1]
Zaire	51[3]	7	27 262[3]
Zambia	141	12[3]	6 441
Zimbabwe	606	47	6 919

Notes: n/a = not available.
[1] = Only hotels.
[2] = Visitors.
[3] = 1989.
[4] = 1988.
[5] = 1987.
[6] = 1986.
Source: Compendium of Tourism Statistics, WTO, 1991.

The hospitality industry

Latin America

The provision of tourist accommodation in the traditional areas of the Caribbean has probably reached its peak and further expansion will be limited. A similar situation occurs in Mexico, where there were nearly 8000 hotels in the four- to five-star range in 1988 (Chant, 1992). Cuba is the one area in the Caribbean where new developments can be expected, with plans to increase the accommodation capacity to 28 000 rooms by 1992 and to 40 000 by the turn of the century (Hall, 1992). As regards South America, Rizzotto (1992b) gives a comprehensive analysis of both the history and the current status of accommodation provision. Table 5.5 shows the total capacity in 1980 and 1989, whereas Table 5.6 sets out the figures for the different categories of classified hotel. One of the problems noted is that there is inconsistency in classification criteria and methods of evaluating star ratings, which alter the recorded total capacity of the region. Brazil, for instance, was recorded by WTO from 1985 on the basis of a new star classification system, which appeared to reduce the accommodation provision by half between 1984 and 1985. Rizzotto (1992b) also points out that there has been little growth between 1989 and 1991, due to the region's poor economic performance.

The share of the international hotel chains in the provision of accommodation is given in Table 5.7, with Brazil being the country with most inter-

Table 5.5 Capacity in hotels and similar establishment in South America (000 rooms)

Country	1980	1989
Argentina	108.0	111.7
Bolivia	8.2	9.9
Brazil	225.9	132.3
Chile	14.3	20.4
Colombia	24.2	42.4
Ecuador	8.5	24.5
Paraguay	2.8	4.6
Peru	34.5	51.7
Uruguay	11.1	10.7
Venezuela	45.5	59.9
South America	482.9	470.2
Americas	3 156.0	4 034.7
World	8 529.4	11 120.3

Source: World Tourism Organization, quoted in Rizzotto (1992b).

Table 5.6 Accommodation in South America, 1988 (000 rooms)

	Classified hotels					Classified and similar establishments Total
	5 star	4 star	3 star	2 star	I star	
Argentina (1987)	3.12	9.02	15.04	18.52	25.13	111.72
Bolivia	0.95	0.55	0.81	0.75	1.29	10.10
Brazil	16.33	25.69	37.22	43.34	9.74	132.32
Colombia	3.06	1.82	3.65	3.05	2.52	39.77
Chile						22.35
Ecuador						24.45
Paraguay	0.46	1.55	1.87			4.38
Peru (1984)	1.88	1.11	7.16	6.97	11.92	42.32
Venezuela (1987)	3.04	2.16	5.40	3.63	4.65	59.92

Source: World Tourism Organization, quoted in Rizzotto (1992b).

national hotel groups within its borders, and having three indigenous hotel chains, one – the Othon group – of international standard, ranked 120 in the world. An interesting development is taking place in Chile, in connection with the French-backed development of the ski resort of Valle Nevado, where two hotels with a capacity of 183 rooms each and an apartment hotel of 56 rooms are being built. In Argentina, most of the accommodation is in one- and two-star hotels, reflecting the importance of the domestic market. Only one international chain, Sheraton, has moved to Argentina, but more recently the apparent economic recovery has induced more investment, and both Hyatt and Caesar-Park Westin will open their first hotels in 1992. There is no Argentine group among the top 200 hotel chains.

Table 5.7 International hotel chains in South America, 1991

	No. of rooms	No. of hotels	Countries
InterContinental	3 321	8	Brazil(1), Colombia(3), Venezuela(4)
Sheraton	3 263	7	Brazil(3), Argentina(1), Chile(1), Peru(1), Venezuela(1)
Hilton	3 251	10	Brazil(4), Colombia(2), Venezuela(4)
Accor (Novotel/Sofitel)	2 202	18	Brazil(17), Paraguay(1)
Melia-Sol	732	3	Brazil(1), Venezuela(2)
Meridien	923	2	Brazil
Club Mediterranee	670	2	Brazil
Holiday Inn	615	3	Brazil(2), Chile(1)
Eurobuilding	633	1	Venezuela
Caesar-Park Westin	422	3	Brazil
Total	16 032	57	

Source: *Directory of Hotels of International Chains*, quoted in Rizzotto (1992b).

Africa

The nature of the hotel industry in Africa reflects its colonial past and current economic characteristics (Hubbard, 1989). In colonial Africa there was little need for hotels apart from those serving transit visitors en route to government guest houses, while other tourists were normally visiting friends and relatives. This system produced a number of large colonial-style hotels at one extreme and hundreds of small hotels catering for the domestic market at the other, with little in between. With independence in the 1950s and 1960s, many African countries wanted the prestige of large four- or five-star hotels. These were commonly owned and operated under management contract by companies such as Intercontinental. The success of such hotels is closely linked to the economic performance of the country – at times of high commodity prices, business tourism sustained them; with the collapse of these markets in the 1980s, occupancies fell.

The imbalanced nature of tourist arrivals to Africa is reflected in the level of tourist development and the supply of accommodation in the continent. In total there are over 325 000 rooms in hotels and similar establishments (WTO, 1991), but these are concentrated in North Africa, which has over 40 percent of these rooms and the majority of tourist plant. These North African countries are distinctive in terms of culture and religion to the rest of Africa, and their Arab origins have attracted Arab oil investment into the hospitality industry. In *Morocco*, substantial hotel development took place in the 1970s and 1980s, financed originally by French and local sources, but more recently by 'oil money' (Seekings, 1988). These developments have taken place on the Atlantic coast, with considerable assistance from the government, particularly in middle- and luxury-priced accommodation. Concentrations of bed spaces are found at Agadir, Tangier and Taghazoute, while Club Mediterranee have been active in promoting Morocco as a 'winter sun' destination with a number of holiday villages. There are also small ski developments in the Atlas mountains.

Tunisia, in contrast, has sought the mass inclusive tour market, though development has been carefully managed. Tunisia had a period of hotel construction throughout the 1970s, again mainly with local and French investment. In order to aid competitive inclusive tour pricing, such investment was in the form of large properties, especially around Sousse and Hammamet and on the island of Djerba. Accommodation is now concentrated on the coast and in Tunis – where business tourism is important. Many recent developments are low rise and built in the local architectural style.

Algeria's tourism is more recent and on a smaller scale. Indeed, there were reported shortages of hotel accommodation. Bed spaces are focused on the coast and Saharan oases. In *Egypt*, the tourism industry is based on both the archaeological and the cultural sites, as well as on beach resorts. Most of Egypt's hotel rooms are found in Cairo and the sightseeing centres of Alexandria and Luxor. There are also a number of floating hotels on the Nile. Resorts on the Mediterranean and Red Sea (at Sinai and the new resort of

Hurghada) are also being developed, and conference facilities are encouraged. US aid is funding new bed spaces in Sinai and the Red Sea, as well as contributing to infrastructure development (Wahab, 1992). Again there has been considerable Arab investment in Egypt's hospitality industry, particularly since the Egyptian government's sell-off of its hotels. *Libya*'s hotel industry is virtually nonexistent and in a poor state of repair (Seekings, 1988).

Southern Africa contains almost 20 percent of Africa's hotel rooms. The sleeping giant of African tourism is the *Republic of South Africa* (RSA). As political reforms progress, the country will become a significant destination, and also a source of tourists for the rest of Africa. The RSA has the most developed tourist industry and is the most industrialized and urbanized country in Africa. In consequence, domestic tourism is more important than inbound tourism. The RSA has 16 percent of Africa's hotel rooms, concentrated along the Natal coast, especially Durban, popular with domestic tourists; in the major cities of Cape Town and Johannesburg; and in the eleven national parks where self-catering huts or 'rondavels' are available. In Bophuthatswana, Sun City is a purpose-built 'Las Vegas' style resort and others are planned. Elsewhere in Southern Africa, accommodation development suffers from poor infrastructure and training. For example, the Zimbabwe Tourist Development Corporation has had to take over the running of some hotels in an effort to improve occupancy.

In West and Central Africa, these problems are particularly acute. The region contains almost a quarter of the continent's hotel rooms, but only *Gambia* has consciously sought the inclusive tour market and put into place a purpose-built accommodation sector. This comprises around 5500 beds with major chains and tour operators represented, as well as government ownership of one major hotel (Hubbard, 1989). Elsewhere, leisure tourism has only developed on a small scale. This is complemented by some business tourism activity in major cities. For example, conference facilities have been developed in Lomé in Togo. Other major centers, such as Lagos in Nigeria, have room shortages. The development of Abuja in Nigeria as a new administrative capital has led to some new hotel building (Hubbard, 1989).

In East Africa, wildlife tourism is complemented by coastal developments on the Indian Ocean. The region is dominated by *Kenya*, and accounts for around 15 percent of African hotel rooms. Kenya has 60 percent of its rooms in large hotels at coastal resorts, in contrast to the smaller 'lodges' in the game parks. International chains are represented in Nairobi, where tourism tends to be business/conference and transit visitors. Also in Nairobi is Utalii College which acts as the main hotel school for the whole of sub-Saharan Africa. In neighboring *Tanzania*, some hotel stock is in poor shape (Burton, 1991), but hotel complexes have been built near Arusha and along the coast near Mombasa (in Kenya), almost as an extension of the Kenyan tourist industry. In the early 1990s the main hotel-building programs are in the islands off the coast – the Seychelles and Mauritius rather than the mainland.

Current and future issues

The main issue affecting tourism in Latin America is economic and political instability. Both phenomena are closely related. Another connected problem is the external perception of a lack of security, which Richter (1992) calls the 'fifth S' (after sea, sun, sand and sex). Rizzotto (1992b) states that international chains are staying away from Colombia because of the drug traffic, and avoiding Peru because of terrorism and political tension. The recent decline in international arrivals to Brazil can be attributed to the same causes, in particular reports of violence and lack of safety in Rio de Janeiro.

The constant cycles of hyperinflation and deflation and the arbitrary fluctuations in the exchange rates also contribute to deter tourists from Europe and the USA. Schlüter (1991) mentions also the negative image projected by the media in the originating countries, which only refers to the region in the context of natural and social disasters.

While not strictly a political or economic issue, the unreliability or complete lack of statistical data is a great obstacle to the development and planning of tourism. It is well documented that tourism statistics suffer from serious methodological difficulties (Allard, 1989), but most authors dealing with this region have specifically pointed to the problem of unreliable or absent data (Bywater, 1987, 1989a, 1989b; Morgan, 1987; Rabahy and Ruschmann, 1991; Riegert, 1991; Rizzotto, 1992a, 1992b).

A document prepared by the Organization of American States (Riegert, 1991), lists a series of concerns about the future development of tourism in Latin America. Among the most fundamental are the following:

- The need to generate more foreign exchange, to compensate for the shock of the 'debt crisis'.
- The need to generate more jobs in the tourism sector, to combat chronic unemployment and underemployment.
- Protection of the environment, mainly through adequate education.
- Development of adequate tourism infrastructure to accommodate the expected flows.
- Elimination of entry and exit barriers to the movement of international tourists.
- Skills development in the hospitality industry.
- Greater emphasis on marketing, promotion and research, in particular collection of statistical data.
- Adequate political support.

The same document proceeds to list a series of programs and projects aimed at addressing some of these concerns. If this agenda is taken seriously both by government agencies and private enterprise, the enormous tourism potential of one of the most unexplored and varied regions of the globe could lead to it becoming the growth area of the next millennium.

Similar issues confront the African continent. The obstacles to tourism development include pervading human problems of overpopulation, hunger and social inequity; political instability and in some parts actual civil war; corruption in the public sector; poorly developed infrastructure to support tourism; and health problems such as the emergent new strains of tropical diseases and AIDS. At the same time the physical safety of tourists cannot be guaranteed even in some of the more established destinations. The result is a continent with an unsafe image, few top-quality hotels and a shortage of trained labor.

Even when the decision is taken by a government to invest and encourage tourism, the question of maximizing the benefits to the country and minimizing leakages and negative impacts to the environment and host society is a critical one. Sinclair *et al.* (1992) have examined the problems of the Kenyan hotel industry in this respect and identify two separate but related issues. First, the dependence of the industry upon tour operators means that contractual arrangements are highly unfavorable for the hotels and as a consequence they allocate more rooms than they possess, leading to overbooking. The second issue is the level of foreign investment and ownership of hotels. A number of international hotel chains are represented in Africa. Accor has considerable presence, as do Intercontinental, Hilton, Sheraton and Meridien. Naturally, the pattern of ownership varies according to individual country's legislation and history. In Tanzania the government has been hostile to foreign investment in the past and some argue that this has held back development of the sector – although profits have been retained in the country. In Kenya a majority of large hotels have an element of foreign investment and a minority are owned outright. Here historic ties with East Africa tend to determine the source of investment – mainly UK and German companies, both tour operators and airlines, with corporations such as Lonhro also owning a number of flagship units, such as the Norfolk Hotel in Nairobi and the Mount Kenya Safari Club.

The African tourist industry is therefore in a cleft stick. In order to compete successfully in the international market, the level of quality required demands that investment and expertise are important. Yet this then increases the levels of dependency of the industry and the national economy. Possible solutions including transferring skills and technology (marketing access to central reservations systems) through management contracts. Intercontinental, for example, operates this system as does the domestic Kenyan company African Tours and Hotels (Sinclair *et al.*, 1992). Franchising also involves a much greater degree of local control. However, Hubbard (1989) adds a rider to this by observing that government privatization policies mean that companies operating management contracts in government hotels may, in the absence of other buyers, be pressurized into becoming shareholders. Sinclair *et al.* neatly sum up the situation:

> The roles played by governments of developing countries in the tourism industry are important, and vary across different sectors of the industry. Within the hotel sector, the government may directly own a hotel chain and usually legislates with resort to foreign investment in that sector, thereby influencing the growth of

accommodation supply and the terms on which it occurs. In addition, the government sometimes attempts to influence the terms of contracts made by locally based hoteliers and foreign firms, for example, by attempting to impose minimum prices for accommodation. However, such attempts are usually frustrated. Local hoteliers, faced with competition within the country and from other developing country destinations, are dependent on foreign tour operators, who control the overseas marketing of the accommodation. (Sinclair *et al.*, 1992, p. 61)

References

Allard, L. (1989) 'Statistical measurement in tourism', in S. Witt and L. Moutinho (eds), *Tourism Marketing and Management Handbook*, Englewood Cliffs, NJ: Prentice Hall.

Bell, J. (1991) 'Caribbean tourism realities', in D. Hawkins and J. R. B. Ritchie (eds), *World Travel and Tourism Review*, vol. 1, Oxford: CAB International.

Boniface, B. G., and Cooper, C. (1987) *The Geography of Travel and Tourism*, London: Heinemann.

Burton, R. (1991) *Travel Geography*, London: Pitman.

Bywater, M. (1987) 'National Report No. 142: Argentina', *EIU International Tourism Reports*, no. 4, pp. 27–38.

Bywater, M. (1989a) 'Chile', *EIU International Tourism Reports*, no. 1, pp. 5–17.

Bywater, M. (1989b) 'Venezuela', *EIU International Tourism Reports*, no. 3, pp. 59–70.

Chant, S. (1992) 'Tourism in Latin America: perspectives from Mexico and Costa Rica', in D. Harrison (ed.), *Tourism and the Less Developed Countries*, London: Belhaven Press and Halstead Press.

EIU (1989) *International Tourism Reports*, no. 4: Database pp. 102–3.

Fish, M., and Gibbons, J. (1991) 'Mexico's devaluations and changes in net foreign exchange receipts from tourism', *International Journal of Hospitality Management*, vol. 10, no. 1, pp. 73–80.

Hall, D. R. (1992) 'Tourism development in Cuba', in D. Harrison (ed.), *Tourism and the Less Developed Countries*, London: Belhaven Press and Halstead Press.

Harrison, D. (1992) 'International tourism and the less developed countries: the background', in D. Harrison (ed.), *Tourism and the Less Developed Countries*, London: Belhaven Press and Halstead Press.

Hubbard, D. (1989) 'The hotel industry in sub-Saharan Africa and the Indian Ocean', *Travel and Tourism Analyst*, no. 6, pp. 9–39.

Machlis, G. E., and Costa, D. A. (1991) 'Little Darwins: a profile of visitors to the Galapagos Islands', *Tourism: Building Credibility for a Credible Industry*, pp. 49–53, Proceedings of the Twenty-Second Annual Conference of the Travel and Tourism Research Association, Long Beach, 9–13 June.

Morgan, E. (1987) 'National Report No. 144: Bolivia', *EIU International Tourism Reports*, no. 4, pp. 51–62.

Rabahy, W. A., and Ruschmann, D. (1991) 'Tourism and the Brazilian economy', in C. Cooper (ed.), *Progress in Tourism, Recreation and Hospitality Management*, vol. 3, London: Belhaven Press.

Richter, L. (1992) 'Political instability and tourism in the Third World', in D. Harrison (ed.), *Tourism and the Less Developed Countries*, London: Belhaven Press and Halstead Press.

Riegert, T. (1991) 'Regional tourism policy concerns: Latin America and the Caribbean', in D. Hawkins and J. R. Brent Ritchie (eds), *World Travel and Tourism Review*, vol. 1, Oxford: CAB International.

Rizzotto, R. A. (1992a) 'Brazil', *EIU International Tourism Reports*, no. 1, pp. 53–67.

Rizzotto, R. A. (1992b) 'Hotels in South America', *EIU Travel and Tourism Analyst*, no. 1, pp. 33–54.

Ruschmann, D. (1992) 'Ecological tourism in Brazil', *Tourism Management*, vol. 13, no. 1, pp. 125–8.

Schlüter, R. (1991) 'Latin American tourism supply: facing the extra-regional market', *Tourism Management*, vol. 12, no. 3, pp. 221–8.

Seekings, J. (1988) 'The hotel industry in the Arab world', *Travel and Tourism Analyst*, no. 5, pp. 15–31.

Sinclair, M. T., Alizadeh, P., and Onunga, E. A. A. (1992) 'The structure of international tourism and tourism development in Kenya', in D. Harrison (ed.), *Tourism and the Less Developed Countries*, London: Belhaven Press and Halstead Press.

Wahab, S. E. (1992) 'Egypt', in J. R. B. Ritchie and D. E. Hawkins (eds), *World Travel and Tourism Review*, vol. 2, Oxford: CAB International.

World Bank (1992) *Atlas*, volume 24.

World Tourism Organization (1991) *Compendium of Tourism Statistics*, Madrid: WTO.

Part 2

Business formats in the international hospitality industry

A feature of the hospitality industry, whether on just a domestic or an international basis, is the range of alternative business formats adopted by firms operating in the industry. This section looks at four main formats – direct ownership by chains, franchising, management contracts, and consortia – and examines the effect that operating internationally has on these formats.

A common feature of the section is the extent to which international development adds *complexity*. This complexity derives from a number of sources and expresses itself in a number of ways. Sources of complexity include major differences in the legislative framework from country to country, social conditions, economic and financial factors, and market conditions. Such complexity has resulted in innovative responses to these challenges. Olsen and Merna explore the extent to which both the strategy and organization structures of international firms have developed in response to this. Khan identifies the great importance of a wide-ranging feasibility study prior to restaurant firms franchising their operations internationally. And Barge explains the increasing number of types of contract that international hospitality contract management companies now operate under. This is also reflected in hotel consortia, as discussed by Byrne, which were relatively easy to categorize into four types in the early 1980s, but which are very much more diverse today.

A second common feature is the *speed of change* within each of these areas of activity. Things happen quickly among international hospitality firms, including wholesale changes in the ownership of hotel properties, social and political revolutions, economic instability, and so on. Despite the turbulent environment, the pace of change and development appears to be speeding up rather than slowing down as international firms seek to gain competitive advantage and new firms seek to expand internationally for the first time.

One of the ironies of this section is that it highlights the extent to which the historic differences between business formats are no longer obvious. International hospitality firms may directly own and operate some properties; manage others on a contract basis, even under some other brand name; and have some of their properties which may not fit their brand as members of a consortium. Even the view that hotels are managed on contract, while restaurant or fast-food chains are franchised, is breaking down. International growth to date has most certainly not led to a standardization of business methods or management approaches. It appears that the reverse is true.

6

The changing character
of the multinational
hospitality firm

Michael D. Olsen and Katherine M. Merna

The 1980s represented for the hospitality industry one of the most tumultuous decades in its history. The free-wheeling development days of this decade were driven by the creative investment packages put together by all the constituents of the global capital market community. These packages were based upon a mistaken belief that inflation will continue unabated, thus making real estate development one of the most attractive investment opportunities available to those with capital to loan or invest.

During those cavalier days of the 1980s, many hospitality firms engaged in expansion beyond their national boundaries as they tried to take advantage of what they believed to be the investment bonanza awaiting them. They engaged in many forms of growth such as joint ventures, master franchising agreements and strategic alliances (discussed in detail in the next chapter). It seemed that there was almost a corporate footrace to see who could join forces with whom, regardless of the form of business agreement. Most of these agreements were driven more by what seemed to be a need not to be left out of this phenomenon than by anything else. In addition, little was done during this period to determine what was the best match between a firm's strategy and its structure. In fact, most expansion of this nature took place without changing much of the organization's structure.

The realities of low inflation, global recession and a crash in the real estate market in the early 1990s brought an abrupt end to the heady days of reckless growth and expansion. Multinational firms were required to rethink their strategies and alliances, along with their operational and balance sheet performances. Investors the world over began calling for greater accountability and more thorough planning by hospitality executives as they tried to preserve the asset values of their investments. Today, the multinational hospitality firm is engaged in developing what it hopes to be the right business format for the remainder of the decade. In so doing, it must deal with several major concerns that continue to vex international expansion. These are matching strategies to environments, creating the correct structures globally and locally, properly diagnosing important environmental threats and opportunities, and effectively dealing with cultural diversity. It is our purpose here to discuss some of these issues and the experiences of multinational hospitality firms as they push forward with international expansion, and to look at what the implications are for the future.

Strategies, then and now

There are several ways to look at how firms conduct business on an international scale. The generic management literature on multinational firms is rich in ways to describe reasons for international expansion, as well as strategies used by firms as they compete in the international marketplace. These will be detailed below.

According to Hamel and Prahalad (1985), companies that are global or international have distribution systems in key foreign markets that enable cross-subsidization strategies (use of financial resources accumulated in one part of the world to fight a competitive battle in another), international retaliation, and world-scale volume. They state further that businesses 'go global' because the minimum volume required for cost efficiency is not available in the company's home market.

Kim (1988) states that, structurally, multinational firms can operate in related business segments, either abroad or on the multinational corporation's home turf, and can operate in the same business segment but in different geographic regions. According to Yip (1989), strategies change as a firm internationalizes. In order for firms to remain successful in this effort they find it essential to develop a total worldwide strategy in three stages. First, they develop the core strategy which is the basis of sustainable competitive advantage, usually developed for the home country first. Second, the core strategy is internationalized through international expansion of activities and through adaptation. Finally, globalization occurs as the international strategy is integrated across countries. The forces behind the changes in industry globalization are market factors (homogeneous customer needs, global customers and channels, transferable marketing), cost factors (economies of scale and scope, learning and experience, sourcing efficiencies, favorable logistics, differences in country costs and skills, product development costs), environmental factors and competitive factors.

Porter (1980) defines a number of basic strategic alternatives in globalization efforts, but first suggests that the firm must choose 'to compete globally or ... find niches ... to compete in one or a few national markets'. The alternative strategies are as follows:

- Broad line global competition – competing worldwide in the full product line of the industry and taking advantage of the sources of global competitive advantage to achieve differentiation or an overall low-cost position.

- Global focus strategy – targeting a particular segment of the industry in which the firm competes on a worldwide basis.
- National focus strategy – taking advantage of national market differences to create a focused approach to a particular national market that allows the firm to outcompete global firms.
- Protected niche strategy – seeking out countries where governmental restraints have excluded global competitors, which requires a high degree of attention to the host government's activities.

In 1984, Leontiades defined two types of strategy found in international industries, 'big-league' and 'little-league', the word 'league' being used here as a definition of vastness of geographic and financial scope. Big-league strategies were characterized by targeting high-volume mass markets defined on a multinational basis, maximum use of economies of scale and accumulated volume, and use of internationally integrated approaches to product/technology/geography/partnerships/joint ventures, maximum use of national strengths in distribution and sales, and avoided competition with big-league firms. Global organizations were the focus in 1986 when Leontiades suggested four global strategies.

- Global high-share strategy – geared toward high-volume, global market segments.
- Global niche strategy – to gain competitive advantage through specialization because financial resources prevent the firm from adopting a high-share strategy.
- National high-share strategy – for a firm to achieve a national competitive advantage such as high volume and low cost, through economies of scale and established distribution channels, for example.
- National niche strategy – to capitalize on the firm's specialization advantage at the national level.

Depending upon resources and products, firms could choose one of these strategies put forward by Leontiades to position their firm in a global or an international framework.

Hamel and Prahalad (1985) stress that global competition requires anticipation of competitive moves and use of new strategic concepts and plans rather than 'precooked' generic strategies. Three competitive methods were mentioned to improve market share valuation. Achieving worldwide cost competitiveness refers to the minimum world market share a company must capture to underwrite the appropriate manufacturing-scale and product-development effort. Retaliation refers to the minimum market share the company needs in a particular country to be able to influence the behavior of key global competitors. Finally, home country vulnerability refers to the competitive risks of national market share leadership if not accompanied by international distribution. Market leadership at home should not be seen as invulnerability.

According to Fayerweather (1981), strategy formulation for the international firm is fundamentally the same as for any firm in an industry, but he emphasizes that attention should be paid to the economic and political factors in the environment. Additionally, assessment of firm strengths and weaknesses in the areas of resources, technology, managerial skills, capital, labor, raw materials, firm structure and global capabilities is recommended. In this context, four strategy models for international firms are put forward:

- Dynamic high-technology model – gives the firm a strong power base, specifically targeted to host countries with interest in future technological innovations. Structural requirements include a strong R&D emphasis and supportive capital resources.
- Low- or stable-technology model – results in a relatively weak power base, depending on the value of the firm's technology and competition, with no guarantee of firm viability for the long term. Technology is typically unsophisticated and has a slow rate of innovation.
- Advanced managerial skill model – infers a high competence in marketing or other management fields, but operates from a weak power base because of lack of demand, unless national benefit is perceived from the skills involved.
- Unified-logistic labor-transmission model – operates from strong power base due to high priority for exports in producing countries, but in an importing country this strategy would be less powerful. Requires low-cost production sites, global marketing, product standardization and integrated control of operations.

Ghoshal's framework of global strategy (1987) is classified into three strategic objectives: achieving efficiency, managing risks – macroeconomic, political, competitive and resource – and achieving internal diversity directed toward innovation, learning and adaptation. Using national differences, scale economies and scope economies are the suggested means and sources of competitive advantage.

Hout et al. (1982) emphasize a change in mentality about how a firm envisions and operates a global company, using pre-emptive strategies. They advocate management of the global firm interdependently – not independently based on conceived 'boundaries' – using economies of scale and other synergistic activities. Effective strategic control is achieved through a central product-line-oriented organizational structure and reporting relationships, with greater centralization as the firm becomes global. Finally appropriate financial policies and strategies should match competitive realities.

Franko (1989) in a longitudinal study of major changes over the period 1960–86 in the world market shares of the world's leading American, European and Asian corporations based in fifteen major industries found that one principal determinant of the firms' global growth rates and gains and losses in world market share was related to corporate research and development intensity, suggesting that investment in technology should be an important factor in determining and maintaining strategic, competitive advantage.

As the above review of the literature on global strategies suggests, a firm must make several decisions regarding how it plans to compete and then decide what unique capabilities it possesses in order to succeed in its globalization efforts. In examining the strategies that have been employed by multinational hospitality firms it can be seen that they have subscribed to at least three of the generic strategies suggested by the literature. They are as follow:

- Exporting a core technology that has been well developed in the home country. Examples include McDonald's, Accor, Forte, Marriott, Oberoi, Choice, and Club Mediterranee. This core technology approach is often referred to as *branding*.
- The belief that the international customer has homogeneous needs and reasons for travel. This suggests a broad-based competitive positioning by most multinational hospitality firms. However, current approaches suggest that a focus or niche approach is now emerging, as is evidenced by the movement of such firms as Day's Inn into India and Accor's Formule 1 throughout Western Europe.
- The exporting of management expertise. The continued practice of hotel multinationals to sell their management capability with little or no capital investment adequately describes the current competitive approach of lodging firms.

Since the service industry has been recognized as differing from the manufacturing industry in several ways (Olsen *et al.*, 1992), further examination of the approaches that multinational hospitality organizations have taken toward development of effective global strategies yields the following additions to the above list:

- Strategic alliances that are characterized by joint ventures, management contracts and master franchise agreements (Olsen *et al.*, 1991).
- Destination/location advantage. This approach is designed to maximize the firm's presence in as many key areas as possible throughout the world. This has especially been the case for those lodging chains which have been strategically aligned with airline companies such as Air France, Swissair and Lufthansa. Beyond this strategic linkage, firms have attempted to locate in primary destination markets in order to have presence in as many market areas as possible, regardless of the competition.
- Technological advantage. As firms have attempted to compete in an increasingly combative environment, they have begun to rely upon technology as a way of differentiating themselves. Firms such as Holiday Inn, Choice International and Hyatt have invested, in some cases, in excess of US$50 million on the development of technology designed to maintain control over the capacity of their rooms inventory, and to improve customer service and overall operations (Langton *et al.*, 1992; Hazard *et al.*, 1992).

The strategies used throughout the 1980s could best be grouped under one heading: real estate development. Developments in the 1990s suggest that the multinational firm will be significantly challenged in its need to ensure that available investment dollars are directed toward maintaining assets which are now ageing; spending considerable effort to develop a technological differential; establishing a clear superiority in management capability; and demonstrating an effectiveness in generating business that has hitherto been unparalleled.

Judging by the difficulties that most multinationals are having today, it would seem that successfully developing these competitive methods is proving to be extremely challenging. Progress is being made in developing technology, but no one appears to be achieving an advantage in this area. Firms are trying to market their management expertise and are increasingly touting their capabilities in trying to grow through management contracts, but few stand out as being different in this regard, especially when two- and three-star hotels are considered. Interest in the use of the management contract as a 'new' strategy is limited beyond the nonhotel sector. It does exist but primarily in airline catering, health care and business and industry settings. Here again, no superiority has emerged.

Regarding the ability to generate capital for reinvestment, most multinationals are failing. Few firms are able to produce sufficient capital from internal sources to keep assets current, and it is mostly wishful thinking to imagine that they can get new investment capital. In fact, due to pressures from the capital markets, many firms are having to cut back on basic asset maintenance expenditures in order to meet return expectations. Few firms are able to find the external capital to support the growth expected by the capital markets. Finally, given the competitive and mature nature of the hospitality industry today, few firms are able to claim a marketing differential that allows them to say that they are able to generate more business than their competitors.

To conclude, it appears that multinational hospitality industry organizations today are struggling to find the right combination of competitive methods to succeed in the environment of the 1990s as they did in the 1980s. As external environmental forces continue to shape the strategies of tomorrow, it is the astute executive who will give the hospitality multinational life throughout the 1990s and beyond.

Multinationals do not look the same

The structure of multinationals today is often characterized as lean and decentralized. This change from the traditional hierarchical structure is partly a function of the hard times that have affected hospitality firms across the globe and partly a recognition that, while these firms may be able to market globally, they must be able to function within a local environment that is often very different from those that they are familiar with. This decentralization process has not come easily for the industry.

In the late 1980s and early 1990s most multinational firms have changed their structure. 'Structure' here is defined as the degree of centralization, formalization and complexity that exists in firms. Centralization refers to the locus of control and power relationships in the firm; formalization refers to the policies, rules and regulations that are employed to keep the organization moving toward its goals; and complexity refers to the degree of specialization of tasks within the firm.

Changes in centralization

One of the major changes is that multinationals are performing with fewer layers between the unit manager and the chief executive. This change is dramatic since there is less oversight by corporate and regional management of the day-to-day decisions that must be made by management in the field. This is especially true in the operations area. The only managerial responsibility areas that appear to be remaining under the tight control of corporate headquarters are the development, finance and, in some cases, marketing functions – the marketing function only as it relates to global programs. Overall corporate strategic planning and legal affairs are also maintained at that level. The handling of corporate human resources matters, which are generally minimal, remains centralized; the rest is decentralized.

To meet the need for improved decision making and quality control in a decentralized structure, most firms are putting more responsibility and control into the hands of unit management and fewer regional personnel. While this approach is generally a welcome one for people in the field, it has resulted in several problems. First, it is difficult to encourage unit managers, who have been accustomed to taking orders and following strict guidelines, to think differently. In fact, one of the most significant problems is how today's manager, who has been performing in an environment that often required a minimum amount of thinking, can be developed into one who can think and respond quickly to changing market conditions, and do all this without checking with his or her immediate supervisor. This is especially problematic for those firms which have expectations that unit-level managements should develop comprehensive strategic plans for their units.

The second major problem is that top management is impatient with the slowness with which unit-level managements adapt to these new demands and changes. This impatience is often the result of the anxiety of the investment community, which wants to see change immediately. It is also due to the inability to recognize that changes like this must be well orchestrated and timed, and often take many years to complete in large complex multinationals. In the case of one multinational hotel chain, the CEO did not expect to see a significant difference in unit management understanding and performance for three years, and had designed a training and development program which took this into consideration.

A third problem often encountered by firms going through this decentralization process is communication, which is compounded by the number of nations a firm does business in. In highly structured firms the flow of information is well understood. But in the case of downsizing, it is often this well-developed communication system that is the last to be adjusted. This usually results in considerable uncertainty among all management personnel up and down the hierarchy, since they may be using old communication channels to deal with new situations to which these old channels no longer apply. However, one positive evolution found to exist in the communications area among some multinationals is the utilization of electronic mail to transfer information from distant places around the globe. Through the use of reservations systems and other forms of electronic media, unit-level managers are now in better contact with headquarters personnel. Performance data, critical information needs and general correspondence are now being handled using modern technology. As events in the industry environment become more uncertain and complex, this positive development in communications should be of extreme importance to both the unit manager and headquarters personnel.

Changes in formalization

The uncertainty stemming from the changes associated with pursuing an international strategy while decentralizing result in changes in the degree and extent of formalization of the firm. Generally, fewer procedures exist that prescribe management interaction between the headquarters and the unit level. However, more policy guidelines are established that guide decision making at the unit level. The policies, procedures and rules that are developed are designed to provide the unit-level manager with sufficient guidance to run his or her business so as to achieve the results called for by the firm's headquarters.

The strategic planning process has become more formalized. In many multinationals today, unit-level managers are required to develop very thorough strategic plans. This is a change from the past where a business plan, which was mostly a budgeting effort, was required. Now managers are expected to begin the planning process six months prior to plan submission. Often firms provide the basic planning framework in the form of a diskette. This guides the manager through the process by prodding him or her with a series of questions designed to stimulate thinking and action. The final plan is then submitted to regional or corporate personnel weeks in advance of a formal defense of the plan by the unit manager. During this review period the plan is looked at in depth by appropriate corporate personnel. The unit manager normally makes an oral presentation of the plan to a team of executives representing various functional areas of the firm, such as finance, marketing and human resources. These executives rely upon their earlier critique to query the manager about the reasons for specific activities, goals and implementation schedules. The final plan is usually a product negotiated between the unit manager and upper management, and serves as the guide for management action for the forthcoming business period. Generally, the unit-level manager's performance evaluation and subsequent compensation are based upon how successful he or she is in achieving the plan's goals.

The overall change in formalization activities can best be described as a shift away from specifics regarding how activities should be done. Instead, the decision-making process is more formalized, allowing unit-level managements to decide for themselves how to perform activities in order to achieve the results called for in their strategic plan.

Changes in complexity

During the 1980s a perusal of the help-wanted advertisements in industry trade literature would have revealed numerous position vacancies that required specialized skills. The increased degree of specialization in headquarter-level positions resulted from the rapid growth in the industry and the accompanying cash flow required to support these specialists, and it created increased complexity in the firm. This was true of many multinationals which felt the need to strengthen the corporate headquarters with individuals who were capable of understanding and managing new international ventures. In some cases the specialists were also employed in the field in regional offices. They covered a range of positions from international law and finance to engineering and design.

The downturn that occurred during the late 1970s and early 1980s affected the degree of complexity in much the same way as it affected the centralizing process. The specialists could no longer be afforded in organizations experiencing financial difficulties. Consequently, in some organizations entire departments were eliminated or greatly reduced in staff. While operations personnel were retained in the field, headquarters specialists found their numbers dwindling. Those who remained were more likely than not to have strong capabilities in such functional areas as finance and marketing. In numerous multinationals many of the functional specialists who remained possessed little actual experience in the industry and had been educated in the well-known business schools. This suggested that the industry was beginning to utilize highly skilled functional specialists in key top-management positions. This trend continues today as a reflection of the increasing complexity of the industry as it reaches maturity.

To conclude this section on changing industry structure, it can be said that the greatest challenge which has faced the multinationals in a changing environment has been effective decentralization. Firms have had to learn how to function with fewer personnel at all levels. They have responded by decreasing formality in corporate control of field operating units, but increasing policy-level guidelines to assist the unit manager in making timely decisions. Accompanying this have been increased expectations regarding unit-level management performance and more in-depth evaluation of that performance by highly qualified functional specialists at corporate headquarters.

Changes in the way the environment is viewed

The business environment defies accurate prediction, especially in the long run. It is made up of many factors and can be arranged into categories in which events take place, such as the economy, technology, sociological-cultural changes, political changes and ecological matters. Managers in all types of firm must learn to develop skills to facilitate their gathering of information on events taking place in the environment, to evaluate and analyze their potential impact and then to take corrective action. For firms operating in a single nation and a narrowly scoped environment, the process of scanning the environment, identifying trends and determining the probability of their occurrence and their subsequent impact on the firm is difficult enough, but for firms operating globally, this difficulty is multiplied by the number of countries and locations within each country. Despite this difficulty, it is essential that firms develop the capability to scan the environment effectively and to determine the threats and opportunities presented by it.

When considering the environment, one of the first issues to be considered is: what would be present in the environment to encourage a firm to 'go global'? In other words, what are some of the environmental triggers that cause firms to globalize? Porter (1980) discusses environmental triggers and strategic innovations as stimuli for globalization. Environmental triggers include increased scale economies; decreased transportation or storage costs; rationalized or changed distribution channels; changed factor costs – labor, energy, raw materials; narrowed national economic and social circumstances; and reduced government constraints – for example, the European Community promoted a major increase in US direct investment in Europe. Strategic innovations which stimulate globalization are product redefinition; identification of market segments; reduced costs of adaptations; design changes leading to more standardized components; deintegration of product; and elimination of constraints from resources or perception (Porter, 1980).

Shanks (1985) discusses three environmental factors which have driven domestic corporations to seek international markets: the maturation of the economies of industrialized nations, such as the slackening of economic growth/GNP in the USA, Canada, the UK and Germany which occurred in the 1970s (although political changes in Europe now offer markets with significant growth potential); the emergence of new geographic market and business arenas, particularly the Pacific Rim and Europe; and the globalization of financial markets, beginning with the International Monetary Fund in 1945, the United Nations promotion of freer world trade, the World Bank, the creation/transformation of multinational financial institutions, and so on. Fannin and Gilmore (1986) state that a single-nation firm can generally divide its concerns into two environmental arenas: internal (assessing resources available to the firm and the capabilities of the firm to use them) and external (market opportunities and threats).

However, the multinational firm faces more decision arenas and four are proposed by Fannin and Gilmore (1986):

- Company's internal arena – productive capacity, technical expertise, marketing ability, management ability, financial resources.
- Home nation state – culture, economics, politics.
- Host nation state – culture, economics, politics.
- Global arena – exchange rates, geopolitics between nations, economics of operation.

Leontiades (1984, 1986) points out that the key initial tasks for a company which is considering 'going global' should be changing perceptions about competitors and markets, losing the idea of compartmentalization along national lines, and integration of management's vision of opportunities and threats to a global level – geographic scope cannot be assumed to be either stable or readily ascertainable over time.

The context of the above discussion suggests that management generally views the globalized environment from a corporate home nation perspective. There are in the hospitality industry equally compelling arguments to view the environment from the perspective of the single-unit operation. Put differently, it is the local environment that creates most of the threats and opportunities for a majority of hospitality firms. Thus, it is not only essential that unit-level multinational firms scan the international environment for corporate-level purposes, it is also essential that unit-level managers possess the capability to do the same for their individual units.

Environmental scanning, while important, is still a relatively little used management activity in many multinationals. Environmental assessment practices of foreign corporations were studied by Klein (1984) to determine the extent of use. The largest 500 foreign industrialists from the Fortune 500 listing were surveyed; 95 percent reported the existence of a corporate planning unit, 51 percent used formal environmental assessment practices, and 41 percent had a formal environmental assessment unit or department in the firm. Forecasting techniques included trend extrapolation (72 percent), but only 29 percent went further with trend impact analysis. Scenarios and brainstorming were the next most popular methods of forecasting, with 61 and 52 percent of firms involved, respectively. Klein also determined that corporations are shifting toward longer time frames for strategic plans, and are using internal corporate forecasts from economists and staff, and purchased environmental information from outside agencies almost equally.

Preble (1989) studied environmental scanning processes of US-based multinational firms and found that several US firms have responded to environmental changes such as greater internationalization of the marketplace and an unfavorable business climate for US-based firms. Some 5.3 percent of the firms stated that they had an environmental scanning unit tied into the planning process, with computer databanks. Scanning involved most countries in which they operate and integrated environmental information on a worldwide basis. Typically, these were the largest and most successful firms. Some 48.4 percent of respondents indicated that they had at least one employee continuously conducting environmental scanning on the countries in which they operated. Internal sources (61 percent) were more relied on than external sources (39 percent) for environmental information.

Finally, Utterback (1982) states that assessing single future trends and changes through environmental monitoring is quite accurate and comprehensive; however, the usefulness in practice is constrained because prediction of the effects and impacts of trends is much more difficult to make.

These research efforts focused mostly on multinational firms in enterprises other than those involved in hospitality. Our own case study investigations suggest that it is no different in the hospitality industry. Most multinationals do little in the way of formally scanning the environment; nor have they done much to prepare individual unit managers in the field for this activity. The problem expressed by most executives when questioned by the authors about their scanning activities was that it was difficult for managers to think in such abstract ways. In other words, many found difficulty in trying to discern trends or patterns from a maze of activity going on in the environment. This problem is compounded further if managers have not been scanning and analyzing the environment before. In order for management accurately to identify and assess trends it needs first to have some way of classifying the environment, and then needs to monitor activity in each classification scheme over time to see changes and patterns taking place. Thus, it takes time, practice and discipline to engage in this activity. Since most unit-level management personnel are busy with day-to-day matters that need immediate attention, they are less likely to develop and fine-tune scanning skills.

This problem generally manifests itself in several ways. First, without someone looking critically at the local environment it is quite probable that activities in either the threat or opportunity category will be missed, or that, in the best case situation, the recognition of them will be out of step with the unfolding of the events. This leads to the second problem, which is that management is always in a reactivating mode. This is an unsatisfactory situation in a highly turbulent environment. While many multinationals recognize these problems, few have designed ways to overcome them. This continues to be one of the most perplexing management problems faced by multinationals.

An additional problem arises when an attempt is made to try to blend environmental information provided by individual operating units with information obtained at the corporate level. In many cases there are important events that are observed at the local/national level which are important early indicators of potentially significant threats or opportunities. However, few firms have yet been able to develop approaches which allow this information to surface and be used for corporate strategic planning purposes. In only one case with which the authors are familiar did the multinational's headquarters seek to accomplish this important synthesis of information. The CEO believed that the only way this could be accomplished was to bring together all the managers from approximately twelve countries around the globe. This was done on an annual basis. While several items of business were conducted at these meetings, environmental scanning reports were required and this was built into the activities of the meeting. The same CEO required rather extensive written environmental analyses from each unit manager as part of their strategic plan. The practice is just feasible for a small multinational firm which has the cash flow to support the expenses associated with such an endeavor. However, for firms with hundreds of units throughout the world, this approach is not financially practical.

It appears that most large firms are trying to deal with this problem by providing very structured planning guidelines that require the collection, analysis and reporting of environmental information. The results to date are so far mixed. It appears that the greatest problems still associated with environmental analysis are those articulated by Lawrence and Lorsch (1968), which are a lack of clarity in the information about the environment which is obtained by the organization; uncertainty of causal relationships which exist between the environment and the organizations, and the differing variables of the environment itself; and the unpredictable nature of the timespan of feedback regarding the results associated with efforts to manage the environment. Multinational executives must somehow solve these problems if they are effectively to improve the performance of their units in each nation. In this day of turbulent global change and uncertainty, environmental scanning is an area in which management is trying to do something but is struggling to achieve anything positive.

The diversity issue

As we have seen, managing globally requires adjustment to the needs of the local environment (discussed in detail in Chapter 15). One of the most perplexing issues faced by the multinational as it expands is the overall adjustment that must be made from a cultural perspective. This is especially critical in working effectively with the local workforce and in marketing to local clientele.

The principal issues surrounding the workforce norms are based upon: the ideological base of the country; religious issues regarding work; local work ethic; laws and regulations; and indigenous biases regarding gender and race. In general, the multinational can do little about these deep-seated cultural norms. Thus, it is more important for the multinational to learn to understand, monitor and remain flexible in regarding behavioral issues associated with the workplace.

Equally important is the need to factor these differences into the cost of doing business in each country. The labor costs of a caterer doing business at airport operations in Paris, New York and Moscow are vastly different. Also unique are the laws which govern and protect the worker. These are basic elements of doing business in each country that for the most part cannot be changed. Thus, the role of the local manager is to know them and learn to operate within the parameters they dictate.

Regarding behavioral issues, most firms are trying to sensitize both head-quarters and field personnel regarding cultural diversity matters. Various educational programs have been offered by firms, but this effort is in a fairly immature stage at present. While the need for more behavioral education is increasingly recognized as an important issue that multinationals must deal with, as yet there is no consensus on how this can best be accomplished. Thus, it is an issue which continues to challenge multinational firms as they expand into new locations.

Marketing to local clientele also presents diversity challenges. The local norms regarding entertainment, food consumption, dress and interrelationships must be considered in every interaction between the guest and the customer. In some cases these norms are laws emanating from either a religious or a legislative base. The local manager must know not only what they are, but also the rationale for their existence. In many situations it is more problematic if a manager disregards the intent rather than the actual letter of the law. While market research can solve some of these types of problems, it is an activity that is not always permitted, and in many cases it may not yield reliable and valid results.

Summary

As firms move from a national base of operations to a global marketplace, they encounter several challenges. These include the adoption of the correct strategy to drive the expansion, the need to address the changes in structure that are likely to result from it, the problems associated with trying to develop and improve managers' scanning of the environment and implementation of the chosen strategy, and lastly, improving the ability of the firm and its management to address the issues of cultural diversity that emerge in each new nation that the firm begins its business activities in.

The hospitality industry is unique in the fact that it does business on a very local level even though it may claim to be multinational. Thus, it must address two sets of managerial challenges: those that exist from a multinational perspective and those that exist at the local level. Effective management will have to develop the appropriate strategy to deal with this situation if it plans to succeed in the long run. It must also recognize that the balance of strategy and structure will change quickly and on a nation-to-nation basis. Thus, developing the appropriate structure to react quickly to the threats and opportunities in the environment will continue to be one of the most important challenges the multinational firm will face.

References

Fannin, William R., and Gilmore, Carol B. (1986) 'Developing a strategy for international business', *Long Range Planning*, vol. 19, no. 3, pp. 81–5.
Fayerweather, John (1981) 'Four winning strategies for the international corporation', *Journal of Business Strategy*, vol. 2, no. 2, pp. 25–36.

Franko, Lawrence K. (1989) 'Global corporate competition: who's winning, who's losing, and the R & D factor as one reason why', *Strategic Management Journal*, vol. 10, pp. 449–74.

Ghoshal, S. (1987) 'Global strategy: an organizing framework', *Strategic Management Journal*, vol. 8, pp. 425–40.

Hamel, Gary, and Prahalad, C. K. (1985) 'Do you really have a global strategy?', *Harvard Business Review*, July–August, pp. 139–48.

Hazard, Robert C., O'Rourke Hayes, Lynne, and Olsen, Michael D. (1992) 'Going global – acting local: the challenge of Choice International', in R. Teare and M. Olsen (eds), *International Hospitality Management: Corporate strategy in practice*, London: Pitman.

Hout, Thomas, Porter, Michael E., and Rudden, Eileen (1982) 'How global companies win out', *Harvard Business Review*, September–October, pp. 98–108.

Kim, W. Chan, and Mauborgne, R. A. (1988) 'Becoming an effective global competitor', *Journal of Business Strategy*, vol. 9, no. 1, pp. 33–7.

Klein, Harold E., and Linneman, Robert E. (1984) 'Environmental assessment: an international study of corporate practice', *Journal of Business Strategy*, vol. 5, no. 1, pp. 66–75.

Langton, Bryan, Bottorff, Celeste, and Olsen, Michael D. (1992) 'The strategy, structure, environment coalignment', in R. Teare and M. Olsen (eds), *International Hospitality Management: Corporate strategy in practice*, London: Pitman.

Lawrence, P. R., and Lorsch, J. W. (1968) *Organization and Environment*, Division of Research, Graduate School of Business Administration, Harvard University, Boston, Mass.

Leontiades, James (1984) 'Market share and corporate strategy in international industries', *Journal of Business Strategy*, vol. 5, no. 1, pp. 30–7.

Leontiades, James (1986) 'Going global: global strategies vs national strategies', *Long Range Planning*, vol. 19, no. 3, pp. 96–104.

Olsen, Michael D., Crawford-Welch, Simon, and Tse, Eliza (1991) 'The global industry in the 1990s', in R. Teare and A. Boer (eds), *Strategic Hospitality Management: Theory and practice for the 1990s*, London: Cassell.

Olsen, Michael D., Tse, Eliza, and West, Joseph (1992) *Strategic Management in the Hospitality Industry*, Chapter 1, New York: Van Nostrand Reinhold.

Porter, Michael E. (1980) *Competitive Strategy: Techniques for analyzing industries and competitors*, Chapter 1: The structural analysis of industries; Chapter 2: Generic competitive strategy; Chapter 13: Competition in global industries, New York: Free Press.

Preble, John F. (1989) 'The environmental scanning practices of multinational firms: an assessment', *International Journal of Management*, vol. 6, no. 1, pp. 18–28.

Shanks, David C. (1985) 'Strategic planning for global competition', *Journal of Business Strategy*, vol. 5, no. 3, pp. 80–9.

Utterback, J. (1982) 'Technological forecasting and strategy; environmental analysis and forecasting', in Michael L. Tushman and William L. Moore (eds), *Readings in the Management of Innovation*, London: Pitman.

Yip, George S. (1989) 'Global strategy ... in a world of nations?', *Sloan Management Review*, Fall, pp. 29–41.

7

International restaurant franchises

Mahmood Khan

In the emerging global economy, franchising will play a very significant role in the forthcoming century. The question most franchisors are faced with is not whether to enter international markets, but rather how and when to enter with the best chances of achieving success with fewest problems. Franchising is considered as a continuing relationship in which the franchisor provides a licensed privilege to do business, plus assistance in organizing, training, merchandising and management in return for a consideration from the franchisee (International Franchise Association, 1990).

This method of conducting business is distinctly different and is based on a symbiotic relationship between franchisors and franchisees. In a foreign land, the task of organizing, training, merchandising and management can become a nightmare, particularly when the complexities in restaurant business are considered. Among the types of franchising arrangement, business-format franchising, as opposed to product-and-trade-name franchising, is common in international restaurant franchises. In business-format franchising, since the success of the entire concept is involved, the opportunities in foreign markets can be both exciting and frightening.

The process of translating a franchise concept so that it will be successful in a different environment is the most difficult task. Restaurant franchisors and franchisees are faced with unique cultural, political, social and economic challenges. For example, when McDonald's opened an outlet in Moscow, restaurant patrons took home the plastic, paper, and styrofoam trash. Localizing the franchise concept in an international market involves more than legal and financial challenges. The United States of America, pioneer in the field of franchising, continues to be the leader in restaurant franchising. American franchisors continue to expand to foreign markets throughout the world. In this chapter American restaurant franchises will be used as examples, but the concepts discussed are also applicable to international franchises generally.

Restaurant franchises in international markets

According to the International Franchise Association, a total of 374 business-format franchisors operated outside the USA during 1988. A total of 35 046 American franchise outlets were distributed all around the world. The largest number of outlets were in Canada, followed by Japan, Europe, Australia, the United Kingdom and Asia. According to the report by the Association:

> American franchisors enter foreign markets using a variety of methods, including franchising directly to individuals and operating company-owned units, joint ventures or franchising. Selling a master franchise is the most popular, cheapest and fastest technique. Of the 374 franchisors operating outside the US, 88.2 percent sold their units either directly or through a master franchisee who received the right to develop the franchisor's system in a foreign country. (International Franchise Association, 1990)

The report also notes that entering foreign markets can be difficult, and that the success (or failure) of international franchising depends on several factors, including the franchisor's domestic market position and its ability to expand its expertise and adapt to countries that may have cultural and language differences. Some of the major factors that have an impact on expansion in foreign markets are discussed later in this chapter.

American franchises are lucrative for foreign franchisees, since they not only offer opportunities for local ownership of a foreign business, but also provide American business methods, knowledge and technology. As shown in Tables 7.1 and 7.2, of the different types of US business-format franchise, restaurants had the highest number of outlets. The total number of outlets is close to 7000, or 20 percent of all business-format franchises. Except in parts of Europe and Canada, 20 percent or more franchises in all regions surveyed were restaurant franchises. It can be rightly said that the most rapid and successful expansion of US business has been in the area of restaurant franchising. The largest number of restaurant franchises is in Japan, which

Table 7.1 Restaurant franchises in international markets

Region	No. of units	% of total restaurant franchises	% of total franchises
Canada	1338	19.1	14.0
Mexico	146	2.1	21.3
Caribbean	213	3.0	36.8
UK	726	10.4	25.5
Other Europe	772	11.0	15.5
Australia	750	10.7	26.2
Japan	1827	26.1	20.4
Other Asia	546	7.8	26.0
Other	678	9.7	27.2
Total	6996	100.0	20.0

Source: *Franchising in the Economy*, 1988–90, International Franchise Association (1990). Reproduced with permission.

Table 7.2 Location of international establishments, 1988

	Total	Canada	Mexico	Caribbean	UK	Other Europe	Australia	Japan	Other Asia	Other
Total – all franchising	35 046	9 544	684	579	2 843	4 975	2 858	8 975	2 097	2 491
Total – business-format franchising	35 046	9 544	684	579	2 843	4 975	2 858	8 975	2 097	2 491
Restaurants (all types)	6 996	1 338	146	213	726	772	750	1 827	546	678
Hotels, motels and campgrounds	518	238	22	19	28	77	13	9	31	81
Recreation, entertainment and travel	327	194	0	1	17	25	34	41	0	15
Automotive products and services	1 708	683	25	31	15	505	128	143	49	129
Business aids and services	5 851	2 762	8	8	459	732	776	890	103	113
Construction, home improvement, maintenance and cleaning service	2 813	1 188	0	7	502	104	27	647	17	321
Educational products and services	5 583	520	124	7	106	183	262	3 673	665	43
Laundry and drycleaning services	27	21	0	0	1	0	0	0	5	0
Rental services (auto-truck)	5 548	553	268	265	378	1 682	417	579	471	935
Retailing (non-food)	3 574	1 378	78	9	548	720	429	227	81	104
Retailing (food non-convenience)	2 101	669	13	19	63	175	22	939	129	72

Source: International Franchise Association, 1990. Reprinted with permission.

amounts to 26.1 percent of the total restaurant franchises. The other regions are Canada (19.1 percent), Europe (11.0 percent), Australia (10.7 percent) and the United Kingdom (10.4 percent). Restaurant franchising is gaining popularity in almost all parts of the world. Since franchising is predominantly present in the United States, international franchising will be discussed from the point of view of US franchising entering other foreign markets. Although the discussion is heavily slanted toward the US franchise restaurant industry, the factors involved have universal applicability.

Many of the franchisors who are entering foreign markets have been very successful in franchise business in the United States and have the necessary expertise in restaurant franchising. Although some attribute international expansion to the saturation of the local markets, there are scores of other reasons that can make foreign markets lucrative. The most important factors are outlined and discussed below.

Factors related to the expansion of restaurant franchising

In a survey conducted by Walker (1989), the major benefits perceived by franchisors from international expansion were based on achieving financial, market or general growth. The benefits cited by more than 10 percent of the respondents were:

- Additional growth/expansion.
- Added revenues/profits, improved return on investment, or direct financial gain.
- Larger market, more market penetration, or more market share.
- International identity and greater recognition.

On the other hand, the major drawbacks cited by more than 10 percent of the respondents were:

- Lack of control/accountability.
- Difficulty of supporting/ servicing franchisees, and operations challenges.
- Cost/expense involved.
- Distance and time differences.

Culture and language differences and the difficulty of judging local needs were indicated by 9.5 percent of the respondents. The top four reasons why companies do not have franchises outside the United States were given to be:

- Concentrating on the USA, occupied with current franchise activities.
- Company is too young and has not reached that stage of development.
- Need to expand further within USA.
- Lack of capital or financial resources.

A discussion of some of the reasons for international expansion in restaurant franchises now follows.

Expanded market

International markets provide new dimensions for the expansion of restaurant franchises. Increases in population, which are rapid in some countries, and the rise in available disposable income, have created a market for restaurants. The combined market size and potential demand for franchise restaurants (both product and service) is much greater in some developing countries than in many of the developed countries. Demographics in countries such as China, Japan, Korea, Malaysia, India and Indonesia are changing very rapidly. The financial status of the populations in these countries has changed for the better. Economically, some of the countries are getting more resources due to the export of natural products and finished goods, and domestic industrial expansion is taking place simultaneously. All this has resulted in large pockets of the population that would like to avail of restaurants.

Economic and demographic trends

Some notable trends which favor the increase of restaurant franchising in foreign markets include the following:

- Increased educational levels of the local population.
- Technological advancement, facilitating travel and intercultural cooperation among countries.
- The willingness of the younger generation to try new products and unconventional types of food.
- Rapid development of rural areas and concentration of population in urban and industrial areas.
- Increased disposable income of the population.
- Increased number of women in the work force and of two-income families.
- Increased emphasis on convenience.
- The popularity of take-out or home-delivered menu items.

A closer look at the above list shows that they are the very factors that led to the popularity of franchised restaurants in the United States.

Increased travel and tourism

Increased travel and tourism for business or pleasure has positively exposed the successful and rapidly growing restaurant franchise industry to visitors worldwide, primarily the quick-service industry and a variety of food products that are offered through them. Business people on international travel are picking up the idea of franchising and are getting interested in investing in restaurant franchises. Foodservice franchising lends itself to duplication and brand recognition, both considered to be an asset in obtaining repeat business from consumers.

Quality of product/service

Restaurant franchises, such as McDonald's, Kentucky Fried Chicken and Hardees, are known for the quality of their products and services, which are regarded very favorably in many countries and serve as a selling point for franchised products. In many instances, consumers have a good expectation of products and services as well as a degree of food safety assurance. The standardization process that is used by many franchise concepts lends itself to quality assurance and consumer satisfaction.

The demand for products offered by some US franchise restaurants in many countries has far exceeded their franchisors' expectations, although this may not be true for all countries. A good example is the demand for products like hamburgers, fried chicken and pizza in addition to Pepsi and Coca-Cola and some of the other foods currently being offered by franchised restaurants in foreign markets. As further evidence, the international operations of McDonald's Corporation are its fastest-growing business, contributing 21 percent of the company's pre-tax profits in 1986 (*Restaurants USA*, March 1989).

Acceptance of food is also based on the 'taste development' for a particular product. Acceptance of new food items normally requires frequent exposure and eating occasions. Once the taste is developed and the product is accepted then it may lead to its popularity. This may be the case for many menu items which are popular in the United States but will take some time to gain popularity overseas. There will always be certain areas of the world where food product acceptance will remain a problem. Thus restaurant franchisors will have to plan their strategies carefully and target sections of the world in which there is good potential for achieving the acceptance and popularity of their product. Variations in menu items may be necessary to achieve this. Also, the quality and safety standards set by American franchises make the products and services offered consistent in quality and above all of high safety standards.

Restaurant franchises achieve certain standards and status both nationally and internationally. Strange as it may sound, in some countries eating at a western country's franchise restaurant is considered as a status symbol. Consumers base their expectations on what they have seen abroad or on television – for example, standard products, fast service, well-lit and air-conditioned dining areas, clean restrooms and a social atmosphere. In Taiwan, younger consumers consider eating at an American franchise restaurant a special social occasion.

There is a willingness among individuals in the younger generation to try new and unconventional food products, with the result that foods offered by American franchises are more acceptable now than ever before, in almost all parts of the world. Nutritional concerns related to foods in the United States may not necessarily be valid in other countries where undernourishment rather than overnourishment is the major concern.

Technological advancement

Technological advances, especially in information technology, have led to more sophisticated controls and management techniques being implemented all over the world. This has made it easier to implement the concept of a franchise system. A spinoff of these technological advances is an enormous increase in the movement of population from rural to urban and industrial areas, resulting in convenience becoming much more important. Restaurant franchises focus heavily on consumer convenience and a fast and efficient service. Increased use of computers, videos and other electronic devices is modifying behavior and hence creating needs that are unparalleled in the history of humankind. The concepts of 'eating away from home', 'drive-ins' and 'home-delivered' meals are gaining in popularity. Franchise restaurants are equipped to serve many of these needs and consequently are increasing their demand worldwide.

Business management

Many countries have already borrowed the American way of conducting business, in which franchising plays a very important part. American entrepreneurship and the role that the multi-billion-dollar quick-service industry plays in the US economy have attracted many foreign entrepreneurs to seek replications in their native countries.

There are several significant factors that provide restaurant franchising with a fertile ground, such as the relative availability and/or lower costs involved in securing human resources, ingredients and products in foreign markets. Also, the sales volume required to break even and/or to offset any possible losses may be much smaller. Expenses, such as on advertising and training, may also be relatively less, thereby increasing the profitability of the venture. A word of caution is necessary at this point: not all countries offer these advantages. For example, the extraordinarily high costs of start-up, occupancy, labor and food in Tokyo are blamed for delayed or non-existent profits. It may be easier to get human resources in countries such as India and Indonesia, but the available disposable income may be low, making the menu items unaffordable for an average person. Thus there is a need to balance carefully all the positive and negative factors. Although finding this balance is difficult, it is not impossible. Above all, the products offered by restaurant franchises and their very functionality have been successfully tried and tested to such an extent that it makes sense to use this apparatus elsewhere, making modifications as necessary.

In some countries it is easier to manage restaurant facilities if resources are easily economically available. With the advancement of technology, educational standards and economic conditions in many countries, there are a growing number of management-oriented entrepreneurs available, who have enormous potential to be successful in the operation and management of franchised restaurants. Also, multi-media teaching tools, publications and computerized programs can be used effectively for management training purposes.

Trade and monetary balance

The international financial system has changed dramatically in the past few years. The import and export balance in many developed and developing countries has changed drastically. These changes have facilitated the investment of foreign currencies in international markets with a decent return on investment. However, fluctuating currency values remain a major concern for foreign investors and play a role in the decision to invest at home or abroad.

Political climate

The unification of the European countries and more openness among the countries of the Eastern bloc has created a curiosity in those countries and tremendous potential for the growth of franchise restaurants. Such political changes, if long term, can provide opportunities unparalleled in the past. The chances of establishing a flourishing franchise concept in places where none exist now are much greater and should be utilized to a maximum extent by all franchisors considering whether to enter foreign markets. The political climate has moved considerably towards creating an environment that favors

Table 7.3 US franchise restaurants in Europe

Restaurant	Country	Number of units
McDonald's	United Kingdom	320
	Germany	319
	France	115
	Spain	28
Burger King	United Kingdom	163
	Germany	70
	Spain	39
	France	18
Pizza Hut	United Kingdom	228
	Germany	41
	Spain	14
	France	3
Domino's	United Kingdom	42
	Germany	3
	Spain	3
	France	1
KFC	United Kingdom	271
	Spain	16
	Germany	10
TGI Friday's	United Kingdom	5
Taco Bell	United Kingdom	2
Sbarro	United Kingdom	1

Source: *Restaurants and Institutions* (1990).

business ventures on foreign soils. Currently there are several US franchise restaurants in Europe (see Table 7.3) and this number is growing rapidly. All predictions are that the unification of Europe will result in the favorable development of franchised restaurants as a result of the following:

- Free movement of goods, services, people and capital resources within the Community.
- Centralization of purchasing and distribution functions.
- Pooling of human resources.
- Uniform codes, specifications and regulations.
- Uniform currency and monetary regulations.

These changes are bound to have a profound impact on the franchise businesses being conducted or planned for the future.

Points to consider in international franchising

Restaurant franchising has tremendous potential in the international market. However, in order to be successful several factors have to be considered. Some of these factors are explained below, illustrated with examples of existing franchises from selected parts of the world.

Political environment and legal considerations

Political stability and the nature of legal restrictions are important considerations prior to entering any of the foreign markets. Political changes may have adverse effects on methods of conducting business. Political stability in a country is often hard to gauge, but past history and the present political environment may provide good indicators.

Legal restrictions may also make it very difficult for foreign franchises to function. For example, the French government has created a historical classification aimed largely at protecting the traditional flavor and atmosphere of the French restaurants. This will restrict the use of bright lights and the atmosphere normally prevalent in many fast-food restaurants. In order to conduct business, terms and conditions of contract have to be written in such a way that there is room for future adaptation to unfavorable situations.

Associated with the political environment are the monetary restrictions and tax policies of a country. There may be a long trail of bureaucracy involved, or it may be difficult to get money out of the country. On the other hand, there may be certain countries which may provide incentives for foreign investors and provide special concessions.

Developing countries with stable political and economic situations, such as Malaysia, Taiwan, South Korea, Indonesia and Singapore, are good candidates for foreign restaurant franchises. Also, the greater openness of the Eastern bloc countries has made them more inviting to restaurant franchisors. It was reported that when McDonald's became the first fast-food chain to open a restaurant in Moscow, people stood in line for hours to sample

American burgers! Similar scenes have lately been witnessed in several other countries. Pizza Hut and Baskin-Robbins have plans to open outlets in the former Soviet Union, while McDonald's is planning to have joint ventures in Hungary and Yugoslavia. Other franchisors are planning to enter Poland and Hungary.

Clearly, politics play an important role in the franchise operation. No matter what the economic significance of a franchise to a particular country, it is considered to be of symbolic importance. So there may be occasions when some restaurant franchises become targets of physical or non-physical attacks by government or the public in general. Such situations arose for American restaurant franchises in China, Beirut and Nicaragua, where businesses have had to be closed. It was reported that Kentucky Fried Chicken had temporarily to shut its two Beijing units, one of which is in Tiananmen Square, out of concern for employees' safety. Insurance against such risks is hard to obtain in foreign countries. It must also be remembered that some countries do not honor the integrity of copyrights, trademarks and logo types.

Two political events that are being watched particularly carefully are the return of Hong Kong to China and the economic cooperation of European countries in 1990s.

Language, culture and traditions

Language plays a very important role in the successful operation of a franchise system in foreign countries. A good working knowledge of the language of the country is essential primarily for three purposes:

- For effective communication with the franchisees or master franchisees, and for the complete interpretation and comprehension of the philosophy, strategy and functioning of the franchise system.
- For developing and implementing a successful training program for the employees and management personnel.
- For providing details of operations and an operations manual to the franchisees.

Countries where English is spoken and understood, such as the United Kingdom, Australia, Hong Kong, Malaysia, India, Indonesia and Singapore, present no language problems. Moreover, language should not be a deterrent where profitability is warranted, since in countries like Japan and Taiwan US franchises have functioned successfully. Also, certain franchises like McDonald's have training centers overseas. McDonald's also has Hamburger Universities in England, West Germany and Japan. Foreign training centers follow the same format as in the countries of origin with the necessary intellectual and cultural adaptations for a particular host country.

Some aspects which might be thought minor may be stumbling blocks in a foreign environment. For example, even the trade name and trademark may have different meanings in other languages, which may be indecent and unacceptable in some countries.

Cultural food habits have an enormous impact on food selection, acceptance and popularity. There are certain countries where food items such as beef, pork and pork products, and alcoholic beverages are not acceptable. Other animal products or combinations of certain ingredients may not be acceptable in some countries. This rules out the sale of products such as sausages and bacon, and the use of lard as shortening. Consequently, it poses a problem for the selection of breakfast items by some foreign franchises. Thus the popularity of breakfast in American restaurant franchises does not necessarily translate into profitability in other countries. Also meal timings vary considerably, and eating out for breakfast may not be popular in some countries. Eating styles may also be distinctly different. Many people do not like the idea of holding burgers in the hand (without knife and fork) and biting with the mouth wide open! There are many such minor considerations to be taken into account.

Menu items and service

Not only the types of menu item but also the variations of an item should be considered. Tastes vary from population to population and this should be taken into account. For example, the fried chicken served by Kentucky Fried Chicken in Taiwan, Mexico and Malaysia is considerably spicier than in the United States. Also chili sauce is provided in Mexico and South American countries. Such modifications become necessary to satisfy the needs of local populations.

The popularity of menu items becomes a top priority for many restaurant franchises planning to expand overseas. In the Pacific Rim area, where fresh fish and fish products are readily available and popular, frozen fish products may not be popular. It should also be noted that salads are not very popular in many countries. McDonald's in Malaysia uses the local type of popular dried meat in burgers and has sugar cane juice on the list of beverages sold. It also has beer as one of the beverage choices in Germany. Other tropical fruit juices and toppings should also be considered for inclusion on the menu.

Exposure of the food concept may be a time-consuming process. Hamburgers and fried chicken are not native foods in many countries, and may require frequent exposure to gain familiarity and acceptance. An example is the growth of the pizza market in the United States. For pizza to gain popularity in Japan, a period is needed for taste development.

Similarly, there are differences in the style of service required based on the attitude of the local population. In countries where eating at the dining table is popular, take-out and delivery systems are not popular. In some countries chinaware and silverware are used rather than paper or polystyrene packing. In others, trays and soiled dishes are left on the table for staff to clear, even in quick-service restaurants. The cleanliness and air-conditioned atmosphere of American restaurant franchises are a top priority among customers in foreign countries.

The arrangement of a country's transport network is another factor to bear in mind when considering delivery of service. For example, travel through highways may not be as popular in other countries as it is in the United States. On the other hand, train traveling may be very popular. Site selection for a restaurant becomes an important criterion, and it becomes necessary to draw up a new set of guidelines for each country.

Demographics and economic data

An accurate demographic study of the target population is essential before and/or during the operation of franchised restaurants on foreign soils, and can be undertaken as a part of the feasibility study. The age, sex and available disposable income of the target families should be carefully evaluated with special emphasis on the potential for changes in the near future. This type of study helps in the planning and management of operations.

Demographic changes may be important and rapid in many countries. Educational status and working conditions have generally improved with the growing number of educational institutions. Large segments of populations may have migrated or may be expatriates in some countries, particularly in the Middle East. All these changes make 'eating out' facilities very significant. The development of industrial centers, malls and shopping complexes provides an opportunity for the development of restaurant franchises. In many countries where franchise restaurants were built in such locations, business is flourishing. In fact, some franchise restaurant units have the biggest sales in their respective countries and regions.

Menu prices and cost control methods have to be adapted to particular situations. The value of the dollar and the cost of the ingredients may make the overall price of the menu items too high for the average person.

Availability of resources

An important element in international franchising is the availability of resources and the possibility of conformation to the standards set by the franchisors. For example, chicken or tomatoes (as per the specifications of the franchisors) may not be locally available or, if available, may not be in sufficient quantities to keep pace with the demand. It was reported that McDonald's put meat, potato, and other processing operations under the same roof when it opened its unit in Greater Moscow. This type of arrangement may be necessary in some countries in order for the franchising to be successful.

Compounded with these problems is the fact that indigenous products and ingredients may not function as expected when combined together, thus affecting the finished quality of the product. For example, in the case of fresh biscuits, flour and other ingredients obtained from local sources, when blended, may not result in the same quality of product. Seasonal variations, varietal characteristics (particularly in the case of vegetables) and the availability of items become important considerations for foreign franchisors.

Equipment availability and performance may also vary, which can have a serious effect on the quality of the product. In certain countries, the power supply or water supply may be regulated which may also affect the quality of the product and services. Storage facilities and temperatures may dictate the extent to which products can be stored. In short, the potential for the conformation to the standards and specifications of a franchisor needs careful scrutiny. Another major problem for many restaurant franchises is the preservation of and compliance with their proprietary rights.

In conclusion, it can be said that consideration should be given to all of the factors outlined in this chapter with particular emphasis on the political and economic climate of the country. Of course, common business sense is required to assess the potential return on investment, future growth potential, market demand, expense and cost estimates, and overall business functionality. In short, a good feasibility study should be conducted prior to entering any international market and regular evaluations of the business performance should be made in order to obtain the necessary feedback to maintain a competitive edge. Despite the diversity of approaches, there are some common denominators that can serve as guidelines for restaurant franchisors who are planning on foreign locations. Looking at the current trends, all the indications are that restaurant franchising in international markets is the wave of the future.

References

International Franchise Association Educational Foundation, Inc., and Horwarth International (1990) *Franchising in the Economy, 1988–1990*, Washington, DC: International Franchise Association.

Restaurants and Institutions (1990) 'Europe: the new foreign market', vol. 100, no. 16, 13 June, pp. 114–18.

Walker, B. J. (1989) *A Comparison of International vs Domestic Expansion by US Franchise Systems*, Washington, DC: International Franchise Association.

8

International management contracts

Peter Barge

The international hotel industry has gone through at least two management eras in the last one hundred years, during which time the operating philosophies and values have clearly shifted. The industry is currently in transition from the present era (that of management efficiency, practiced and dominated by American companies) to one as yet still indistinct. Accompanying these shifts have been far-reaching changes to the hotel operating environment – its extent, complexity and competitive parameters being remodeled within a shaky world economic, commercial and political framework.

The first era: the European hotelier

The era of the modern hotel and the first era of modern hotel management began about the mid-1800s in Europe. Around this time large numbers of travelers began to tour for leisure. Up until that time the volume of travel was relatively scant, largely for vocational and business purposes, and was confined to small roadway inns and similar hostelries. This increase in travel was tied to the industrial revolution, which created a traveling class of wealthy business and industrial people, in addition to the landed aristocracy. From the mid-1800s, Europe became the playground of the landed gentry, and 'grand' hotels were constructed which were palatial villas with suites of rooms designed to provide private accommodation for entire families.

With the advent of mass tourism, travel between countries and continents became a leisurely pursuit. Railroads and steamships developed to service the needs of the expanding middle class. As travel increased, Interlaken became the centre of the fast-growing hotel industry in Switzerland. This country became the birthplace of both great hoteliers and the first era of modern management. The hotels of this period were independent, family-run enterprises with names that became synonymous with luxury. Eventually, some of the operators went international. In Lucerne, for example, Maximillian von Pfyffer Altishofen built the Hotel National, an Italian palace-style building. It was in this hotel that the young César Ritz began his famous career. The tradition of excellence and luxury associated with the name and career of Ritz has survived to this day.

Along with the success of the grand hotels evolved a concept of hotel management which has been labeled the *hotelier*. It was a style which emphasized the concept of guest rather than customer, for these hotels were more like homes than hotels, and they were run with service and personal reputation rather than profit as the major measure of success. Most were accustomed to providing rooms without thought of payment until the room had been occupied. Labor was cheap, food was plentiful and a 20 percent occupancy was sufficient to keep the establishment solvent. The guest's needs could be paramount.

Through the late 1800s the glories of the grand Swiss hotels were enjoyed by an ever-expanding cross-section of society traveling on package holidays. Meeting this growing demand, however, became increasingly difficult over time, given the limited number of the existing grand hotels and their design and construction on a lavish scale with family suites. Breaking these suites down into rooms, however, they could accommodate several hundred guests, and thus the hotel as a cyclical, capacity-constrained business was born. However, the concept of hotelier did not change immediately as the business environment changed. The demise of this first era had begun, but it would not be recognized for some time.

As time progressed, increasing pressures were felt through scarcity of staff, rising food prices and the demands of foreign tour operators that prices should fall, in return for which they promised more customers. Caught in a spiral of rising costs, Continental hoteliers recognized the need for more rooms, in new buildings, on borrowings which added a new burden of loan interest to already increasing costs. They went in search of new markets and payment in advance from their customers. The pace quickened and many hotels merged or were swallowed up by conglomerates which appointed executives to manage ever-larger establishments. More and more, hotel management became a business and not the reflection of a family/guest experience.

The second era: the efficient manager

In North America, early accommodation for travelers followed a similar development pattern as in Europe until the early 1900s, but without the tradition of family involvement so prevalent in hotel operations on the Continent. Hotel development in America was spurred by the opening of new rail lines and, as such, emphasized leisure hotels. But eventually the industrial development that gave rise to the great American cities in the East and Midwest provided the impetus for the development of commercial city hotels. The great American hotel operators who systematized management efficiency and clarified the second era of management were in their heyday at this time.

The early hotel magnates such as Paran Stevens, Eugene Eppley and Ezra Statler, the owners of hotel chains, paved the way for later giants like Conrad

Hilton, Ernest Henderson (Sheraton) and Kemmins Wilson (Holiday Inn), who were each to take the concept of management efficiency and add to it in profitable ways: from Hilton, revenue maximization and use of space; from Henderson, ways to measure results and an expansion orientation; and from Wilson, concept standardization for operational control and consistency of guest experience.

Ultimately, purpose-built hotels began to appear across North America in a boom-and-bust cycle, following expansion of the railroads in the nineteenth century, the prosperity of the 1920s and then the near collapse of the 1930s. Beginning in 1939, however, US hotels enjoyed an uninterrupted period of growth, expansion and evolution in hotel development, fueled primarily by the explosion in travel between countries and continents after the Second World War.

The growth of hotel management systems

Expansion during the 1950s and 1960s occurred largely through hotel companies franchising or investing their own capital. It was not until the 1970s that management contracts became popular with major North American hotel operating companies, both in North America itself and in their operations abroad. In the 1970s the major hotel chains grew up. Prior to that, lodging properties on both sides of the Atlantic were generally operated by their owners. Leasing of properties to major hotel operators became popular in the late 1940s and remained so until the early 1970s when the management contract evolved primarily as a growth and financing vehicle. The first such contract is attributed to Inter-Continental Hotels. It offered flexibility and allowed Inter-Continental, then a fledgling company, the ability to extend into new markets with reduced financial risk. Hotel operators developed distinctive brand images and recognized the value of operating standards and management systems that allowed them to promise consistency to the guest experience and a critical mass in the form of a staff management pool and reservation and referral capabilities.

Eventually, the chains exported these systems to Europe, Africa, the Middle East and Asia. The chains provided 'insurance', through the manager's skills and know-how, to local investors with little hotel experience. Developers did not have these skills and lenders were not experienced in hotel financing. The management philosophy of consistency, while still delivering the profit, made the United States chains the best source of management expertise. These chains discovered that they had something to sell overseas; indeed, the demand for these systems was greater than the supply, as many US chains did not see a need to expand overseas. The USA itself was a large market and companies like Marriott saw more than enough opportunity at home.

Those companies which did launch management systems overseas invariably found that they held contract negotiating advantages. Taking an 'all care and no responsibility' approach to management agreements, the operators sold expertise and sales networks in return for a share of revenue and profit. This was normally in the range of 3 to 5 percent of revenue and 8 to 15 percent of gross operating profit. In addition, the operator charged fees for group services such as marketing and reservation network, and these tended to be around 3 percent of gross rooms revenue. Additional charges were made for reservations secured, head office visits and, in some cases, head office training levies.

Developers and owners ultimately found that they did not understand hotel operating models and the effect of fluctuating rates, inflation and occupancies on an owner's return. They soon discovered that their management company was only partly a real partner – one who had not provided equity and one who, via operating agreements, extracted a large proportion of profits in good times while continuing to draw significant fees even when hotels traded unprofitably. Eventually, hotels came to be perceived by owners as poor investments. Many operators with little investment were driven to expand their chains, usually under the guise of reaching a strategic size, or opening new markets or increasing segmentation. As new markets opened up, operators were able to convince developers and lenders in these new countries to enter into what was in many instances a one-sided agreement. It was the operators who now drove the projects, not the developers.

The 1980s pose new problems

The 1980s brought changes to the form and style of the hotel industry and its management. A boom occurred in international tourism, hotel building and operator profitability. An oversupply of hotels gradually emerged and returns were souring. Owners had become more sophisticated, having been exposed to competitive information and specialist consulting and appraisal firms. Competition for management contracts increased as numerous operators ventured outside their traditional markets. In addition, new operating companies emerged, particularly American, European and Asian chains, set up specifically to target the expanding international tourism market.

Until the 1980s the established stable of truly international operators seemed to have the world as their platter. Global expansion remained the domain of relatively few international hotel-operating companies, Hilton International, InterContinental, Hyatt International, Sheraton, THC and Holiday Inn. In the 1980s, however, with the increased opportunities for international hotel management came the new contenders, such as Regent International, Beaufort International, Ramada International, Meridien, Marriott, Mandarin, Nikko, Grupo Sol, ANA Hotels, Ritz Carlton, Four Seasons, Accor, Quality (Choice) and Westin. The swelling in the ranks meant that the 1970s 'take it or leave it' attitude towards hotel operation was rapidly replaced by the 'let's make a deal' approach of the 1980s. All of the major companies trading internationally in the 1980s were being fueled by an expansion philosophy. The more properties in the chain, the stronger the group's clout in terms of referral capability, marketing impetus, regional dominance and an established tourist feeder network.

New forms of contract emerge

The lessons of the past had been learned and hotel owners had 'graduated' to a different view of how their properties were to be managed. No longer were they interested solely in the security and insurance offered by management contracts. They understood the contract's strengths and weaknesses and they were now familiar with the hotel as a business. These were boom markets, and competitive bidding by operators increasingly resulted in innovative deal structures and offers being presented to owners. Unlike many situations before, offers began to include the following:

- Equity participation of around 10 to 15 percent.
- Guaranteed performance, i.e. if the property did not perform to a determined level of profit, the operator would make up the shortfall.
- Joint venture development.
- Leases providing a rental return based either on a set amount or on a combination of base rental and a share of profit.
- Franchise.
- Stand-aside provisions resulting in the withdrawal of incentive fees for unsatisfactory performance results.

In an era of easy financing and booming economies, the deal structures enabled funding packages to be put in place easily. The unprecedented growth of new hotels and refurbishment was experienced in all regions of the world, particularly in Asia and, latterly, Eastern Europe in the late 1980s.

Those international operators of long standing, and which were tied to only one fixed brand were forced to compete with smaller chains establishing in niche markets, particularly at the top end. These new chains were designing specific products to cater as much for the new ownership desires of the emerging Asian investors as for the intended hotel guest. The only established chain which successfully mounted a challenge was Hyatt International, which segmented its brands by introducing Grand Hyatt, Park Hyatt, Hyatt Regency and, to a lesser extent, Hyatt suites. Others generally clung to the generic 'five-star international' positioning – a product with little differentiation anywhere in the world. To take advantage of the many management opportunities, operators established a network of development vice-presidents who traveled the world seeking out opportunities and negotiating management agreements. Most companies established regional development offices in centers such as London, Hong Kong, Sydney, Los Angeles and Frankfurt. Those quick to establish a staffed regional office tended to succeed in acquiring new agreements. Companies such as Marriott which approached global expansion using development staff based largely in head office in Washington had little success until regional offices were established.

In many instances, the signing of the contract was the easiest of the stages.

Many overseas hotel developers had little experience of hotel development and required extensive technical support and pre-opening marketing backup. Catering to these needs required the chains to expand their regional infrastructure further. As expansion continued, the medium- to long-term potential for profitability increased, even though overheads were growing disproportionately to profit. This was rationalized on the basis that the average agreement spanned 20 years and that super-profits were earned traditionally in the late half of the contract with the pre-opening and first three years placing the major burden on head office resources.

Many chains found that the infrastructure necessary to acquire agreements was very expensive. Rapid expansion outside the national boundaries often required capital and management input to the detriment of the home market and life-blood cash flow. In many instances, the skills necessary to operate successfully in France or Canada could not be applied, without major adaptation, to India, Indonesia or the Bahamas. To overcome these difficulties a number of groups which were committed to internationalization pursued the acquisition route. The abundance of capital in the latter part of the 1980s meant that quantum leaps were possible for a small group of operators. The Pritzkers, owners of Hyatt, beat Trusthouse Forte and Accor to the Pacific prize of the Southern Pacific Hotel Corporation, and in one step established a dominant position for the group in the Pacific in the five-, four- and three-star markets. With this base and regional infrastructure, the brands of Hyatt, Parkroyal and Travelodge are now expanding rapidly into Asia. Accor's acquisition of Motel 6, and New World's takeover of Ramada International, are other examples.

This was also the beginning of the end for the second era of management philosophy. The American hotel operators which had perfected this philosophy and taken it abroad found that it could no longer 'ensure' profits. With increasing competition, management performance needed to emphasize revenue as well as efficiency. This also ended the dominance of the Americans. But it would be some time before the end of this era would be recognized. During this period of change, operators were enticed further to expand their base outside traditional markets. This was due, first to a world boom in travel that was both business and tourist driven, and second, to the need to diversify geopolitical risk and even out demand cycles.

New markets emerge

Hence, two geographical markets with considerable new potential have emerged: Europe and Asia. Some of the reasons for the renewed interest of management companies in extending further into Europe and Asia are as follows: Continental Europe at this time was essentially devoid of hotel chain domination; air passenger travel on the Continent was three to four times higher than in the USA; Europe reaped 75 percent of the world's tourism receipts; and finally, the strong economies of the region, it was thought, would only improve with the advent of economic union in 1992. Subsequently the wild card of a democratic Eastern Europe has emerged as a further enticer. The second area that emerged during this time as having great potential was Asia. This region had become a major business and tourism destination; it had growing affluence; the gross operating profit for hotels had been far higher by percentage than for comparable US hotels; and, most importantly, by the year 2000 visitor arrivals to Asia were projected to swell by 120 percent.

While these regions were seen as fertile, they were not virgin. They were boom markets, but securing market share and profit from the opportunities meant that an operating company needed four critical elements. These were a strong capital base; friendly accounting standards (located in not overly litigious environments) which would allow recognition of goodwill, the value of the brand and the value of the management agreement; strategic vision; and a network or critical mass in the form of a large number of hotels, geographically dispersed with possible interfacing to major reservation systems. Most US firms possessed the vision and the critical mass. Others at that time, such as Marriott, had the capital base but not the other critical elements.

Mergers and acquisitions

Some owners whose core business was not in hotels, but who had been dabbling in hotel ownership/operation, saw a great opportunity. They soon recognized that they had three elements for success and could acquire critical mass. As a result, a rash of acquisitions broke out, as illustrated in Table 8.1. All of these companies had the necessary capital base and a friendly accounting system.

A major change in ownership patterns occurred at this point. Today there are three groups driving hotel development and, indirectly, industry operations. The first are those hotel developers found in all regions which have no intention of owning and operating, and are merely building to sell. For them, brand name is as important in the sale process as are operator guarantees, and anything else that will help achieve a sale. The second group driving hotel development today are the large chains themselves which, with seed capital, can control projects and secure management. The third group just now emerging as a development force are the air and travel groups, especially in Asia. Once before the US airlines had moved into the hotel development business as a strategic ploy but found they did not have the technology, or the interest, or in the end the available capital base to make it work. Today the interest of air and travel groups is driven by the need for integration in a very competitive industry, and the hard and soft technology is now available to make it work.

Table 8.1   Major hotel group mergers and acquisitions, 1987–present

Hotel	Date	Purchaser	Vendor
Hilton International	1987	Ladbroke Group plc	Allegis Corp
Westin Hotel & Resorts	1987	Aoki Corp	Allegis Corp
InterContinental Hotels	1988	Seibu Saison	Grand Metropolitan
Southern Pacific Hotel Corp	1988	Hale Corporation	Tan Sri Khoo Teck Puat
Holiday Inn International	1988	Bass plc	Holiday Corp
InterContinental Hotels (40%)	1989	SAS	Seibu Saison
Regal Aircoa Companies	1989	Regal Hotel Holdings	Aircoa Companies
Ramada Int	1989	New World Development	Ramada Int
Ramada USA	1989	Prime	Ramada International
Thistle Hotels	1989	Mount Charlotte	Scottish & Newcastle Breweries plc
Omni Hotels	1989	World Int'l & Wharf Ltd	Aer Lingus
InterContinental Hotels (40%)	1990	Seibu Saison	SAS
Southern Pacific Hotel Corp	1990	Pritzker family	Hale Corp
Mount Charlotte/Thistle	1990	Brierley Investments Ltd	Mount Charlotte Investments plc
Norfolk Capital	1990	Queens Moat House plc	Norfolk Capital plc
Crest Hotels	1990	Forte plc	Bass plc
Embassy Hotels	1990	Jarvis Hotels	Allied-Lyons plc
Motel 6	1991	Accor	Kohlberg, Kravis, Roberts & Co.
Deutsche Interhotel	1992	Groenke & Guttmann GmbH	East German Government
Metropole Hotels (30%)	1992	Libyan Arab Foreign Co	Lonrho
Regent International (60%)	1992	EIE International	Robert Burns
Regent International (20%)	1992	Four Seasons	EIE International
Guest Quarters Hotels	1992	G.E. investments Hotels	Westinghouse Credit Corp
Posadas de Mexico Hotels	1992	International consortium	Posadas SA
Park Suites	1992	Embassy Suites/Promus	Procordia AB
Commonwealth Hospitality Ltd	1992	Trans American Inc	Bass plc
Day Inns of America	1992	Hospitality Franchise Systems	Days Inn
Wagon-Lit Hotels	1992	Accor	Wagon-Lit

Source: JLW TransAct.

The future

Today we are in a transition period. The management systems which were so successful in providing consistency of experience and efficiency all over the world have contributed as much as they will be able. Management expertise has been transferred and is now widely available to all players in a very competitive, global industry. Large computer-based referral/reservations systems have endless interface opportunities, and what was once only available to be delivered by a handful of well-known operators is now available to many.

What management philosophy will be necessary to succeed into the next century? Clearly, the evolution in the industry has been toward more complexity, absorbing the contributions to be gained from finance, marketing, accounting and human resources management as well as the emerging discipline of information technology. No longer is there the outdated view of the customer–hotel relationship evidenced in 'mine host' and coupled with a management focus on monitoring costs. The new owners of these companies have a strategic view of the business, understanding that value requires operations ability and investment acumen.

9

International hotel consortia

Andrew Byrne

The focus of this text is on the international hospitality industry. At first sight, therefore, it may appear to be a contradiction to look at consortia, since they are made up of independently owned and operated properties. These individual hotels, by their very nature, are location specific and cannot operate in more than one country. But it is for this very reason that consortia grew up. Consortia are the best means for a single hotel to operate effectively in the international marketplace while still retaining a high degree of independence.

A feature of consortia is the fiercely independent nature of many of the member hoteliers. It would be possible, for instance, for these owners to invite hotel management contractors to operate the properties on their behalf. Such a contract would give the hotel all the advantages of 'chain membership' and relieve the owner of the actual management of the property as well. That owners do not choose this option but prefer consortium membership indicates their commitment to managing their own hotels. Often these properties are owned by individuals or families and have been so for more than one generation.

Type of consortia

Housden (1984) has defined hotel consortia as 'independently owned units which voluntarily affiliate ... seeking benefits from access to significantly greater resources than would be possible on their own'. Litteljohn (1982) adds that '[their] aims will often be achieved though the setting up of a centralised office whose activities will be financed through a levy/subscription on member hotels'. The principal activity of such consortia is marketing with the aim of increasing revenue for member hotels. In addition, there are some consortia that enable members to reduce costs through group purchasing arrangements and/or coordinated human resource services, such as recruitment and training.

Slattery *et al.* (1985) distinguished four basic types of consortium:

- *Full consortia*. These organizations provided not only marketing expertise and services, but also assistance with regards to human resources and purchasing. Such consortia tended to operate domestically, rather than internationally.
- *Marketing consortia*. These consortia provided marketing expertise as described in detail later in this chapter. An example of this type of consortium is Small Luxury Hotels of the World.
- *Reservation systems*. These provided a central reservations system, usually based around a single, toll-free telephone number. Utell was an example of this.
- *Referral consortia*. These were affiliations by hotels with airlines and their reservation systems. In this case it was often chains rather than independent hotels that affiliated with the airline, such as JAL World and Golden Tulip Worldwide Hotels.

As hotel consortia have grown internationally, it has become increasingly difficult to distinguish between the four types. Utell, for instance, originated as a reservation system, but during the mid-1980s it began to provide corporate marketing services to its members. To this complexity are added three other factors. First, a single hotel may belong to more than one consortium although most consortia now try to restrict this as part of their membership agreement. For instance, in 1985 two well-known UK hotels were cited (Slattery *et al.*, 1985) as belonging to three consortia – namely, Leading Hotels of the World, Prestige and Relais et Chateaux. The rationale for this was that at this time there were relatively few consortia that were worldwide; most were uninational or very much focused in one geographic region. Since then, many consortia have developed internationally, including Prestige and Relais et Chateaux, so that multiple membership of consortia in order to ensure the right sort of worldwide exposure is less likely.

Second, although it was originally the case that consortia were created to serve independent hotels, as defined by Housden, it is more and more the case that chain hotels, either separately or collectively, have membership of consortia. For instance, among Forte's Exclusive brand are hotels such as the Plaza Athenee in Paris and the Ritz in Madrid. Both of these hotels are also in consortia. Likewise, the referral consortium mentioned above encourages chain affiliation.

Finally, just as the business format of chain hotels has become complex with the development of various types of management contract, franchise and joint venture, so has the business format of consortia. Smaller consortia tend to be relatively informal, member-controlled organizations. They agree on the policies, rules and regulations of the consortium, often regulate these through a committee of elected members, and as such have few if any formal, legal links. As the consortium grows larger, it is unlikely to remain in this simple form and will move to become limited companies or corporations, perhaps retaining the elected members as a sort of board of directors.

Moreover, rather than employing the executives and 'head office' staff directly to run the consortium, some consortia have contracted this out to a management company. Clearly these differences in constitution affect how the consortium operates, in particular with regards to the level of power exerted by individual members.

Size and scale of consortia internationally

The pace of change in international hospitality is so great that it is difficult to obtain reliable data about the industry, and even more difficult to be sure that it will not be out of date very quickly. What is very clear is that internationalization of consortia is a major trend. According to Baum (1992), 'Looking ahead means looking globally – beyond national and regional boundaries. Voluntary chains and associations are doing that by seeking members in new geograpfiic areas'. Examples of this internationalization include an Australian consortium – Flag International – planning to set up a chain in Europe; the expansion by Minotels into North and South America; and the merger of Prestige with Small Luxury Hotels. Table 9.1 provides summary data about ten of the world's largest hotel consortia.

Reasons for the development of consortia

Just as there are uninational and international hotel chains, there are also uninational and international consortia. The same sorts of environmental pressure and internal need cause a consortium to move from operating solely in one country to operating in the international arena as those which drive chains to do so. But the relative importance of these influences is different. First, international consortia tend to comprise hotel properties that have a

Table 9.1   Ten largest international hotel consortia

Consortium name	Head office	Rooms 1991	Hotels 1991	Countries of operation	Grades of hotel
Utell International	London	1 300 000	6 500	144	2, 3 and 4-star
JAL World Hotels	Tokyo	180 000	366		
Supranational Hotels	London	117 168	628	52	Mainly 4 and 5-star
LRI Grande Collection of Hotels	New York	105 000	441	46 / 10	3, 4 and 5-star / 4 and 5-star
Leading Hotels of the World	New York	70 000	260	61	5-star
SRS Hotels Steigenberger	Frankfurt	60 000	270	50	3, 4 and 5-star
Golden Tulip Worldwide	Hilversum	54 000	270	59	4 and 5-star
Foremost Hotels International	Montvale, NJ	37 378	687	49	3, 4 and 5-star
Minotels International	Lausanne	30 000	700	20+	Mainly 3-star
Prima Hotels	New York	29 190	230	25	3 and 4-star

Source: *Hotels Magazine*, July 1992.

history of attracting an international clientele. Such hotels therefore need to belong to a consortium that will assist them to promote and market themselves to their existing international client base. Second, the general growth in tourism and business travel has encouraged independent hoteliers to look for new markets, and membership of an international consortium enables these hoteliers to promote themselves to customers who previously they may not have been able to reach individually. Third, consortium membership not only provides marketing expertise but does so at a reasonable cost, due to the economies of scale that derive from membership. Consortia therefore create a critical mass sufficiently large to support increasingly essential marketing tools such as international sales offices and central reservation systems. Fourth, independent hoteliers are not unaware of the nature of competition from large chain operators and the strategies they employ to gain business and sustain customer loyalty. Consortium membership enables the independents to employ some of these same strategies, especially with regards to creating a *brand* image. And finally, consortia pursue growth just as chain operators do. Within any single country there is a limit to the number of hotels that meet the membership criteria of each consortium and if the organization is to grow it must move into the international marketplace.

Consortia activities

Essentially consortia engage in marketing on behalf of their members. In many respects this marketing activity mirrors the marketing activity of chains, but there are some significant differences. The similarities relate largely to the marketing activities of promotion and distribution channels (or 'place' as it is referred to in the 4Ps of the marketing mix).

Typically consortia engage in the full range of promotional activities. This includes clearly defining a brand image, which is achieved through establishing the brand name and image through logos and tag lines, print media and other forms of communication. The problem that confronts consortia directors is that because the organization is made up of independent hotels, the size, design, location and other significant characteristics of the various properties may vary quite widely. It is for this reason that many consortia establish a brand around a specific image rather than detailed product characteristics. They also promote as an advantage the fact that, although belonging to a 'brand', a feature of their hotels is their individuality and uniqueness. Three consortia brand names illustrate this: *Leading Hotels of the World* says nothing about the characteristics of the properties but strongly conveys the message that these are individual properties with established reputations in prestigious locations and with a great deal of style; *Relais et Chateaux* also conveys a message about the properties being historic, romantic and beautiful, even though many of them are not actually Chateaubriand as such; while *Small Luxury Hotels of the World* is quite explicit in defining the nature of its hotels. Other promotional activity includes the development and delivery of advertising campaigns; the operation of sales offices; the production and distribution of consortium brochures and other print material; and the management of sales conferences and visits.

As well as managing all the usual distribution channels to encourage hotel sales, such as travel agencies, conference and event planners, tour operators, tourist boards and agencies, airlines and so on, the main function of the international hotel consortium is often to set up and operate a central reservation system.

However, there are two elements of the marketing mix that a consortium does not manage in the same way as a chain: namely product and price. We have already seen that consortia usually make an asset out of the individuality of the member hotels. However, since these are independently owned and operated, there is little or no control over the 'product', i.e. the hotel property itself. Such control as there is, is exercised through the criteria established for membership, usually based on a detailed inspection of any hotel applying for membership. Such criteria will vary from consortium to consortium but may include location and surroundings, physical characteristics of the property and accommodation, staffing and service levels, and other aspects of the hotel such as the cuisine and recreational features. In addition, hotels are regularly inspected to ensure that the consortium's standards are being maintained and that the contractual obligations are complied with. For instance, Small Luxury Hotels of the World requires its member hotels to display the name of the consortium on a brass plaque at the main entrance to the hotel. In the event that members do not meet the requirements of the consortium, the elected board members may revoke that hotel's membership.

Likewise, most consortia do not have direct control over the pricing policy of individual members. One of the main reasons for joining is to take advantage of marketing economies of scale and scope without giving up individual control over the operation. Consortia have two basic approaches to using price as part of the collective marketing strategy. First, the consortia can put together specific marketing packages that all members participate in according to their individual terms and conditions. So a consortium might offer a weekend break package targeted at a specific customer segment, but each participating hotel would have its own conditions with regards to the level of discount offered. The second strategy is to put together a specific package at a standard rate and to invite members to participate in the promotion if they wish. So, for instance, a consortium may develop a single, discounted corporate rate for a large client, but not all member hotels would necessarily be part of the package.

As well as these very important external marketing activities, another feature of consortia management is the importance of internal marketing. Consortium executives are very aware of the fact that membership of the consortium also needs to be marketed. Existing members need to be satisfied that membership is of continuing value. New members need to be introduced to the consortium in order that they can get the best out of membership, while at the same time they comply with the consortium's policies. And new members need to be attracted in order to enable further scale economies and growth. Consortia are therefore in a similar position to hotel management contractors in terms of having to satisfy their clients that the service they provide is worthwhile. The best way to do this is to meet the expectations of members in terms of the quality of external marketing, and more importantly to translate this into actual increased sales revenues for the members. To demonstrate this, consortia establish clear reporting systems that enable members to identify the extent to which membership is effective. For instance, Small Luxury Hotels of the World provides member hotels with monthly reservation reports detailing a wide range of information, such as telephone call volume, conversion rates, cost per reservation and so on, as well as sales reports every two months detailing the activities of each member of the sales force.

Other internal marketing that consortia engage in includes regular communications from the head office, often weekly, of a variety of kinds including memoranda, formal letters, *ad hoc* reports, press cuttings and so on. In addition, consortia tend to encourage the members to meet both formally in business meetings and socially. Small Luxury Hotels has a European and North American conference in the spring and a full international meeting of members over three or four days every November.

Issues for international hotel consortia

There are a range of issues that confront a consortium when it moves from being uninational to international. First, it has to modify its approach to marketing to reflect its new product base and any markets it wishes to attract. Many uninational consortia have a history of working closely with their national tourism agencies in promotional activities outside their home country. For instance, the former UK-based Prestige Hotels worked closely with the British Tourist Authority. There was therefore a tendency to promote the destination, in this case Britain, rather than the consortium as such. Once this company merged with a US consortium to form Small Luxury Hotels of the World, such collaboration and destination marketing ceased and the focus switched to the promotion of an international brand, but without the financial support that government tourism agencies could give. Internationality also impacts on marketing in terms of ensuring that corporate designs of logos, print material, brochures and so on are also appropriate for the international marketplace.

Decisions also have to be made concerning the lingua franca of the organization. This is much more of a problem for a consortium than for a chain due to the independence of the members. Operating in more than one language to satisfy the various constituencies clearly adds to the cost in terms of recruiting and employing suitably qualified personnel, translation and interpretation costs, printing costs and transaction costs. But operating in a single language may make the internal marketing that is so important within a consortium very much more difficult. Consortia work best where there is full and voluntary participation in the organization. Such participation may be hindered by linguistic and cultural barriers.

The same sort of thought has to be given to the financial transactions of international consortia. Just as one language may be needed, so one currency may need to be selected as the commonly agreed means of communicating financial information to membership. Such information includes citing membership fees, drawing up budgets, writing financial reports and the internal accounting carried out by the consortium's executives. Added to this are the implications of the movement of funds from one country to another in terms of transaction costs, exchange rate fluctuations and legal constraints of the movement of funds.

International consortia also need to become expert in the legal practices of all the countries they have members in as well as the legislation of these countries that may affect their activities. Examples of this are trademark registration, contract negotiation and the settlement of disputes. However, the legal position of the consortium is very similar to that of a supplier of any kind of service to the individual hotels that are members.

Conclusion

Just as other business formats are growing in complexity, so are consortia. In an increasingly sophisticated marketplace, equally sophisticated marketing is needed to sustain occupancy and reach new customers. Individual properties have neither the expertise nor the level of investment needed to develop reservation systems, national and promotional campaigns, and all the other activities that a consortium can provide. A consortium offers the opportunity for independent hoteliers to join together to operate in the global marketplace.

References

Baum, C. (1992) 'Consortia expand sales: reservations efforts', *Hotels*, July, pp 88–94.

Housden, Janet (1984) *Franchising and Other Business Relationships in Hotel and Catering Services*, London: Heinemann.

Litteljohn, D. (1982) 'The role of hotel consortia in Great Britain', *Service Industries Journal*, vol. 2, no. 1, pp. 79–91.

Slattery, P., Roper, A., and Boer, A. (1985) 'Hotel consortia: their activities, structure and growth', *Service Industries Journal*, vol. 5, no. 2, pp. 192–9.

Part 3

Functional management issues

It is generally agreed that there are at least four main functional areas of management: namely, operations, human resource management, marketing and finance. At the level of the firm these are synthesized into corporate strategic management. This section asks specialists in each of the four areas to discuss the impact internalization has on that function. Corporate strategy is not specifically explored, partly because it has been discussed in the previous section and partly because it is is explored fully in a companion volume, *International Hospitality Management: Corporate strategy in practice*, also published by Pitman.

Jones identifies the fact that hotels, and probably every other kind of hospitality operation, perform differently from one region of the world to another. This is a result partly of local circumstances, but also of strategic choices made by international firms. These choices relate to the service concept, concept development, country and site selection, and resourcing operations. How operations are then managed internationally varies widely from firm to firm, in particular with respect to the degree of discretion local managers have. Managers at unit level share similar problems irrespective of their international location, and operations need to perform well with respect to a common set of key result areas. Jones suggests, however, that effective management action will need to vary from one location to another in order successfully to respond to the different challenges each manager faces from one country to another.

Goss-Turner too identifies the extent to which different international locations may have an impact on human resource policy. He argues that human resource specialists are reviewing their role in a number of ways, with regards to their image, specialist expertise, team development and cultural awareness. Human resource managers are adopting a much more strategic role within international hospitality firms, particularly with regards to their role in management development. They also face great worldwide challenges resulting from a potential lack of suitable people to work in the industry.

Renaghan argues that many, if not most, international hospitality firms engage in sales rather than marketing. Operating on an international scale presents marketing professionals with a number of problems relating to control of quality and costs, locus of marketing decision making, organizational communications, staffing, evaluation of marketing efforts, and the use of technology.

For Kreul, internationality also presents challenges for finance and accounting functional specialists. He too discusses economic, political and cultural factors affecting the practice. In addition, there are some technical and legislative differences across the world. The key concerns are the consolidation of operational results, currency translation and conversion, transfer pricing, and management accounting practice. He offers some hope that, at least in this area, there may be some global uniformity.

10

Operations management issues

Peter Jones

Operations management has been the Cinderella of the hospitality industry. Academics and others who write about the industry have tended to ignore this area. Marketing, human resource management and corporate strategy have been considerably more researched and written about. The interest in these subject areas is due to the fact that they have direct relevance in a wide range of industries; there is an agreed or at least well-defined body of knowledge, which is well researched and documented, and hence there are clear definitions and analytical structures. Operations management on the other hand, as a discipline, originated in manufacturing so that some of its analytical frameworks are not directly applicable in a service business such as hospitality. Furthermore, the specific operational activities of the hospitality industry – that is, the provision of accommodation and meals – are regarded as industry specific rather than generic. There has been a gradual change in this attitude over the 1980s, when quality has emerged as a key issue for service industries. Nonetheless we continue to have a relatively poorly defined discipline with few analytical frameworks with which to explore the impact of internationalization.

Corporate strategy and operations management

Essentially operations management is the transformation of inputs, through processes into desired outputs, as illustrated in Figure 10.1. The particular configuration of processes for a given operation can be defined as a 'service delivery system' (SDS). Pickworth (1988) defines an SDS as 'an operation in which products/services are created and delivered to the customer almost simultaneously'. Thus, for example, a fast-food store has a particular location, design, technology, operating procedure and so on, all focused on producing the fast-food product. These features may vary slightly in detail between a McDonald's, Taco Bell or Kentucky Fried Chicken, but essentially the service delivery system is the same.

These in turn have to be consistent with the corporate strategy and

Figure 10.1 Systems model of a service operation

marketing plan of the firm. Johnston (1989) proposes a model that explains this link between strategy and service delivery systems. This is illustrated in Figure 10.2. It is clear that when a hospitality firm moves from its domestic market many of the key elements change. The *company* itself may change its perspective, shareholders' expectations may be modified, it may have been necessary to restructure financially, and so on. The nature of *competition* is also likely to change by bringing the firm into competition with other

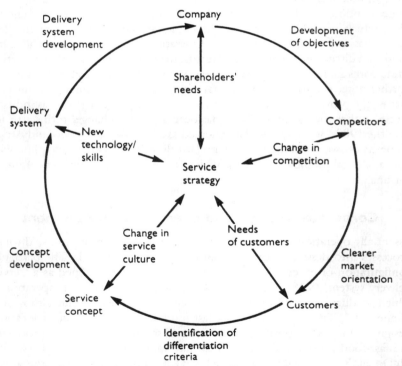

Figure 10.2 A service strategy development framework
Source: Johnston (1989).

hospitality firms for the first time. The *customer* base will also expand, by definition. The *service concept* may also be modified, along with the *service delivery system*. For instance, the firm may have to adapt its technology or introduce new technology into its operations when located in more than one country.

Johnston argues that in developing a service strategy, there are five stages that integrate these key elements: revise corporate objectives, clarify market orientation, establish differentiation criteria, adapt if necessary the service concept, and modify the service delivery system. The operations strategy will then derive in particular from the specification of the service concept, and operational management behavior will be related to design of the delivery system.

Commonly cited corporate goals of international hospitality firms (Economist Intelligence Unit, 1991) include cash flow, customer loyalty, guest satisfaction, profitability, employee morale and growth. All of these clearly have an impact on key result areas. For instance, to achieve some of these corporate goals a major marketing trend is strong branding. The impact of this for the operations manager is greatly to increase the need for standardization in the two key result areas of service and quality. Likewise the decision by Forte Hotels to fix room tariffs at advertised prices has a major impact on the key result areas of capacity and income.

In this chapter we are explicitly concerned with the nature of operations management when carried out internationally. We are concerned with the extent to which service concepts and delivery systems are identical worldwide or modified to match local circumstances. We shall also investigate if the behavior of operations managers varies from one country to another, whether such differences are planned or unplanned, and whether it affects successful performance. For a variety of reasons it is extremely difficult to answer these questions. But what we do know is that *actual* operating performance does vary from one country to another. Pannell Kerr Forster's annual report *Trends in the Hotel Industry* records such differences.

Some key operating statistics from international hotel chains in 1989 are given in Table 10.1. In all sorts of ways, there are major differences from one country to another and from one continent to another. Occupancy is high in the Pacific Basin but much lower in the Middle East. In Mexico and the Caribbean a very high proportion of room sales are from double occupancy. Hotels in Mexico spend significantly more as a percentage of revenue on marketing than those in Africa. Now it might be the case that an international hotel chain builds identical properties throughout the world and manages them in exactly the same way, but that performance varies from continent to continent simply because the cost of inputs such as raw materials, labor and energy vary from one economy to the next. In other words, this international variance in performance might be due to external, environmental factors. The five chapters in Part 1 of this text clearly identify the extent of major differences between geographic regions of the world.

Table 10.1 International comparison of hotel operating ratios, 1988

	Average for all hotels	Canada	Mexico	Latin America	Caribbean and Bermuda	Europe	Africa	Middle East	Pacific Basin
Average number of rooms	255	250	281	287	224	201	199	257	463
Percentage occupancy	69.8	70.3	65.1	66.2	71.3	69.7	66.5	51.7	77.3
Average daily room rate (US dollars)	79.50	65.88	57.37	66.78	96.58	93.99	56.84	66.77	81.10
Revenues (%)									
Rooms	53.8	57.6	57.4	57.7	55.2	54.4	47.1	40.4	51.3
Food – inc. other income	26.4	25.8	23.3	22.6	24.0	26.4	29.2	32.3	27.9
Beverages	10.8	10.3	11.8	11.1	8.2	11.4	11.8	10.1	10.2
Telephone	3.8	2.5	2.8	4.1	1.4	3.8	6.2	6.7	4.0
Other operated departments	3.5	2.3	2.4	2.4	7.2	3.0	2.8	6.7	4.5
Rentals and other income	1.7	1.5	2.3	2.1	4.0	1.0	2.9	3.8	2.1
Departmental costs and expenses (%)									
Rooms	12.6	15.6	10.7	9.9	15.2	14.2	7.9	10.1	10.1
Food and beverages	27.7	29.8	21.9	22.5	25.9	29.0	28.9	29.2	26.8
Telephone	2.7	2.5	1.8	2.8	1.4	2.5	4.6	4.6	3.0
Other operated departments	2.0	1.4	1.3	1.2	5.8	1.8	1.5	3.1	2.6
Total costs and expenses	45.0	49.3	35.7	36.4	48.3	47.5	42.9	47.0	42.5
Undistributed operating expenses (%)									
Administrative and general	8.2	7.6	10.5	10.6	11.0	8.4	11.6	10.4	5.9
Management fees*	2.8	2.8	3.5	2.9	10.9	1.4	4.1	3.1	3.7
Marketing and guest entertainment*	4.5	5.2	7.0	6.1	6.9	3.6	3.0	4.1	4.6
Property operation and maintenance	5.3	4.8	8.2	7.4	7.3	4.9	8.9	6.7	4.5
Energy costs	3.6	3.4	3.9	3.4	5.0	2.9	6.3	3.9	4.4
Other	0.3	–	0.7	0.7	0.5	0.1	1.5	0.8	0.5
Total undistributed expenses	24.7	23.8	33.8	31.1	41.6	21.3	35.4	29.0	23.6

* Not all establishments reported data
Source: Pannell Kerr Forster (1989), pp. 11–12.

However, we know in fact that hotels are not identical. The same study reports for instance, that hotels in the Pacific Basin are on average much larger than in the rest of the world. It is clear therefore that, as well as being affected by external influences, international hospitality organizations make some strategic decisions about their operations.

In order to explore the impact of internationalization on operations, this chapter is divided into three sections. We shall look first at strategic issues in operations management relating to the service concept, and hence the nature and type of decisions made at corporate headquarters. Second, we will consider the organizational implications of these decisions. And finally, we will examine in detail operational management at operating unit level. In the main, from an operational perspective, it does not matter if outlets are directly owned and operated, franchised or managed on a contract basis. If the nature of the business format does result in different operational responses, we shall identify these as they arise.

Strategic issues in international hospitality operations management

Essentially, strategy in an operational sense refers to all those decisions and activities carried out at corporate level that affect the individual service delivery systems in the chain. These will vary from sector to sector and from chain to chain, but broadly they are likely to include:

- Defining the service concept.
- Developing or adapting the service concept.
- Locating the concept.
- Resourcing the concept.

Defining the service concept

It would seem relatively easy to define or specify exactly the nature of a given service concept in the hospitality industry. In some sectors this is the case. In the hotel sector, the various guides all have specific criteria for classifying hotels into their various categories. Likewise in the fast-food industry, the layout, design, organization and performance of any given outlet will be defined precisely. McDonald's for instance, has several clearly specified categories of store that relate to the floor area and seating capacity of the outlet. Some hospitality operators have a high degree of strategic control over defining exactly the service concept for three main reasons. First, most if not all such firms operate globally with a strongly branded competitive strategy. Second, investment costs of some types of hospitality business, such as a fast-food store, are relatively low when compared with hotels. This is especially true if growth is achieved through franchising, so that most if not all outlets are built from new. Finally, the essence of some concepts is to minimize complexity. For instance, in the fast-food industry the thing that makes it 'fast' is having a simple menu, based around a few core products with a dedicated SDS and standardized procedures.

It is therefore much more difficult to define/specify the concept corporately or strategically where these conditions do not apply. Hotels are generally more complex than food service outlets and there are instances of poor concept specification or respecification to match changing environments. In the hotel industry there is a broad range of possibilities. A hotel consortium, for instance, almost by definition, consists of individual properties, rarely if ever built from new, marketing an image rather than a brand as such. This makes concept definition difficult. Hotel chains that grow through acquisition or management contract systems may also face challenges to ensure consistency of the concept. On the other hand, some new concepts such as Accor's Formule 1 and Forte's Travelodge chain are built on green-field sites with very strong and defined specifications. So concept definition is most difficult when firms do not own their own properties, especially in the case of contracts, and have not built them from scratch.

New concept development

As Johnston's model suggests, service strategies need to be dynamic to reflect changes in the environment. So as well as defining the service concept, hospitality firms need also to review their concepts continually. Such review frequently results in incremental changes to parts of the concept. The extent to which new concept development will be significant in the international hospitality firm may well depend on the corporate strategy of the organization. A US study reported in 1990 (West and Anthony, 1990) found six strategic groups in the foodservice industry, only one of which was based around product/service innovation and development. This comprised focusing on innovation in menu development, new product development and offering a broad menu. This strategic group appeared to be significantly outperforming the other five groups. However, the nature of this innovation is likely to be through adoption rather than original research (Wan, 1992). That is to say, companies will be introducing new concepts or products adopted from other firms, either as a straight copy or in an adapted form.

Most large, international hospitality firms have a corporate research and development department, although they will not always call it by that name. For instance, Kentucky Fried Chicken has a staff of 50 in the USA and four in the UK engaged in this activity. Other chains, however, such as Wimpy International, work with and use their suppliers on product development. The role of such departments is continually to review and modify existing product lines in order to match changing consumer tastes. McDonald's, with 12 000 outlets worldwide, has been significantly engaging in such activity, especially in its home market. In response to adverse publicity, it has improved the 'healthiness' of its products by introducing 100 percent vegetable oil for frying, frozen yogurt and low-fat milk shakes, and low-fat items such as apple bran muffins. It has also developed its first non-100 percent pure beef hamburger. The McLean Deluxe is a 91 percent fat-free hamburger that includes carrageenan, a seaweed derivative, to help retain moisture. As well as developing its existing product range to respond to changing tastes, McDonald's has also been introducing new products on test trial in the USA, including pizza, fajitas and burritos, sandwiches, spaghetti and meatballs, and bone-in chicken.

In the international context, R & D departments have another main function. They need to be able to advise on whether to change the concept when moving into new international markets. For instance, McDonald's is believed to have experimented with the recipe for its hamburger buns before moving into the UK, believing that the bun may contain too much sugar for the British taste. In fact it eventually made no changes to the product. Likewise hotel companies have found that they need to reconsider the design of their hotels when building in the Middle East. In these Muslim countries there is much less need for public spaces, since alcohol consumption is prohibited and therefore there are no bars, and social activity in public is constrained and therefore there is less need for lounges.

Location and site selection

Johnston (1989) might argue that the location decision is not related to the service concept, but is a facet of the service operation. However, it can be strongly argued that in the hospitality business location is fundamental to the concept. It is regarded by some as the most important corporate operational decision, as witnessed by Conrad Hilton's often quoted comment concerning 'location, location and location'. In the international arena, the location decision refers to which country and then which cities and towns to select for expansion into, while site selection relates to precise decisions on the exact position of an outlet.

There is no doubt that the decision criteria for deciding in which countries to locate a new hotel or restaurant can be clearly established and structured. The reality is that, historically, few firms have used these criteria for actually developing their international operations. In a study of US franchised restaurant chains (Go and Christensen, 1989) the decision concerning the location of the first outlet outside the USA for many of the firms was not a rational choice based on proximity to home market or political/social stability in target country or similarity to home market conditions. For nearly half the firms, 59 in all, the decision to expand internationally was the result of a prospective franchisee approaching the chain and asking to build an outlet in its country. In Europe in the 1980s there was also a tendency to develop a presence in a high-profile city, often the capital, in a number of different countries. In many cases this has been unsuccessful, since fast-food operators in particular need strong marketing support through television advertising, which is uneconomic if there are only four or five outlets in each country. Many European operators have now retrenched and focused on certain countries to achieve the necessary critical mass to support advertising before moving on to the next location. Likewise, chains, especially in the hotel sector, have developed operations in new countries through the acquisition of other chains, rather than by planned strategic growth based on locational decision criteria.

Although in the past many firms have become international in an unplanned way, they do tend to begin to apply more rational criteria once established. It would also seem likely that in the future firms contemplating expansion will tend to use the emerging models of locational decision making. 'When transnational corporations (TNCs) decide to expand internationally they need to decide what form that involvement will take – that of developer, supplier of technical expertise (through management contracts), capital investor or combination thereof' (Go *et al.*, 1990). Go *et al.* suggest that this decision and the hotel accommodation requirements in the target or host country are the two most important criteria. There then usually follows a detailed analysis of the business environment. The type of criteria used in this scanning include: economic factors, such as repatriation of capital or profits, stability of inflation rate, GNP and so on; social factors, including crime rate, demographics and language; political factors in terms of stability, frequency of elections (if any), and government attitude and policies; technical and physical factors, such as climate, transportation infrastructure and construction costs; and industry-related factors – wage rates, market size and level of competition.

The same sort of sophisticated analysis is now taking place with regards to site selection in those geographic regions where there is maturity and saturation. This is the case in the USA where increasing real estate prices, changing consumer lifestyles and increased competition have significantly changed the way in which restaurant chains select new sites. The data analyzed for a given location now focus on a smaller area (as customers are reluctant to travel too far) and include demographics, pyschographics, census data, traffic pattern analyses and consultants' appraisals. An ideal location would have a mix of both residential and commercial activity, with high visibility and good growth projections. But such sites are rare.

One impact of this is that US restaurant chains are now locating their outlets on nontraditional sites. Kentucky Fried Chicken plans to expand from 5000 to 10 000 outlets in the USA by 1999, largely by building limited-menu express stops and kiosks in areas such as food courts, schools and colleges. Burger King in Europe has several basic concepts that enable them to fit whichever style of operation is most suitable into a range of different sites. These concepts are high street, drive thru (*sic*), drive to, double drive thru and kiosk. Likewise, in the UK, roadside dining chains are also modifying their site selection criteria as competition increases, planning constraints restrict access, and sites become harder to find. One chain, AJs, is building slightly smaller units and working with major petrol companies in order to locate its restaurants on petrol-filling station sites, a relatively new trend in this country.

However, site selection criteria will vary widely from one country to another. Few markets are as saturated as the USA, and therefore different factors may be taken into account. McDonald's decision to place its first outlet in the former Soviet Union in Moscow's Red Square probably broke every one of its established site selection criteria. But this unique location and site has been a huge success in terms of the high public profile it has generated both in the local market and internationally.

Resourcing the concept

Once the concept is defined, the firm needs to check out that it can be resourced. For instance, a roadside dining chain that decided to develop an identical concept in a new country might find that the availability of suitable sites, building regulations, building materials and so on may actually prevent that concept from being developed in the way that the firm would like to. Hotel operations are a capital-intensive business, as are restaurant operations, although not to the same extent. The nature of architecture, building practices and regulations will vary from country to country, and this type of capital investment may well rely on regional expertise to support development. But those companies which define their concept rigidly and attempt to standardize their operating units worldwide will tend to procure their plant and equipment from international suppliers as much as possible (see also Chapter 16). For instance, Hobart, manufacturers of kitchen and dish-wash equipment, have a network of agents throughout the world.

There is clear evidence suggesting that a feature of international hotel and restaurant chain expansion is the role of information technology (see also Chapter 16). In this particular area, it is most likely that international firms will 'single source' – that is to say, standardize their IT provision around one single supplier. Since most if not all major suppliers operate globally, this makes a great deal of sense. Forte Hotels, for instance, meets all its IT needs from IBM.

As well as being able to set up the concept through capital investment, there is then the issue of supplying the outlet with all the consumables it may need, such as food, beverages and other items. The extent to which the supplies needed are identical to those purchased in the home country depends on the basic strategic decision the firm has made concerning the concept. If a firm makes a decision to maintain its concept exactly as it originated, there are likely to be huge problems with the supply of certain fairly basic goods. The availability of certain types and cuts of meat varies widely across the world, often due to religious differences. Flour, a prime ingredient of many foodstuffs, also varies widely according the type and strain of cereal used. For instance, there is a marked difference between bread products in France and England. Even such a basic commodity as water may vary widely in terms of its quality. Fast-food companies, even in European countries, have not one but two water purifiers in each of their stores. This is largely to ensure the consistentcy of taste of their soft drinks. The purchasing of supplies may also present problems where the characteristics of the supply chain vary from one country to another. Deliveries may be unreliable, with greater or lesser time lags between one delivery and the next. This may require the firm to invest more heavily in storage space and infrastructure than it might have done in its home country.

Procurement tends to be a relatively highly centralized function in most hospitality firms. In one study (Riegel and Reid, 1988), foodservice chains typically had a vice-president of purchasing with a department of seven specialists. This department had responsibility for all high-expense purchases of consumables, notably meat, poultry and groceries. Highly perishable, lower cost items, such as dairy products, were more likely to be purchased at a regional or local level. These departments also tended to establish national or regional supply contracts with major suppliers and to approve suppliers.

Procurement has two features: selection of suppliers and supplies, and the actual purchase of the goods. This clearly presents a challenge for international companies if long-established suppliers of products in the home market do not operate internationally. Hospitality firms have reacted to this in three main ways. First, they have instigated rigorous reviews of local suppliers in their new markets in an effort to establish the same sort of consistency that they achieve elsewhere. Second, they have encouraged their suppliers to expand internationally along with themselves in order to ensure continuity of supply. And finally, they have backwardly integrated into the supply chain in order to influence or even directly control their supplies. Those chains that have grown through franchising face some restrictions with regards to procurement in Europe due to EC laws on restraint of trade. Although most fast-food chains, for instance, have a principal supplier of a particular foodstuff, under this legislation franchisees are free to purchase from any supplier so long as it meets the franchisors' very tight product specifications. However, the franchisors' preferred supplier is usually able to secure the supply to most franchisees on the basis of being the lowest-cost supplier.

Organizational issues in international hospitality operations

Organizational variation exists even among firms operating in single countries. Firms develop alternative structures depending on the age of the company, its ownership, geographic spread, speed of growth and so on. There is also the view that the organization structure of a firm should reflect its strategy, and we have already seen that different firms may adopt very different operational strategies when they operate internationally. It is therefore logical that international hospitality firms will organize themselves in a range of different ways. In this section we shall briefly consider four aspects of organization as they relate to operations management: namely, alternative organization structures, the degree of formalization, the extent of centralization and the nature of organizational culture.

Alternative organization structures

There is little or no evidence concerning how hospitality firms organize their operations. The basic assumption is that it is largely on a geographic basis. That is to say, area managers are likely to report to regional directors, who in turn would report to an operations director or vice-president. In addition, this senior manager may also have specialist departments reporting to him or her, such as the R & D department, purchasing department and strategic development (site selection and feasibility) department. We have already discussed these three specialist functions in the previous section. For instance, Forte Hotels, Hilton International, Burger King and many other international firms have a centralized, corporate department responsible for making decisions on expansion into new countries and selecting appropriate sites.

Area or district managers are typically appointed to look after a number of operating units, be they hotels, restaurants or fast-food outlets, grouped together on the basis of their proximity to each other. In 1988 it was suggested in the US food service industry (Umbreit, 1989) that managers at this level might be responsible for on average 6 outlets. Wayne Calloway, the CEO of Pepsico, when talking about Taco Bell, Kentucky Fried Chicken and Pizza Hut, indicated in 1990 that their area managers were responsible for 12 units, but that within two or three years this would increase to about 24 units.

Burger King, Europe, Middle East and Africa, have adopted essentially a matrix structure with three vice-presidents of sales and service responsible for operations in different geographic regions, and vice-presidents of marketing, human resources, finance, and quality and costs managing across the whole company. Each regional vice-president has two types of manager reporting upwards: area managers, who are responsible for between 15 and 20 directly managed outlets; and franchise sales and service managers, who work with the owners of franchised outlets.

Formalization

Although the concept of area managers is a well-accepted one, the role that such managers play is not always well defined (Umbreit, 1989). On the basis of this research it is suggested that in foodservice there are three important roles. The restaurant operations role enforces consistent company standards, systems and procedures; evaluates product quality; implements new systems overseas; ensures delivery of positive customer service; supervises new product introductions; and monitors unit management activities. With respect to human resources, the area manager typically supervises effective orientation and training; teaches unit managers how to manage people; provides quality feedback; and develops promotable managers. Finally, the financial management role maintains the profitability of units by monitoring performance, preparing budgets, developing forecasts, authorizing expenditures, controlling costs, and reviewing results with unit managers. It is likely that area managers in hotel companies will have similar responsibilities to these. The idea of formalization refers to the extent to which such responsibilities are clearly laid down and defined, and the extent to which performance is measured against such criteria.

Centralization versus decentralization

The extent to which a hospitality firm is centralized or decentralized tends to be affected by the level of internationalization, but it is not solely dependent on this factor. Queens Moat House has been aggressively expanding its operations outside the UK throughout the 1980s, and has continued to operate in a highly decentralized fashion. This reflects the management style, operating philosophy and organizational culture of this particular firm. Other firms, particularly in the fast-food sector, adopt highly centralized control over their operations.

Organizational culture

In a service business such as hospitality, the culture of the organization can be an important aspect of effective service delivery to customers. Although not often explicitly engaged in promoting the culture of the organization, operational managers inherently rely on there being a context in which customer satisfaction is supported by all that the company does. Since the basis of culture is the concept of *shared* values, internationalization clearly presents a challenge to ensuring that managers and employees do share common goals and values. Ideas that have been successful in one country in terms of encouraging or motivating employees may not work in another (see also Chapters 11 and 15). One way to respond to this challenge is to increase the internal marketing activities of the firm. Forte Hotels, for instance, has a director of corporate communication whose role is to address this very issue. There are also implications for the incentive schemes that firms use to encourage employee performance. At least one fast-food chain does not automatically utilize all its incentive programs in all European countries, but selects those it feels are most appropriate for the culture of that country.

Management at operating unit level

As well as considering the strategic and organizational implications of operating in the international hospitality business, we must also consider the impact this has on individual managers in individual operations. The service concept and the service delivery system explain *what* the operations manager has to manage, but they do not adequately describe *how* the manager successfully carries out his or her responsibilities. Merricks and Jones (1986) and Lockwood and Jones (1989) propose that an examination of outputs, which they call key result areas, is the most effective framework for understanding this. They identify seven such key result areas, as illustrated in Figure 10.3, for which standards of performance must be set and against which success or failure can be judged. Just as there are many different types of service concept within the industry, ranging from fast food to haute cuisine and from budget motels to luxury resorts, so there are 'sets' of specific key result areas appropriate for each type of operation. While key result areas will loosely match service delivery systems, hospitality firms will have a high degree of discretion over the exact standards of performance they expect in each. For instance, the service/income levels in a Travelodge, Formule 1 or Super 8 motel may vary according to the strategic or competitive position of the firm, even though the SDS is essentially similar. The role that the operations manager plays in the firm is to ensure that there is a complete fit between the service concept and each of the key result areas.

Managing employee performance

It is clear that interaction between management and employees will vary from one country to another due to the cultural and social norms of that country and the abilities and experience of the workforce. It is therefore likely that

Figure 10.3 Model of key result areas in hospitality operations
Source: Lockwood and Jones (1989).

how a manager leads, motivates and communicates with employees will reflect this context. We shall not examine this in detail as at least two other chapters (Chapters 11 and 15) deal with aspects of human resource management and the multicultural workforce.

Managing assets

This key result area refers largely to the routines and procedures unit managers must follow in order to assure the safety of employees and customers and the preservation of property, equipment and stock. Lockwood and Jones (1989) suggest that assets can be divided into low-value items, such as small items of stock or equipment, and high-value items, such as employees, customers and property; and the level of threat to these assets into low and high categories. They suggest that control procedures are typically adopted to respond to low-threat/low-value assets, while assurance strategies are necessary for high-threat/high-value assets.

The implication of operating internationally is that the relative position of assets in terms of both value and level of threat may change from one country to another. For instance, a high-value/low-level threat would normally be the terrorist bombing of a property. However, in certain parts of the world, such as Belfast, Beirut or Sarajevo, this becomes a high-level threat and extra precautions need to be taken. Likewise, hurricanes are more of a threat in Miami than Montreal; flooding is more likely in Venice than Vancouver; and forest fires are more prevalent near Nice than New York.

Normally, hotel and food service chains attempt to assure the safety of their customers, employees and property through a combination of good design, standard operating procedures and effective contingency programing. But even a firm's ability to do this may be constrained by the country in which it is operating. Thus the infrastructure of the country may make it impossible to rely on automatic warning or fire-fighting equipment due to the unreliability of either electricity or water supplies. Local planning laws and regulations may also prohibit, change or limit the way in which the firm designs its properties. Likewise the cultural norms of a country may modify the extent to which employee or customer behavior threatens assets through non-deliberate acts of negligence or conscious acts of pilferage and theft.

Managing capacity

Managing capacity refers to the concept of matching supply and demand at the operating unit level. There are four variables over which the manager has some control: volume, the total demand for the product/service; variability, the extent to which volume fluctuates over time, sometimes called seasonality; variety, the extent of the product/service range on offer; and variation, the change in demand for different items of the product/service range over time. It is apparent that in different parts of the world these four Vs exhibit different characteristics within the same sector and even within the same branded product due to structural differences between regions.

In Part 1 we have seen how the *volume* of tourist activity varies from one country to another. In some countries, demand is relatively stable over time. But in others it is highly *variable*, either on a cyclical basis due to seasonality derived from fashion or climate, or randomly due to specific circumstances, such as political, economic or social upheaval.

The foodservice and hotel sectors of the industry have different characteristics with regards to the management of capacity. Most restaurant chains serve only local markets and hence unit managers have a high degree of control over capacity. Many hotel chains, however, serve international markets and therefore the locus of control in this business moves away from the unit towards the center, especially with the introduction of central reservation systems. For instance, Choice International's strategy is based around the creation and management of such systems tied into its specific marketing approach.

Managing income and profitability

Most international firms accept that performance of individual operating units will vary from one country to another due to local circumstances. Therefore, although they use standard criteria across all their units to assess performance, they adapt the parameters to reflect location. The extent to which this is clearly established will reflect the level of formalization within the firm. In fast-food chains, the unit managers will normally have to achieve a performance consistent with the concept and marketplace in which they operate. In the four- and five-star hotel business, locational variation is usually built into the annual business planning exercise undertaken by each hotel general manager, so that performance is measured against the forecast.

Managing productivity

The effective management of productivity is based essentially on achieving operating efficiencies consistent with the specified level of service. Since the hospitality industry has relatively high labor costs, managing the workforce is a key feature of this. In most cases, hospitality firms will have established criteria for staffing levels based on their experience of operating their type of operation. However, internationally these criteria may need to be adapted for a variety of reasons. First, the cost of labor is likely to vary quite widely. In those countries where labor is relatively cheap, managers may schedule more staff than 'normal' either because they may feel the expertise of employees is relatively low or because customer expectations in that region are higher. For instance, it is common in hotels in India to have an employee on each floor of the hotel to act as a server/porter as required. Second, the educational background, experience and expectations of employees may vary widely. Third, the social context may prevent the operator from implementing its typical pattern of staff scheduling. For instance, female employees may have family obligations with regards to their husbands or children that prevent them from working at some times of the day.

Managing service

In the context of key result areas, service relates to the interface between the customer and the service worker. Once again, cultural differences from one part of the world to another may require the manager to adopt entirely different approaches to managing this key result area (see also Chapter 15).

Managing quality

Quality in many respects derives from the successful management of the other key result areas. Two broad strategies can be adopted: namely, quality *control*, especially back-of-house; and quality *assurance*. There seems to be little doubt that firms tend to modify their approach to quality management internationally on the basis of whichever of these strategies appears to be most effective. Thus there is a trend in hotel firms in the USA and Europe to adopt quality assurance, whereas they continue to exert high degrees of quality control in other parts of the world. There is also a greater reliance on providing direct feedback to hotel general managers on the results of customer satisfaction surveys. For instance, Hilton International introduced in 1992 its guest satisfaction tracking system. Hyatt has revised its guest comment card system so that results are now analyzed by each property before they are sent to head office. And Stouffers Hotels has a guest satisfaction index derived from guest comment cards, follow-up cards, unsolicited telephone calls and an operational survey report.

In the fast-food sector there is greater reliance on control and standardized procedures worldwide to check on conformance. For instance, Burger King has developed a brand delivery index which it applies to all its restaurants worldwide. So all BK outlets are mystery shopped every month, quality assurance audited every three months, and reviewed against measures of customer satisfaction derived from a toll-free number available to customers who wish to comment on their experience.

Conclusion

There is no one 'right' way of managing international hospitality operations. This chapter argues that the successful firm will be the one that develops an integrated service strategy and concept, supports this through appropriate organizational forms, and empowers its managers to manage their operations through key result areas.

References

Economist Intelligence Unit (1991) *Competitive Strategies for the International Hotel Industry*, Special Report No. 1180.

Farrell, K. (1991) 'Sites and Saturation', *Restaurant Business*, 1 July, pp. 72–80.

Go. F., and Christensen, J. (1989) 'Going global', *Cornell HRA Quarterly*, vol. 30, no. 3, pp. 73–9.

Go, F., Sung Soo Pyo, Uysal, F., and Mihalik, B. J. (1990) 'Decision criteria for transnational hotel expansion', *Tourism Management*, December, pp. 297–304.

Johnston, Robert (1989) 'Developing competitive strategies in service industries', in P. Jones (ed.), *Management in Service Industries*, London: Pitman.

Lockwood, Andrew, and Jones, Peter (1989) *The Management of Hotel Operations*, London: Cassell.

Merricks, P., and Jones, P. (1986) *The Management of Catering Operations*, London: Cassell.

Pannell Kerr Forster (1989) *Trends in the Hotel Industry*.

Pickworth, J. R. (1988) 'Service delivery systems in the foodservice industry', *International Journal of Hospitality Management*, vol. 7, no. 1, pp. 43–62.

Riegel, C. D., and Reid, R. D. (1988) 'Food-service purchasing: corporate practices', *Cornell HRA Quarterly*, vol. 29, no. 1, pp. 24–9.

Umbreit, W. T. (1989) 'Multi-unit management: managing at a distance', *Cornell HRA Quarterly*, vol. 30, no. 1, pp. 53–9.

Wan, L. (1992) 'Look who's innovating: an investigation into the management of innovation within the fast food and related industries', unpublished dissertation, University of Brighton.

West, J. J., and Anthony, W. P. (1990) 'Strategic group membership and environmental scanning: their relationship to firm performance in the foodservice industry', *International Journal of Hospitality Management*, vol. 9, no. 3, pp. 247–67.

I I

Human resource management

Steven Goss-Turner

I was first introduced to international human resource management in the hospitality industry when working in this function in the late 1980s. Within a week of introducing a new bonus scheme for managers and staff in all the chain's international hotels, two general managers had contacted me to discuss the scheme. The first GM telephoned from Guyana to explain that locally inflation was at 120 percent per annum and our scheme would be of no value in that country. He suggested that bonuses should be paid not in money but in kind. Managers should receive an emergency electricity generator (as power supplies were uncertain) and staff should receive good quality shoes and umbrellas (as most of them had to walk to work in tropical rain storms). The second GM contacted me from Malta. He was worried about the tight-knit, family-orientated community of that island. Virtually all his staff were in some way related to each other and the scheme could cause upset among relatives – some doing well, others not so well.

These conversations date back to the mid-1980s, within the then Trust-house Forte Hotels organization, now known as Forte. As an individual I was a head-office-based personnel manager, grappling with overseas responsibilities recently added to my London remit. As a company we were on that learning curve that takes a centrally based, one-culture, one-country firm into a truly internationally sensitive organization. As a human resource department, we were responding to an overall business strategy of international expansion, and we were being confronted by many of the issues which will be considered in this chapter.

Primarily, we had to consider the implications for and impact upon human resource management (HRM) of international expansion. We had to analyze the role of HRM within the company's strategy and business plan. Finally, we had to consider how we could add value as a key specialist activity, and contribute significantly to long-term success.

Decentralization and flexibility

The postwar history of the international hospitality industry is exemplified by famous brand names of mostly American origin. Hilton, Holiday Inn, Hyatt and InterContinental were synonymous with quality across a five-star hotel globe. Their burgeoning success, particularly through the 1960s, was based on providing consistent service in a consistent product under strong central control. Such control has been a feature of an American style of managing multinational businesses, not only in the hospitality industry. But Barham and Rassam (1989) suggest that today's successful and progressive companies are 'groping towards a new way of managing complex multinationals, turning their backs on the American way – for so long the role model – which has often been based on strong central control'.

Barham and Rassam conducted a far-reaching research program within some of the largest international companies. Their findings show that senior managers are convinced that they need to be more and more multicultural, incredibly flexible and highly adaptable to local conditions and practices. They call this approach a more flexible 'European style', citing BMW and IBM as examples, as well as the rapidly expanding French hospitality group Accor. A leading Accor executive is quoted as saying, 'We do have an Accor way of doing things, in finance, in marketing, and in our philosophy of management, but it must be adapted to the local culture'.

The essentially macro issues of a company's management philosophy and style must be clear and foremost in the mind when organizing and directing an international human resource (HR) function. HR must be a proactive, involved contributor at the strategic level, not just a reactive administrative support service. HR must have significant input into strategy; into the organizational structure; into the development of management style, as well as into the traditional and highly influential HR technicalities of recruitment training and management development. John Watson, director of human resources and information management for British Airways, recently supported this view by saying that the HR department 'must continue to be more strategic and less operational. We must add real value to everything we do rather than just be a basic bureaucratic utility' (quoted in *Personnel Management*, June 1992).

The hospitality industry has changed its world profile considerably in recent years. European companies are achieving an enhanced and impressive eminence. Ladbroke Hilton, Bass Holiday Inn and Accor are three prime examples of recent acquisition and development. The methods of growth and expansion are also more diverse, with the trend being towards joint ventures, franchising, lease-back arrangements and management contracts (as discussed in Chapter 8). Ownership is increasingly international, as with that famous name 'InterContinental', now part-owned and operated by the Scandinavian firm SAS and part-owned by Japanese company Seibu Saison. All these organizations are faced with decisions on business strategy across many geographical locations. To centralize or decentralize is often the question. The human resource function must be fully integrated with the outcomes of such strategic considerations. HR must itself be flexible and responsive enough to be able to provide the level of input and influence required. The department also has to ponder its own structure and strategy in line with the total business plan, and the next section looks at the alternatives available.

Human resource strategic alternatives

My early experience in international HRM clearly demonstrated to me the simple fact that you cannot continue to manage in the ways of the past when you move to a world-scale organization. Within the fast-changing hospitality business today, HR managers need to be even more aware of the alternative strategies that could be adopted. There can be no one 'blue-print' approach, for each organization has its own characteristics and history and is at a unique stage in its development. Each company must analyze its own corporate image and culture, and follow a course of action which is appropriate. Johnson and Scholes (1988) refer to this combination of unique characteristics that make the organization what it is, as the 'recipe'. This 'recipe' is a complex blend of interrelated factors, which include the structure of the organization, its control systems and power structures, and the company routines, symbols, myths and rituals.

The reaction of Forte in the late 1980s to the 'shoes and umbrellas' scenario was to restructure on the basis of regionalization. There was agreement that some level of decentralization was necessary for the management to be closer to the action, understanding the issues affecting a particular region of business. With Guyana in mind, one example of this process was Caribbean regionalization, with a regional vice-president installed in the Bahamas, supported by a small team of specialists, and with access to an HR regional manager who specifically covered the area.

Other companies have taken the decentralization process further. Accor, Campanile and Queens Moat House are firms which have devolved more autonomy and decision making to the level of individual units. They look at each hotel as a small unit. 'Accor prefers to talk of itself as an enterprise rather than a company organization' (Barham and Rassam, 1989). This approach leads to HR involvement in many of the currently high-profile management theories, such as empowerment, performance management and total quality management. These are all 'people issues' of a strategic and highly influential nature, providing challenges and opportunities for HR professionals.

Watson and Litteljohn (1992), have provided a concise and practical model of alternative human resource strategies, developed from the earlier work of Perlmutter (1969). This framework is useful in the assessment of both the current position of an organization and the direction that it should be moving in. Table 11.1 summarizes their analysis into three categories: ethnocentric, polycentric and geocentric. The ethnocentric type of organization is characterized by the central control approach, with strategies and procedures

Table 11.1 Human resource management strategies

	Ethnocentric	Polycentric	Geocentric
Definition	The same strategies and practices are employed in all countries	HRM is decentralized on a country-by-country basis	HRM is managed on a global basis
Characteristics	A high degree of authority and decision making at head office	Authority and decision making devolved to take account of local environments	Harmonizes the overall management of HRM while at the same time responding to local environmental factors
Management Development	Managers are recruited and developed in the company's home country, for anywhere in the world	Local managers are trained and developed for key positions within own country	Allows for the development of the best person within the company as a whole

Source: Watson and Litteljohn (1992).

virtually identical across the entire company. The polycentric organization is typified by regionalization, HRM being decentralized on a regional or country-by-country basis. The geocentric approach is truly global, involving the total merger of HRM and overall business strategy with the fundamental ability to be flexible and adapt to localized circumstances and factors.

Most organizations will find themselves somewhere between categories, but wherever it currently lies and wherever it intends to lie, there are significant implications for the HR function. The implications for management development are particularly important, as here the future of the company is at stake. We will look at this crucial area in detail later in the chapter. However, before promoting the HR product, we must make sure that the product itself is fitted to the needs of the company and the strategy. The HR department must review its own structure and capabilities.

Development of the human resource function

If the HR function is to change its role and purpose, to become a fully integrated part of the business plan, proactive and strategic, then it must analyze the internal change and development that may be unavoidable. HR must look at its own corporate image, its own culture and its own capabilities, from administrative expertise to the interpersonal skills of the team members. Within an international company, the HR function should reflect the very internationalism that the company as a whole is striving to create. My own experience with Forte Hotels addressed this issue, and we attempted to achieve an international transformation by addressing four aspects of the HR function.

Image

Human resource departments need to move from a 'bureaucratic utility' to a customer-oriented, market-driven enterprise. The employees of the company need to become customers. This premise has to invade the HR philosophy and influence its every action. This entails considerable change. In Forte, an early and symbolic change was the new name of the department, which was changed from 'London and Overseas Personnel Department', to 'Human Resources – International'. A logo was created to sit alongside the new name, as were new letterheads, a policy on print-style and promotional literature. A splendid training center was built, 'fully loaded' with the most advanced technology and training equipment. The center was based in the United Kingdom, but deliberately at a Heathrow Airport hotel to facilitate the coming and going of overseas delegates. Its name, 'The Academy', was itself internationally acceptable and understood, and much of its literature, course material, even signage, was translated into a number of languages.

Specialist expertise

In order to develop a truly international HR function, it is necessary to develop additional skills within the team. This can be achieved partly through training, and partly by recruitment. Forte needed expertise in the area of information technology, a vital ingredient for any multi-unit, multinational organization. We had to install a new computerized personnel information system to be able to provide a fast, responsive service to our managers. We needed expertise in choosing the most appropriate, cost-effective system. Administration generally was reviewed and made more 'customer' friendly, rather than being a convenient bureaucracy of most value to the HR team itself. With international transfers more and more frequent, we had to determine new policies and procedures to ensure that such moves were successfully administered. This involved close examination of the nuts and bolts of the transfers, from the contents of expatriate contracts, to compensation and benefit packages, relocation plans, personal fiscal and tax issues, and other family-oriented matters such as housing and schooling.

Team development

The profile of HR team members is typically one of ex-hotel operators who have specialized in personnel and training, working in the industry, or even the same company, for most or all of their career. This is still an important strength but international firms now need more. In Forte, over a period of time, it was necessary to change this profile of human resource professionals. Specific criteria were established for all future recruitment into the HR department. Expertise was 'bought in' with regard to information technology and also overseas transfer administration; expertise from a service industry background, not purely hospitality. Recruitment and training strategies for the department were adopted which stressed cultural awareness, language ability and overseas work experience. There developed a team of people with a variety of nationality and culture. The interpersonal skills of the team became multicultural and highly influential, as personal relations between overseas managers and the company improved dramatically. Members of the team spent time in the regions, in the hotels, training and advising, always supporting as a colleague and not arriving on an 'inspection' from head office.

The cultural awareness factor

The HR team needs a more sophisticated and educated approach to being an international organization. External consultants were hired in Forte to run training courses on cultural awareness, aimed at specialists like ourselves and also at senior line management and management trainees. We also realized that we had to tackle the issue of information and briefing of managers within the international transfer arena. Research by Scullion (1991) into the expatriate success or failure story suggests that 'the main reasons cited for poor expatriate performance ... are ... family related problems, the managers' inability to adopt to a new culture, selection problems, inadequate preparation of managers, and lack of experience in international transfers'. Specialist organizations were used, such as the Centre for International Briefing, Farnham Castle in Surrey, and we became a subscriber to Employment Conditions Abroad (ECA), which provided an updating system of information for every country in our company's portfolio.

This four-pronged attack, embracing changes of a symbolic and procedural nature, was necessary to nudge the organization from an essentially ethnocentric culture to a more regionalized, polycentric model. The difficulty with such models is, of course, that they are not in a static environment. The business of international hospitality firms has been particularly fragile and has been subjected to dramatic global effects. In the last few years we have seen the effects of recession, political upheaval, the Gulf war, civil wars and terrorism. The financial consequences for tourism-related and hotel companies has caused expansion to be reviewed and curtailed, and has forced managers to question overall strategic direction. In this turbulent and uncertain environment, multinationals are also reviewing their position on the key issues of decentralization and devolution of decision making. As an example, the petrochemical giant Shell has felt it necessary to 're-centralize' some of its activities which have been devolved to operating units, believing that such empowerment had led to inefficiency and fragmentation of effort. The next section looks at how a proactive, responsive HR department can find a crucial role in assisting companies to avoid these dangers.

The role of human resource management in international corporate strategy

Barham and Rassam (1989) cite the four key elements which, following their research, seem to dominate the structure of organizations in the current business environment. These four elements, interlinked within a dynamic framework, are strategy; decentralized businesses; information technology; and coordinated activities. By consideration of their model, Figure 11.1, companies could evolve a structure and an operational approach which capitalizes on the value of decentralization on an international basis, without falling into the dangerous trap of fragmentation.

The diamond-shaped diagram clearly illustrates the dynamic interrelation of the four aspects. Beginning at the top of the diamond, *strategy* should be achieved through internationally *decentralized businesses*, which impacts on *information technology* to collate and feedback data to both the centre of the company and the devolved units. IT also serves those activities, such as financial control, which are required to ensure the long-term success of the total organization. Like IT these *coordinated activities* need to feed back to strategy, ensuring update, review and future plans.

However, the example of Shell (*PM Plus* 1992, vol. 3, no. 4) illustrates that decentralization and empowerment on a grand scale can lead to the fragmentation of 'coordinated activities' and is a warning to all organizations bent on such a course. Marketing within Shell became so devolved to operating divisions around the world that the strong, well-established corporate image was being eroded, as varying 'messages' emanated from different sections of the company. Shell also found that specific technical expertise held by personnel at the center was being wasted as the autonomous units became isolationist in their attitude to the company.

It is clear that 'reinventing the wheel' could well prosper in such an organization with particular relevance to research and development, design, planning and indeed human resource management. If a global, geocentric

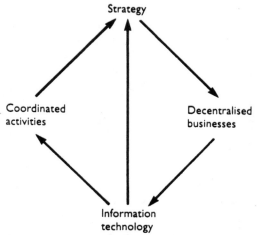

Figure 11.1   Key elements of organization for international firms
Source: Barham and Rassam (1989).

strategy is to lead to enhanced business performance at the bottom line, there clearly needs to be a sensible trade-off between autonomy/empowerment and value/expertise of a corporate organization and culture. Within HRM there can be large and excessive costs involved in training courses run by local management engaging in one-off development activities. There are also very real concerns within management development and company succession planning if fragmentation threatens the future management resource of the overall organization. This area will be treated in greater detail later in the chapter.

The 'coordinated activities' aspect of Barham and Rassam's model is where I believe HRM can play a key role in ensuring that the total strategy of the company is successful. HRM must be the guardian of management style, thus protecting corporate image and culture with regard to people. If, as we are so often told by company chairmen and annual reports, people in hospitality are the most vital asset, then HRM is the coordinator of that powerful asset. HRM has clear and influential inputs, which affect the spread of a company's ethos, principles and management style. HRM has strategic control over recruitment procedures, from the philosophical content of person specifications to the selection methods used to get the right people for the organization. This role of coordinator determines the content and style of induction, training and management development. In an international context we have already considered the importance of HRM influence on compensation and benefits, on terms and conditions of employment, on the spreading of information such as cultural awareness and on management transfers. It also requires HRM to be fully involved in the company's communication process with its workforce, through newsletters, video technology or whatever method is internationally suitable. And as companies need to respond and change more speedily in an ever-changing and unpredictable business environment, so HRM has a key part to play in facilitating the human implications of such change.

Management development

As a coordinating activity, HRM strategy on management development and succession planning is of prime importance in enabling long-term organizational success. Once a style and philosophy has been established, continuity of management is essential in ensuring that each business has periods of sustained growth and achievement of goals. In an international scenario, this means continuity of managers who possess the additional abilities necessary, the flexibility and adaptability to be effective in different countries and cultures. From graduate trainee onwards, HR must be sure that the company's management development programs nurture an appropriate resource for the future. High-quality, focused training linked to performance and potential reviews are means to this end, as is the systematic, long-term succession planning that will aim to secure the right person in the right job at the right time. This company-wide, global approach to management progression is a basic ingredient of the geocentric structure, allowing 'for the development of the best person within the company as a whole' (Watson and Litteljohn, 1992).

Torrington and Hall (1991) describe management development as 'concerned with developing the whole person'. This is particularly relevant for the international manager as we have seen, where business education and cultural awareness are as significant as technical job skills. Irving Borwick, managing director of the Management Executive Centre, warned a lecture audience recently at the Management Centre Europe in Brussells (1989) that management training and development must be totally integrated with an organization's succession planning program. 'No team is forever', is a telling truism often used by Borwick, warning how many fine business plans have been wrecked by the loss of key managers at the most unfortunate stage, followed by the organization's inability to replace effectively and quickly.

This discontinuity of management is a serious risk to any international firm. The gap that often opens up between appointments can at best prevent progress, at worst lead to regression and decline. An international replacement manager needs to be trained, developed and of proven track record to justify the transfer, as well as possessing the crucial personal attributes necessary. There is also the time element needed to give the replacement full briefing and cultural awareness training, and the time to sort out personal affairs. Even relief management can be difficult to arrange, and though many managers profess to desiring international experience, they often find reasons not to go when the crunch comes.

It is clear, then, that international succession planning, and the inherent management development, need to have a long-term approach. Moves may need to be planned two or three years in advance. One principle here is that as soon as a manager is appointed, HR should be planning the successor! Borwick insists that succession planning and continuity are at the heart of business success. He proposes that to achieve company goals, certain 'tasks' (using the term in its widest sense) need to be performed. To carry out these tasks, a company needs people who are trained, developed and ready to take on such work. To ensure such a supply of talent, you need to plan succession well in advance, fed as it is by consideration of future organizational development, by manpower planning needs, by performance and potential reviews, and by the management development programs available.

This approach, indeed the whole principle of management development, is very much geared to growing your own talent, a traditional ethnocentric characteristic. The research by Scullion (1991), referred to earlier, provided some interesting insights into this area. In particular, he found that British companies tended to use expatriate management when expanding overseas, rather than recruiting from outside the company. He found that this was the case with hospitality companies. The reasons for this centered on the fact that management development itself was preparing managers for just such assignments. Other reasons given were a lack of suitable local management, the continuity and knowledge of corporate culture and, rather quaintly, trust or 'peace of mind'. This British approach, largely ethnocentric, varied from the more polycentric stance taken by Japanese firms, which 'rely heavily on expatriates in the early stages of a foreign operation; they then tend to replace the expatriate senior management team with host-country managers'. Hugh Scullion cites Nissan's plant in Sunderland as an example of this HR strategy.

The content of management development programs needs to reflect the special needs of international managers. This may require HR departments to shift the emphasis of the training function away from task-orientated management techniques toward the broader skills required by the 'globally mobile' manager; to exercise more concern with cultural aspects of doing business in other countries, of behavior, of rituals and values in other cultures. The strong behavioral aspect was stressed to me by a highly successful senior hotel company executive, who felt that at the heart of his success in six different countries was his ability to observe and to listen: observing the way other employees and customers behaved and reacted, and listening to what they talked about, and the tone and manner in which they spoke. He also said that gauging the sense of humor of a particular race was most difficult, but once established it could be an invaluable management and social tool.

International companies must also consider the mode of delivery of management development programs. Many overseas locations are isolated outposts, perhaps the only company hotel in the whole country. In terms of development this requires a manager who is self-reliant, self-motivating, innovative and resourceful, and who can take responsibility for some self-development. Thus firms must discover alternatives to costly, time-consuming, centrally run training courses. HRM must review self-learning packages such as the open or distance learning material that is now widely available. The organization should be concerned with providing a range of educational opportunities for the developing international manager, ensuring that he or she has updated knowledge on issues as disparate as economic trends, technological progress, the financial markets, energy and green issues, demographic trends and so on. Horton (1989) summarizes this by saying that 'education, experience and international mobility will be among the qualities they require'.

Resourcing the future

While urging HR professionals to realize their strategic potential in enhancing the success of the organization, it would be wrong in the labor-intensive hospitality industry to omit serious consideration of how hospitality resources itself and the image of the industry as an employer to the international labor force of the future. One of the many changes which seem to be simultaneously affecting the business environment is the composition and aspirations of the national and international labor markets. Moss Kanter (1984) highlights this factor, urging companies to react to demographic change. These changes in the profile of working populations have been much discussed in recent years. The hospitality industry has a high proportion of young people in its workforce, and so cannot be unaware of the implications of the decline in the numbers of such potential employees in the next ten years. Internationally, HRM must get the relevant local statistics and advise local operational managers accordingly. The increasing importance of women in the labor market is also of relevance to an industry that can offer so many opportunities to working mothers and 'returning' mothers. The internal employment market of Europe will be subject to change as the single market takes effect from 1 January 1993. Nobody seems to be too clear exactly what will or will not happen, but international hospitality firms must gear themselves to compete for scarcer and more mobile human resources.

My main concern, however, when looking to the future resourcing of the industry is whether HR influence can really help hospitality organizations to conquer their image problem. At the annual conference of the International Hotel Association in Strasbourg (November 1991), the image of the industry as an employer was still considered the number one issue to be addressed at an international level. Unacceptably high labor turnover, inflexible and out-dated terms and conditions and long hours for poor rewards are regrettably the image that prevails. Whether true or not, whether enlightened hospitality employers are greatly improving conditions or not, image is image, and the perception is what matters. One reason for this may be the specific charac-teristics of the hospitality industry when compared with other industries.

Willman (1989) has looked at the relationship between the style of human resource policies and the characteristics of an industry. He differentiates between 'high contact HR policies' and 'low contact'. The former category embraces all employees within one culture and is active and costly, aiming to gain commitment, reduce labor turnover and absenteeism, and, through staff behavior, enhance the quality of service. He considers that most hotel and catering companies fall into the 'low contact' category. This results in charac-teristics such as accepting the 'presence of relatively low-paid, poorly com-mitted, high turnover staff'. There are enormous if hidden costs of labor turnover and absenteeism. Supervision is close and direct, training is limited, wages are paid at the minimum level and commitment is not actively sought or gained.

Now I recognize that there are many good hospitality employers, and many committed, long-service employees whose life is richer for being in an exciting industry. But I do suggest that there are still too many employers who follow Willman's description, who too readily accept the situation, and who do not seek to innovate or look at alternative ways of running hospitality businesses. Human resource managers must continue to influence companies to review employment policies and practices. They must recognize the long-term prob-lem if the industry's poor image does not universally improve. The Interna-tional Hotel Association is concentrating its effort on improving the quality of training, to reach young people across the world, and to give them skills and opportunities for the future.

This is undoubtedly a valid international response, but I feel that managers must also look at their organizations, at how they run their businesses. Many hotel structures do not seem to have changed since they opened. Structures are hierarchical, traditional and riddled with authority levels, stifling formality and stereotypes. The 'shamrock' organization concept of Handy (1988) could have interesting applications for the hospitality industry in a review of its structural approach. Handy sees this 'shamrock' organization as having three distinctly different types of human resource which could contribute to the company: firstly, a 'professional core' of skilled employees, essential to the existence of the organization; secondly, a 'contractual fringe' of providers of services to the organization; and thirdly, a 'flexible labor force' of varying size dependent on training patterns and demand. This flexibility is not just the ability to call on temporary or casual staff, but is flexibility in resourcing, in work patterns and rotas. Each international location would need to adapt the shamrock to its own set of circumstances, but it begins to invite managers to review the way the business operates. HRM has an enabling role to play here, encouraging managers to question traditional ways of running hospitality units, to innovate and be better prepared to tackle a future of rapid change and unforeseen developments, rather than being victims of it.

Conclusion

As the major hospitality organizations become increasingly global in their representation, they are faced by crucial questions of how to organize and manage their businesses in many countries and cultures. Most see varying degrees of decentralization and empowerment as key answers to these questions. Human resource management is a powerful strategic force in ensuring that such developments are successful.

Therefore HRM is an integral element of strategy and also an influential integrating activity. This role for the function requires it to be proactive and credible, yet less operational as it devolves the more routine activities of personnel management to line management, while ensuring that the latter are well prepared for such responsibilities. HRM must be fully involved with the company's communication process across international boundaries, including the understanding of change and new philosophies. It must be a guardian of all people issues, setting standards that are moral, and that enable strategies to become successful realities.

The HR department must be fully aware of international issues, at a global, national, even local level. It must examine its own image and capabilities, and work to maximize its value and credibility within the total organization. HR managers must work alongside other specialist and line managers to ensure a high level of input towards the making of better decisions.

Finally, HRM must fulfill the role of a coordinating force, developing and influencing management on a wide range of important matters: management styles; management systems; empowerment; cultural awareness, and flexibility. And it can help to prevent the fragmentation of the corporate effort by retaining an organization-wide perspective, through recruitment, training, succession planning and management development.

References

Barham, K., and Rassam, C. (1989) *Shaping the Corporate Future*, London: Unwin Hyman.

Borwick, I. (1989) 'Management continuity planning', lecture to Management Centre Europe, Brussels.

Handy, C. (1990) *Understanding Voluntary Organizations*, Harmondsworth: Penguin.

Horton, B.P. (1989) 'Globe trotters', *Management Today*, February, pp. 5–41.

Johnson, G., and Scholes, K. (1988) *Exploring Corporate Strategy*, Hemel Hemstead: Prentice Hall.

Moss Kanter, R. (1984) *The Change Masters*, London: Allen and Unwin.

Perlmutter, H. (1969) 'The tortuous evolution of the multinational corporation', *Colombia Journal of World Business*, January/February, p. 12.

Scullion, H. (1991) 'Why companies prefer to use expatriates', *Personnel Management*, November, pp. 32–5.

Torrington, D., and Hall, L. (1991) *Personnel Management: A new approach*, Hemel Hemstead: Prentice Hall.

Watson, S., and Litteljohn, D. (1992) 'Multi- and transnational firms: the impact of expansion on corporate structures' in R. Teare and M. Olsen (eds), *International Hospitality Management*, London: Pitman.

Willman, P. (1989) 'Human resource management' in P. Jones (ed.), *Management in Service Industries*, London: Pitman.

12
International hospitality marketing

Leo M. Renaghan

Since academic and business gurus first touted the marketing concept as the success concept for the 1970s, then the 1980s and now the 1990s, in the international hospitality industry the marketing or customer orientation has been slow to take hold. This makes it difficult to discuss how international hospitality firms 'do' marketing because they vary greatly in the degree to which the marketing orientation is part of their corporate culture and drives routine business activities. In fact, many international hospitality companies do not really 'do' any marketing at all. In the 1970s and early 1980s hospitality organizations were quick to adopt the titles and jargon of marketing. Virtually all firms have marketing departments or divisions, and most perform some of the marketing functions such as positioning and market segmentation, but that does not mean that they 'do' marketing. They may call it marketing, but the corporate culture for many firms with respect to revenue management in the 1990s is still that of sales.

It is easiest to think of international hospitality firms as occupying a point on a line with sales anchoring one end and marketing anchoring the other end. Hospitality firms would be placed somewhere along the continuum based on the degree to which their culture, values and activities emphasize one or the other orientation. Firms that emphasize revenue generation through sales, using promotion as the primary vehicle for accomplishment, would be placed towards the sales end. Firms that emphasize revenue generation through loyalty and repeat business, by satisfying customer needs through the offering of distinctive products and services, would be placed towards the other end.

I suggest that most international hotel firms would be placed towards the sales end, indicating that the customer orientation is not prevalent and that revenue generation is driven by the sales approach. For example, international hotel companies initially moved overseas in the 1970s to react to unfulfilled consumer demand and because they found they had something to sell. These chains provided to local investors through their skills and know-how a form of insurance. Developers did not have these skills and lenders were not experienced in hotel financing. The chains discovered that they had some-thing to sell, and the demand for these management systems was greater than the supply as many other chains did not want to expand overseas. Those that did expand found when they moved that they did not need marketing to succeed.

Those companies that did take their management systems overseas found that they held the upper hand in negotiations. Hilton International, for example, in negotiating for the Caribe Hilton in Puerto Rico, its first Hilton outside the United States, was given an exceptional site by the government for which it signed a lease for more than 20 years. Hilton International provided working capital, management and advice in return for 33 per-cent of profits and an exemption from Puerto Rican tax for the first 10 years. Hilton's investment of US$195 000 was recouped in the first two years of operation. These 20- to 40-year contracts with no review were not uncommon. In addition, there was little performance responsibility and no possibility that the operators could be thrown out for nonperformance; they were locked in for the term of the contract. For many companies the major marketing issue was how often to raise rates. The result has been that until recently a marketing orientation never developed.

Restaurant companies, on the other hand, would be placed towards the marketing end of the continuum. Although the initial move overseas for many of these companies was again to meet unfulfilled consumer demand, they had a corporate culture that emphasized marketing due to the com-petitive nature of the chain restaurant industry within which they operated and the consumer product organizations of which they were a part.

Thus, in looking at international marketing practices, one must recognize that it is unfulfilled consumer demand and a lack of competition that drives many hospitality companies overseas in the first place. They do not need a marketing orientation to succeed; they need sales ability. Unless they come out of a corporate culture that recognizes the importance of marketing they will emphasize sales. It is only when faced with strong competition that they begin to move along the continuum towards marketing. When we analyze various practices of international hospitality firms and try to understand them, much of their behavior can be accounted for by the degree to which they need to be competitive to succeed in geographic locations around the world.

In this chapter this idea is explored in detail. We look at what it means for a firm to be marketing oriented and speculate how firms move along the con-tinuum from sales to marketing to focus better on customer needs. We then look at how operating in the international context complicates the ability of firms to use marketing to compete successfully. Finally, we look at the stra-tegic marketing issues that all hospitality firms face in operating inter-nationally, and the possible consequences of the choices they make. By the end of the chapter the reader will better understand the behavior of inter-national hospitality firms and the major marketing issues that each firm must address as it moves outside its borders.

Developing a hospitality marketing orientation

Firms that have become customer oriented are ones that not only understand customer needs but have used that knowledge to focus their resources, energy and efforts in their quest for growth and profit. They all have certain qualities which distinguish them from sales-driven firms. First, marketing-oriented firms are successful not only on the common financial measures of revenue, profit and return on investment, but also on the marketing measures of success: market share, customer loyalty (percentage of repeat customers) and capacity utilization (revenue per available room in hotels and load factor on airlines). This is not to say that sales-oriented firms cannot be successful, but marketing-oriented firms have less variability in their revenue performance under varying economic conditions.

Second, marketing-oriented firms offer the customer a product or a service that is distinctively different from that of the competition. These firms recognize that the customer has a choice. When the customer asks why he or she should patronize a particular brand and not that of the competition, the answer is that the offering is different in some way that is important to him or her. Marketing-oriented companies do not look like and do not copy the competition; sales-driven firms do.

Third, marketing-oriented firms focus on managing revenue not costs. This is a subtle distinction which explains a great deal of management behavior and firm performance in the international hotel industry, and why marketing is still not an important function in many companies. When Hilton International and other hotel companies moved overseas in the 1950s and 1960s there was great demand for their offerings. They did not have marketing departments in the hotels or in the corporate offices; they had sales departments. The role of the general manager was to manage costs, while revenues took care of themselves. Now we are in an era where there is more competition and the focus of companies must be on managing revenues. Yet many of these hotel companies still focus on costs and are thus unable to achieve even their fair share of business in the marketplace. They have still not moved along the marketing continuum.

Fourth, marketing-oriented companies have a corporate philosophy that focuses on success; sales-driven organizations, on the other hand, focus on not failing. The distinction is subtle but important. Marketing-oriented hospitality firms know that customer needs are dynamic and change over time. The same is true for competition. Firms know they must be flexible and innovative to remain successful, but they also recognize the risk inherent in that philosophy. When you are dealing with customers you cannot always be right. Human beings defy being predictable and just because something worked yesterday does not mean it will work tomorrow. Some of the new products and services you offer will fail; some of the new marketing promotions will not work. Marketing-oriented firms accept that risk. They are not afraid to fail. They accept failure as part of the cost of doing business and in so doing win in the long term. Sales-driven organizations are afraid to fail.

They copy the competition; they are slow to change; they do not take risks; they do not innovate. They try to satisfy the customer with yesterday's offering.

Finally, the communication strategy of marketing-oriented firms is two-way. All firms speak to the customer through their advertising and promotion; marketing-oriented firms also listen and react to what they learn. The systems they use to listen are varied, both formal and informal and on-going. They have customer satisfaction monitoring systems, using qualitative and quantitative research, not just comment cards or an occasional survey. Their advertising reflects their knowledge of the customer and what he or she is telling them. They do not show pictures of the restaurant with staged models in their advertising, the empty congress hall set up in schoolroom style with the chairs in neat rows, or the picture of the hotel exterior (what one wag has labeled 'the edifice complex' in hotels); instead they show the product in use by the market segment under consideration.

The rate of speed with which companies move along the continuum is a function of their corporate culture and the level of competitiveness of the industry or the geographic area. As stated earlier, companies are reactive. They change only when necessary. They do not pay attention to the customer unless they have to. It is also difficult to change a corporate culture. Companies, like people, stay with the familiar, with the status quo, even in crisis. Some readers might remember the story of how SAS Airlines went from being one of the worst firms in terms of financial performance and customer satisfaction to becoming one of the best. At the lowest point in the airline's history an executive of the company was flying business class across the North Atlantic and during the beverage service ordered a martini. It was served with two olives stuck to the cocktail stick instead of one. Since the airline was having financial difficulty, this concerned executive wondered why it was necessary to serve two olives when one would suffice (so he believed). Having some free time on this long flight, he calculated how much could be saved if only one olive were served with each martini. His calculations showed the savings to be substantial. He submitted a report which was favorably received and the changes were made.

What is clear from the story is that even in crisis companies will opt for the familiar strategies. Saving on olives was not going to make a real difference in saving the airline, but it was a familiar strategy (cutting costs) and it was without risk. The corporate culture is that powerful. It is only when things become threatening that change is possible. This may happen when companies are on the verge of bankruptcy or when they are sold to owners with different financial and strategic objectives. At these times movement along the marketing continuum may be rapid. Shortly after this event happened, Jan Carlzen took over as the head of SAS and instituted a philosophy of customer satisfaction. His book, *Moments of Truth*, recounts the difficulty of that endeavor. Many recent purchases of international hotel chains have not resulted in value increases in the companies, partly because the new owners did not recognize where they were on the continuum and where they had to move to succeed.

Marketing in the international environment

How does operating in the international environment affect how marketing is accomplished? We have discussed the continuum of marketing behavior of companies. The international context may increase the difficulty of moving along that continuum, or it may create an opportunity through crisis to make the movement more rapid. Those companies that are able to adjust and react will be more successful in the long term. No matter where on the continuum a hospitality company is located, there are a number of strategic issues they must address that will affect the manner and practice of their marketing efforts.

The influence of marketing in the control of quality and cost

Perhaps the most important issue to be resolved by any firm operating in the international environment is the influence of marketing in the firm in the control of quality and costs. Hospitality operations are typified by a high degree of simultaneity of production and consumption: that is, the service is often produced and consumed at the same time. Marketing is responsible for setting customer expectations and monitoring and dealing with customer satisfaction, but it may not have any control or say over the production and delivery of the service. This causes a number of marketing problems. The most obvious is that of consistency of delivery of the expected service. When marketing and operations are not integrated there is often a gap between the expectations of the customer, as set by marketing, by culture and by prior service experiences, and the actual delivery of the hospitality experience. The pressure and philosophy in operations is always to reduce the complexity of the offering, to simplify and to standardize across units, in order to increase the consistency of delivery of the hospitality experience. In doing so this may work against the marketing objective of competitive differentiation and cultural complementarity of the offering. Where one function such as operations rules the other the customer is always the loser. When this is coupled with the fact that customers in many cultures will not complain when they have had a bad experience, it becomes clear why marketing has little influence and why companies move so slowly along the marketing continuum in the international environment.

The issue is less a problem for restaurants than for hotels for a number of reasons. Restaurant companies are less complex operations than hotels, and operate in a much smaller customer trading area and with a much narrower business mix. They are easier operations in which to control quality and cost. That is one reason why quick-service restaurants have been so popular among parent companies to take overseas. Restaurant companies are also brands that are owned by companies in which the marketing orientation is strong. In these instances we see the use of the brand manager concept, which effectively integrates marketing and operations. The restaurants are treated like products and the marketing issue focuses on managing the brand.

Hotels are a much more complex customer experience with a wider business mix, and the control of quality and cost therefore becomes more difficult. The operational problems are daily and immediate, and since hotel companies do not have a tradition of marketing, what you find is operations being paramount in the company and marketing having relatively little influence. The result is that over the long-term the firm loses its competitive distinctiveness as operations makes the offering simpler in order to control quality and cost. The olive incident described earlier is repeated again and again as the offering is changed incrementally. The customer does not complain but just votes with his or her feet by not returning, and eventually market share and revenue begin to decline. Marketing is called upon to reverse the trend, and when new promotions and other activities do not work, marketing is termed ineffective in the company. And that is why international hotel companies have been slow to move along the continuum.

Centralization versus decentralization of the marketing function

One of the key strategic issues faced by international hospitality firms is decentralizing the marketing function. This is a complex issue and one where the practices of companies vary widely. In theory, the marketing function should be decentralized for a number of reasons. First, since production and consumption of the service experience take place at the local level, control is needed there to respond to competitor strategies, to monitor marketing programs, to adjust the operation to changes in levels of customer satisfaction, to adapt to changing local operating and cultural conditions, and to shift the business mix to reflect changes in business conditions. For a hospitality operation the business is determined at the local level.

It might be thought that decentralization would be the norm with companies but this is not the case. There are a number of factors that mitigate against decentralization of the marketing function. The primary one is whether the hospitality company is an owner of the local units or is operating under a management contract. Where the company is running units on management contracts (which is common in the international hotel industry), the company must answer to property owners and thus there is an overriding concern to keep overhead costs down since these are normally charged back to the local properties. Hence, this is a force for decentralization. As might be expected, owners are quick to question what they are receiving in return for incurring these overhead costs. Where the hospitality company has equity control of the local operation, the force is for centralization.

For example, restaurant companies are often either company owned or franchised. The hospitality operating company has much greater power in allocating costs vis-à-vis the units, either through the franchise agreement or through corporate fiat, and is often more willing to centralize those costs at the regional or headquarters level for better operational control. Restaurant companies also have smaller trading areas and the business mix is therefore not as broad as that for a hotel. For these reasons they are less individualistic, more standardized and need less flexibility, making it easier for the marketing function to be performed at the corporate level.

The second factor that operates against the marketing function being decentralized is the lack of marketing expertise available and the cost of placing the marketing function at the local level. Even in instances where firms wish to decentralize it may be impossible to find local staff with sufficient technical marketing skills capable of performing the job. Even if available, the cost may be too high, in relation to unit revenues, to be borne by the local units. The marketing issues may also not be strategic or sufficiently complex to warrant placing the marketing function at the local level. Quick-service restaurants do not have sufficient volume, nor are the marketing issues sufficiently strategic or complex, to warrant placing marketing expertise in the units. Hotels of less than 500 rooms often fall into the same category.

In these instances, and where some flexibility is needed to respond to competition or changes in the local operating environment, companies will put a regional marketing structure into place. This entails having at a minimum one individual who can provide strategic marketing expertise to a number of units. These are normally staff positions with a consultative role to the units and reporting to corporate marketing. The regional organizations may also have a field organization associated with them. Since the majority of international business and leisure travel is within a region, the regional organization of hotel companies, for example, will handle the advertising function for a group of hotels (since you advertise where the customer lives or works) as well as the development of regional marketing programs (for conferences, packages, etc.) and the operation of regional sales offices to prospect and book business. Since regional hotels of the same company tend to have similar business mixes (the group of market segments served), there is a synergy that is achieved through these regional organizations.

For restaurant companies it is a similar situation. The regional marketing organization tends to focus on field marketing which emphasizes the development, implementation and monitoring of sales promotions and the implementation of point-of-purchase and in-store merchandising activities. Regional restaurant organizations tend to have a wider span of control since the restaurants are more standardized than hotels, but the ability of the organization to find the expertise in local staff will also determine the span of control.

Organizational communications

A subtle marketing issue that is often overlooked by international hospitality companies is that of organizational communications. Trying to communicate with a worldwide marketing organization when half the world is sleeping and the other half is working is extremely difficult. It impinges on implementing marketing programs, on sales activities, on training and professional development activities and on the ability of corporate marketing to apply control and guidance to ensure that all units are 'singing from the same hymnbook'. How is the issue resolved? Frequent regional and corporate meetings have been the standard solution, especially in the international hotel industry. But it is not an acceptable solution, especially when business conditions are not good, due to the high cost of meetings caused by travel expenses and the loss of productivity. Meetings take people away from their workplace for long periods of time and they are then not producing for their local organization. This becomes especially visible and annoying with sales and marketing personnel, since their efforts are directly tied to revenue generation in their properties. The direct cost in terms of international airline flights and per diem expenses can also be high. This becomes an acute problem for international hospitality companies as these costs are charged back to the property and owners complain loudly. Some companies reduce the number of meetings and try to shift to technology (phone, fax or satellite net) to handle organizational communications, but the requirements for face-to-face meetings are always there and the issue is never wholly resolved.

Marketing staffing at the local level

Another important issue touched upon earlier concerns hiring marketing and sales expertise at the local level. Using local sales and marketing staff may be required by the management contract, by cultural conditions and even by government regulation, but it may be difficult or impossible to make happen especially as these personnel must usually be multilingual. In many countries the hospitality industry does not have the status or glamor of other industries, and university and business school graduates will therefore not accept employment in it. There may be no marketing training available in some countries due to the lack of educational institutions, or in less developed economies due to a lack of business functions and the fact of the concept of competition just becoming established.

The result is that companies are forced to promote people from within the organization up to their level of incompetence. They may have no choice and thus must rely on centralization of decision making to control the operation; or they may accept the variability in performance of their operations in different parts of the world. Companies have been slow to work with educational institutions to rectify this problem through training, possibly due to a perceived lack of expertise at the most visible international educational institutions. In instances where government and international agencies have become involved, the training emphasis has usually been on technical skill training. This issue will most likely be solved only when companies invest in this training either in a formal manner themselves or in partnership with management education institutions to deliver it through alternative means, such as off-site, in-home or executive education programs.

Evaluation of marketing efforts

All companies must constantly make resource allocation decisions: for example, which of the capital budget proposals from the local operations to fund. Part of this effort requires companies to evaluate how successfully their resources are being used presently. This is not as simple as it appears. All marketing efforts result in business at the unit levels, but how much of those results are attributable to efforts at the local level and how much to efforts at the regional, area or corporate level? Most hospitality companies do not have mechanisms for measuring the productivity and contribution to revenue of these other parts of the organization. They are often tracked as cost centers and charged back to the local units, causing questions and concerns. Depending upon where the marketing power is within the organization, they may even be reduced or eliminated. It is only later that they are determined to be of benefit.

A second area where adequate evaluation mechanisms are lacking is in the evaluation of the revenue and profit contribution of individual market segments in each of the properties. In a hotel, for example, you know the rate a customer pays, but you may not necessarily know the total 'spend' of that customer in the hotel. You may also not know the total cost of attracting that customer to the hotel. This makes it difficult to compare the value of market segments within a hotel and across hotels. It then makes it impossible to compare the marketing productivity of one region of the world with that of another.

This evaluation problem happens for two reasons. First, until recently hospitality organizations have not had the hardware and software technology to capture total purchase data by market segment. This is now available, but hospitality operations have to make a decision whether the information is worth the investment in this generation of technology. This decision is particularly difficult in a period of economic recession throughout the world. The second reason is that hospitality operations are considered high fixed-cost operations. Commonly accepted accounting practices normally track only direct expenses by market segment. Significant expenses are therefore listed as undistributed operating expenses and distort the true costs of realizing the total revenue from a market segment.

A third area of weakness is in the evaluation of marketing and sales promotion programs. Hospitality businesses have cyclical demand patterns and utilize sales promotion activities and special marketing programs during slow demand periods to even out business activity. How should these programs be evaluated? It clearly costs more to get the customer in the door during these slow times, and is it reasonable for a company to look for the same profit percentage then as it does during high demand times? Obviously not, but the concept of contribution accounting or contribution of revenue less direct expenses to fixed cost is not well understood in many parts of the world.

Overall, evaluation mechanisms for marketing efforts are primitive and contribute to the lack of influence of marketing in companies and the trend toward centralization. Technology will help in solving the problem, but that will not be enough. What is needed is better conceptual thinking to determine what the variables are that are critical to marketing productivity, and to devise new measures of effort and productivity that go beyond what is accepted at present.

The use of technology

Technology could prove a boon in the way marketing is conducted in the international environment, for it could solve many of the issues we have been discussing in this chapter. Proper utilization could allow hospitality companies to decentralize the marketing function but to maintain control at the corporate level, by assisting in monitoring local efforts. It would allow companies to control local operations and perhaps reduce the need for marketing expertise at the local level. Finally, it could assist in increasing the productivity of sales efforts.

Yet once again the decision is more complex than a simple return on investment analysis. The major issue is that marketing and operations of hospitality firms operate in tandem, but the technology available that assists these two functions is not integrated. Until recently, reservations and front-office technology in the hotel industry were not integrated. At present, neither of these technologies is tied into the accounting function. The result is that hospitality firms asked to invest in a variety of technologies all of which have limited application. The cost relative to performance is prohibitive.

The second issue with technology is that hospitality companies may be worldwide, but technology vendors often are not. Thus, if companies wish to invest in a particular form of technology, they may be forced to deal with several companies throughout the world. This makes it extremely difficult to develop company standards in marketing and sales. In the area of software, language and technical terminology may be a problem. English may be the language of business, but in less developed countries the lack of language capability may make the use of software impossible. There may also be a cultural bias against the use of technology.

The use of technology is often in conflict with the operations attempt to give good customer service. Customer technology, such as front-office systems in hotels, is not designed to be customer friendly. The use of it shifts the employee's attention from the customer to the computer screen. The result is what I term 'the bald head syndrome' as the customer looks at the top of the employee's head while waiting to be checked in. This is certainly not service with a smile. Technology will be utilized more and more in the international hospitality industry, but only as systems are integrated and customer and employee friendly. Until then, firms will approach technology with a philosophy of minimizing its use.

Conclusion

There are other decisions that international hospitality operations must make that will affect the manner and practice of a company's marketing effort. What we have discussed in this chapter are the major issues that all companies must address. How they answer these is, first, a function of where the firm is on the sales/marketing continuum. This will determine its approach to strategic marketing. The second factor is the degree of competitiveness firms face in their industry segment and in different parts of the world. Marketing will continue to grow in importance in international hospitality firms as the pressure to produce more revenue grows. All international hospitality firms, however, have a long way to go in learning how to 'do' marketing.

13
International finance and accounting

Lee Kreul

One might question why a chapter on international finance and accounting is included in this book on international management in the hospitality industry. From their very first accounting course, students are told that accounting is 'the language of business'. This implies that there is a global universality about the subject that one would think would make a discussion of 'international accounting' redundant and unnecessary. However, in the context of the international arena, it is apparent that accounting is not a universal language that transcends national boundaries. International accounting is a far more complex matter than domestic accounting and it is fraught with problems created by the social, cultural and political differences and physical distances that exist among nations. Some very broad basic concepts, like the double entry approach to record keeping and the logic of the systematic depreciation of assets, are universal concepts that are recognized in one way or another in most countries. However, the accounting principles, practices, rules, interpretations and standards within these universal concepts have developed, like language and law, along national lines. They have developed to suit the needs of businesses, investors, the public and the governments in each country. This is also the case in regard to the taxation practices of governments and the many kinds of financial instrument available.

The growth and problems of multinational corporations

The last 25 years have seen an unprecedented expansion and globalization of trade among nations. Multinational corporations (MNCs) have led the way in this expansion. An MNC can be defined as a parent company and its subsidiaries in foreign countries. In the USA, a precise definition is as follows:

A US multinational company consists of a nonbank US parent and its nonbank foreign affiliates. A US parent is a US person that owns or controls, directly or indirectly, 10 percent or more of the voting securities of an incorporated foreign business enterprise or an equivalent interest in an unincorporated foreign business enterprise. A foreign affiliate is a foreign business enterprise that is so owned or controlled. (*Survey of Current Business*, 1989)

In 1989 US MNCs owned worldwide assets of $6219 billion and had sales of $4400 billion. This compares to $2033 billion in assets and $2060 in sales in 1977. The portion of these figures attributable to United States-based MNCs engaged in lodging and foodservice operations abroad is not well defined in government published data. The figures for foodservice operations are included in total retail trade data. Only hotel and other lodging place data are reported separately from other service industries.

However, despite the lack of collected and published data, it is apparent that during this same 25-year time period the US hospitality industry has become a very visible presence in all areas of the world. There are American-owned or franchised hotels and restaurants operating in all corners of the globe – McDonald's in Moscow, Holiday Inns in Kuala Lumpur, and Kentucky Fried Chicken outlets in Tokyo, to name a few. As a case in point, US Disney has invested US$160 million and its European investors over US$2 billion in the Euro-Disney theme park and resort complex in France. McDonald's Corporation international operations are so successful that it is expected that by 1994 more than half of the company's profits will be coming from its international interests. At the same time the purchase of familiar US hotel and restaurant chains by foreign MNCs, such as Grand Metropolitan and Bass in the UK and Nestlé in Switzerland, is well known and has been greeted with some degree of dismay by the US press and public. According to a survey by *Hospitality Valuation Services* (1992), 'Nearly two thirds of all major US hotels sold in 1991 were sold to foreign investors'. Nikko, Omni, Novotel, Meridien, Swissotel and other hotel MNCs based in other countries have also sought entry into American markets by building hotels in the USA under their own names.

The coming to prominence of MNCs and the globalization of business practices that has taken place in the last 25 years have brought the differences in accepted systems and practices in finance and accounting from nation to nation into sharper focus. Along with this has come a realization that there are differences between the way MNC parents operate and the way their affiliates operate. These differences stem from the differing cultural, social and political environments in which they do business.

In assessing the impact of the global changes in the hospitality industry on the accounting practices of participating business organizations, one immediately finds that the generally accepted accounting principles which in the USA are considered basic, almost sacred concepts governing the approach to accounting and reporting of business operations, may not enjoy the same degree of acceptance and sanctity in other countries. For example, the rules that have resulted from the principle of consistency in both the USA and the UK, in regard to disclosure of changes in accounting methods from period to period, are not required in some other countries. Some countries have very relaxed rules regarding changes in depreciation methods from period to period. The latitude given to businesses in accounting for inventories (direct cost, LIFO, FIFO) also varies, while in some countries the deferral of income tax expenses is considered inappropriate. Until the rise of MNCs, what heretofore were considered unimportant differences from country to country in accounting for business operations, reporting results, financial instruments, etc. have become impediments to commerce and points of major disagreement among accountants. Differences in accounting practices are only a small portion of the many problems confronting MNCs.

To illustrate these differences and the reality of the disharmony of the moment, let us take the situation of a US hotel company carrying on business operations in the USA with a majority holding in an affiliated hotel chain in, for example, a country like Colombia. Not only must the US parent operate the businesses in each country in differing physical, political, economic and cultural environments with major differences in language, and must, by US tax law, communicate the results of the operations of the parent and affiliated company through consolidated statements to individuals, agencies and other entities in the USA. At the same time, the parent must also provide nonconsolidated statements of the affiliates operations to interested parties in Colombia because Colombian authorities do not permit consolidated statements in reporting the operations of Colombian businesses. All of these activities take place in a situation of differences in accounting practices, standards, exchange rates, inflation rates, uniform systems of accounts, etc. in each of the countries. The example outlined is a two-country situation of one parent company and one affiliate. For a company like Pepsico Inc., with affiliates in dozens of countries, reporting the results of the operations of the parent and affiliates becomes an extremely difficult task of dubious value.

Environmental differences

Environmental differences from country to country can, and often do, cause problems. For example, accountants, who are the very people that are charged with communicating the operating results of parents and affiliates, differ very greatly in training, certification, experience and function from country to country. There is no uniformity in these positions. The education, training, licensing and experience requirements to attain the designation of CPA (Certified Public Accountant) in the USA are vastly different from those of people doing the same type of work in France, Spain or Japan. In each country the licensing or certifying body may be different. In one country it may be the federal government. In another country it may be the local, state or provincial government. In another, licensing and certification may be under the purview of a nongovernmental organization similar to the American Institute of Certified Public Accountants (AICPA). There is no international body controlling the certification of accountants or with the complete authority to set international accounting standards or practices.

On the other side of the communication issue lie the users of accounting information – the many individuals, organizations, regulatory bodies and other entities for which information is produced. These users of accounting information are themselves also a very diverse lot, with different interests in the information they desire. For example, information requirements placed on businesses in state-controlled economies are different from the requirements placed on businesses operating in free enterprise economies. Information requirements are also different in nations where credit is the main vehicle of financing, as opposed to countries where equity financing or government financing is the norm. Information generated by businesses about their operations is also different, depending on whether the ownership of businesses is in the hands of a few wealthy individuals or thousands of smaller investors. For instance, in the UK there are a few large multinational companies owned and controlled by a relatively small number of shareholders, often family members. However, the majority of UK companies are financed by large numbers of the investing public. Such shareholders do not have direct access to the information systems of the companies in which they invest, and often feel that the published information available is inadequate. To some extent legislators in the UK have recognized this and have modified the disclosure requirements placed on companies under the Companies Acts of 1985 and 1989.

Cultural differences

Culture also plays a part in making communication difficult. If one society's citizens by nature are generally secretive in their business dealings, or, conversely, if they tend to be trusting and open, there will be a great variability as to how much information is given or desired in financial reports. Another cultural trait, impacting the type of information that is communicated, is the relative importance placed on time by the members of a society. Americans are often (to their detriment) accused of having a short-term viewpoint about business and of placing emphasis on short-term profits when it comes to business activities. This attitude in turn places a greater emphasis on full development of the profit and loss statement, and cash flow information, rather than the balance sheet. In less developed countries there is often an opposite attitude – less concern with near-term success and more interest in longer-term stability. Thus, there is more interest in the development of the balance sheet.

Political risks faced by MNCs

Doing business anywhere entails certain risks. In the extreme, weather, strikes, crime, wars, terrorist actions and dishonest politicians can all present difficulties for businesses either in the domestic or in the international setting. Problems also occur for businesses when governments make changes in laws and regulations, or put licensing difficulties in place. As we will see, the risk inherent in changing exchange rates, which are often the result of political events, is very great. However, two political risks that are ever present are the threat by the host government, through the passage of law or other action, to block the withdrawal of funds from that country or to expropriate the assets of the MNC. An example of blockage occurred in the case of Iraqi assets in the USA in 1991. Assets of Iraqi MNCs were frozen in place when war broke out between the two nations. The blocking of funds may be partial or entire, delayed or conditional. The threat of a blockage of funds in any form reduces the incentive for MNCs to make investments in foreign countries. Expropriation is the outright seizure of assets by a host nation. It is a near certainty when war breaks out between nations.

Even countries like India, which is presently trying to encourage more international investment with a more open economy, may find that deeply ingrained business practices make changing direction difficult. According to the *Wall Street Journal* (1992):

> Translating [Indian Prime Minister] Mr Rao's policy package into practice is not easy. Paring the powers of the Indian bureaucracy is like trying to mow a jungle: It takes many passes before there is much visible headway. For all the regulations he has stripped away, multitudes remain ... anyone registering a new business must still contend with a daunting lineup of state controls over financing, employment, pricing and distribution.

Current international accounting and reporting problems

In addition to the above environmental differences, problems of communication, political risk and nonstandard accounting practices, there are a host of other problems faced by MNCs. We will now explore a number of these problems: the consolidation of results of operations; currency translation; transfer pricing; and capital budgeting. We will also consider the steps that are being taken to achieve more harmony in accounting practices and reporting among nations, and which organizations are involved in doing it.

Consolidation of results of operations

Consolidated financial statements (balance sheets, income statements, retained earnings statements, and statements of changes in financial position) combine the assets and liabilities, revenues and expenses of a parent company with those of its foreign and domestic affiliates into single statements. As stated earlier, US tax law generally requires US MNCs to provide consolidated statements where they have majority ownership interests (own more than 50 percent of the voting stock) of the affiliate and actively exercise control. However, consolidation of activities may not be required if the two entities carry on unrelated activities (e.g. parent operates hotels – subsidiary sells insurance) or the foreign subsidiary is in a country that places restrictions on the withdrawal of assets by a parent.

In the UK, the Companies Acts 1985 and 1989 also require the publication of consolidated financial statements. Whereas the 1985 Act required consolidation on the basis of both ownership and control of the subsidiary, the situation was modified by the 1989 Act which places a greater emphasis on control. This modification was consistent with the European Community's Seventh Company Law Directive. Broadly the position in the UK is that an enterprise is the parent of another enterprise if it holds a majority of the voting rights in that enterprise; or if it is a member of that enterprise and controls alone, pursuant to an agreement with other shareholders or members, a majority of the voting rights in that enterprise; or if it is a member of that enterprise and has the right to appoint or remove directors holding a majority of voting rights at meetings of the board; or if it has the right by contract to direct the operating and financial policies of that enterprise; or if it has at least a 20 percent interest in that other company and in actual fact exercises a dominant influence over it.

The consolidation is accomplished via a line-by-line combination of accounts. If consolidation is not required, parents may account for subsidiaries in one of two ways. One method is via the cost method (if they own less than 20 percent of the affiliate), in which the initial investment in the affiliate is recorded at cost and income from the affiliate is recognized only in the form of dividends received. A second method is the equity method, where income earned by the affiliate increases the equity of the parent and dividends received reduce the equity.

One of the problems with consolidated statements is that they are of limited use to minority stockholders and creditors of the foreign affiliates. All data on the operations of the affiliate are lumped in with the operating data of the parent. This leaves the minority stockholder with little useful information – no way of knowing how his or her investment is doing unless the laws of that country require a separate statement for the affiliate. Creditors also receive no information about the operations of the affiliate and, unless their loans are guaranteed by the parent, are left in the dark about the safety of their loans to the affiliate. When the MNC is a highly diversified enterprise, with interests not only in several nations but also in several somewhat different industries, there is little way for the stockholder or potential investor to evaluate the operations of the business except in a very broad fashion.

Currency translation and conversion

Another problem that comes with the consolidation of statements is that currency values included in the statements must be stated in the denomination of the parent. The term used for this activity is *translation*. Translation of currency should not be confused with currency conversion. To translate a currency is merely to restate it in the denomination of another country. To convert a currency is physically to change it into another currency. Translation of currencies is necessary in recording foreign currency transactions, and reporting the activities of branches, independent operations and subsidiaries in other countries. The basic problem with currency translation in regard to balance sheets, income statements and the like is that the foreign exchange rates upon which the translation is made change over time. These changes make the translation process difficult. Thus the statements that summarize the performance, financial position and cash flows of a business will be different depending on whether a past rate, average rate or current exchange rate is used. The existence of differing exchange rates has meant that different approaches and methods for making the translation have developed. Hence the difficulty in translation of currency.

The methods of currency translation that are generally acknowledged are: the current–noncurrent method, the monetary–nonmonetary method, the temporal method, and the current rate method. Each method has its supporters and detractors, and all four methods are in use in different countries. A full definition of each of these methods is beyond the scope of this chapter. However, let us make these observations about the basic differences and similarities between the methods. First, the first three methods listed employ both historic and current exchange rates to translate the values of different sections of the balance sheet. Only the current method uses one rate – the current rate. Second, all the methods use current exchange rates to translate cash and receivables. Third, all of the methods cause some fluctuations in reported earnings because of realized or unrealized exchange rate gains and losses. Finally, in practice, MNCs use all three methods and some variations of the fourth. There is presently no agreement among nations as to one method.

The current rate method is presently the most popular throughout the world and in the USA. The current method translates revenue and expense accounts into US dollars using the exchange rate in effect when those items were recognized during the period. In practice, an average rate for the period is used. Assets and liabilities are translated using the exchange rate prevailing on the date of the balance sheet. Equity accounts, like common stock and other paid in capital accounts, use the exchange rate in effect on the date the subsidiary was acquired. The exchange rate for the dividends paid account uses the exchange rate existing on the payment date. The retained earnings account ending balance is determined by taking the balance and the rate used at the previous year end plus net income from the present translated income statement less dividends paid.

Transfer pricing

Transfer pricing refers to the prices charged by one segment of a firm for products or services transferred to another segment. For example, parent company ships a part it builds in country A to be incorporated into a product built and sold by its subsidiary in country B. The question of the cost assigned to the part by each of the organizations is very important from a tax, performance evaluation and profit determination standpoint. Generally, the main consideration for a company in regard to transfer pricing is tax minimization:

that is, which price will yield the least tax liability? Each organizational affiliate accounts for its own revenue and expenditure. In practice, the MNC tries to shift profit from the affiliate in a country with a high tax rate to the affiliate in the country with a low tax rate. If the product is being built in one country with a low tax rate then the company will benefit from assigning a high transfer price.

The problem of transfer pricing for MNC hospitality firms is not as great as it is for manufacturing enterprises because hospitality firms generally deal in services, not a manufactured product or component of a product transferred across national boundaries. Also, many of the international linkages in the hospitality business are franchise arrangements, not parent–subsidiary relationships, and thus do not involve the need for consolidation.

Problems in regard to management accounting

Management accounting is a set of techniques and concepts developed to provide relevant qualitative and quantitative economic information to management about a firm's business activities, to assist in planning, organizing and controlling the operation.

Planning is an extremely difficult, often imprecise task, even in a domestic setting. Very often managers must be 'sold' on planning for it to work. The principles of planning on an international basis are no different from those involved in domestic planning. In each case the firm collects, develops and analyzes data in order to forecast the future and plan how to operate in it. While the approach to planning is the same in both the domestic and the international setting, there are vast differences in the practical application of the planning process.

The actual differences in planning stem from a number of problems and complexities that are present in the international arena but not in the domestic. First, the sheer volume of information that must be handled and digested in the planning process increases with the number of countries in which a company does business. The management information system of an MNC, on which the planning process depends, provides qualitative and quantitative, personal and impersonal data. It must not only be able to handle and digest more information than a pure domestic corporation, but it also must be able to synthesize data that come from different cultural settings, in different languages and using different information systems.

Political and economic uncertainties also create difficulties in making predictions upon which decisions depend. Runaway or uneven inflation rates in some countries make projections for raw material costs, labor rates and revenues less reliable. Cultural differences in regard to business philosophies, which extend to views on the value of planning from country to country and what role management should take, also impact the planning process. The question as to whether the planning should be done by the subsidiary or the parent seems like a simple question to be decided by the parent, but differing views on authority and the role of subordinates from country to country may make the interest or fervor with which managers approach the process a problem.

As stated earlier, exchange rates are very difficult to predict. International operational budgeting is complicated by the fact that operational budgets involving intracompany transfers of funds and materials have to be based on assumptions about exchange rates. Exchange rate fluctuations make product costing for budgeting purposes very uncertain. In addition, political changes taking place after budgets are promulgated may limit the ability of firms whose budgets projected the transfer of funds from one country to another actually to make the transfers, thus throwing the operating budget into turmoil.

Changing exchange rates also impact a firm's capital budgeting plans. Capital budgeting is a decision tool in common use for evaluating long-term capital projects. In many ways long-term capital projects are among the most difficult to evaluate and often affect the strategic position of the firm. Most sophisticated capital budgeting techniques (internal rate of return, discounted cash flow, net present value) entail the development of capital budgeting hurdle rates (decision criteria) and estimates to be made of future increases in cash inflows and/or decreases in outflows. Exchange rates that change over time make long-term cash flow projections very unreliable and thus make the capital budgeting process difficult. Until new approaches to capital budgeting are developed, approaches that are not so dependent on stable exchange rates and which integrate country-to-country differences in the establishment of capital budgeting hurdle rates, the capital budgeting process will be difficult for MNCs.

Control is also a difficult problem with MNCs. According to Choi, 'If a well-designed control system is useful to a uninational company, it is invaluable to its multinational counterpart' (Choi and Mueller, 1978). It is an unfortunate fact that as organizations increase in size, the need for centralized control of operations also increases. Global operations generally increase the size and complexity of a business. The same environmental, cultural and political differences previously discussed, which cause planning, operating and reporting problems for MNCs, also make control difficult.

The heart of any control system is uniform accounting and audit procedures, and performance standards. Accounting procedures are usually detailed in accounting manuals, which may lose some meaning when translated from the language of the parent MNC into the language of its subsidiaries. We have also previously discussed the fact that what are regarded as generally accepted accounting principles in one country lose their general acceptance in another country.

Domestic corporations often find that, while control is important, it does have a cost; control over some aspect of the business is often forgone because it would cost more to control than the cost of the potential loss. While control is even more important to an MNC, it also has a cost that is even higher than many domestic organizations face. For example, the international audit unit of an MNC has a much higher cost than a domestic corporation because of the distance and communication difficulties it faces. Consider the audit team costs of an MNC like Hyatt International, which has operations in many countries, as opposed to Red Roof Inns, which does business in only one country.

One must also recognize that control systems are designed to detect and prevent fraud, theft and other criminal activities that could hurt the company and violate the law. Many domestic corporations go to elaborate lengths to institute control systems, audit procedures and spell out behaviors expected by management and employees. Yet, it is a fact that what is a legal and common business practice in one country may be illegal in another. For example, the payment of bribes is unlawful in the USA yet tacitly accepted as a normal business practice in some countries, and the only way to get something done in others. The control system of an MNC has to take these differences into account.

The prospects for global uniformity

The foregoing discussion indicates that a great need exists for greater uniformity in accounting standards. As the world has shrunk and commerce between nations has increased in type and volume, the need for uniformity has increased proportionately. That need continues to grow. Currently there is no worldwide body in existence with the kind of authority necessary to set and enforce worldwide accounting standards. Instead a host of international organizations are trying to bring this about.

Progress is slow because of the differing political, cultural and economic structures that exist in each nation. The International Accounting Standards Committee (IASC), established in 1973, is presently the only body that seems to be making headway in promoting harmony. In the USA the American Institute of Certified Public Accountants (AICPA) is a member of IASC and supports its activities. The Financial Accounting Standards Board (FASB) is a member of the IASC Consultative Group.

The reality of European economic integration through the advent of the single European market, to take place by the end of 1992, gives some impetus to achieving harmony throughout the rest of the world. Harmonization has been a must for the Europeans. They have made it a reality despite the former widely different approaches to accounting standards practised by EC member states.

References

Choi, F. D. S., and Mueller, G. G. (1978) *An Introduction to Multinational Accounting*, Englewood Cliffs, NJ: Prentice Hall.

Hospitality Valuation Services (1992), 'US hotel sales dominated by international investors', Press Release, 20 April, Mineola, NY.

Survey of Current Business (1989) *US Direct Investment Abroad 1989*, Benchmark Survey Results, p. 2.

Wall Street Journal (1992) 'India races toward the free market', 4 May, p. A20.

Part 4

Operational issues in the international hospitality industry

This section looks at a range of selected issues that arise from international operations in the areas of consumer behavior, employee relations and technology transfer.

Crawford-Welch looks at the major trends impacting on the international consumer and concludes that, to be successful, international hospitality operators have to demassify the market, profile international consumers and cater to every one of their 'schizophrenic' needs. He notes the decline in brand loyalty among international consumers, and an increase in their level of sophistication, coupled with a strong demand for 'value for money'. Crawford-Welch's advice to international hospitality firms is to overcome the above difficulties by adopting a value marketing strategy. This can be achieved through (a) offering products/services that perform; (b) offering more than the customer expects; (c) giving guarantees; (d) avoiding unrealistic pricing; (e) giving the customer the facts; and (f) building relationships.

Pizam discusses the issues related to the management of cross-cultural hospitality enterprises and tries to answer the question: does culture count? After reviewing the large body of literature that looks at the effect of culture on organizational structure and organizational behavior, he concludes that as far as structure is concerned, culture has little impact. Therefore hotels of similar type and size will have similar organization structures regardless of the country or culture in which they operate. But when it comes to managerial philosophies, organizational behavior and human resource management practices, culture makes a difference. Therefore a practice that may work in the USA or Germany may not be effective in France or Saudi Arabia, or vice versa.

Pine examines the issue of technology transfer in the hotel industry, with particular emphasis on the human aspects of this transfer. A key resource needed to operate hotels is people. Since the education, knowledge and skills of the labor force in developing countries is limited, there is a need for hotel operators, governments and managers to prepare people for jobs in the industry. Throughout the chapter, the author lists several ways by which this transfer of technology to developing countries can be achieved. He concludes that the provision of a thorough general education plus specific vocational skills development, through vocational education, industry training and work experience, are vital for the continued and successful development of the hotel industry internationally, and particularly in developing countries.

14

The international
hospitality consumer

Simon Crawford-Welch

The hospitality industry of the 1990s is truly an international industry and is rapidly becoming a global industry; an industry which ranks second to none in terms of size and global influence. Global tourism is a $2 trillion industry and employs over 100 million workers. In 1989 there were a record 403 million international tourists worldwide, who spent $208 billion. In the United States for example, travel to foreign destinations, which has not yet reached maturity, is expected to grow at least twice as fast as domestic tourism by the end of the century. The world is becoming one global marketplace. The growth in the number of international consumers is not limited to one geographic area of the world. It is a pervasive trend being experienced in all areas of the globe. The trend, however, is just gaining momentum.

Thomas Staed, of Oceans Eleven Resorts in Florida USA, states that we have not yet scratched the surface of internationalization and that there is a huge, untapped market in Japan and Europe. Ron Evans, chief executive officer of Best Western International states: 'I truly believe the world is getting smaller, that globalization is more than just a trendy word. The lodging chains of the future will be those that are world players ... the national player is going to be more and more disadvantaged' (Gross, 1989). There has been a significant increase in hospitality organizations expanding their international operations in an attempt to cater to the global consumer. Examples include Bass plc with their European Holiday Inns; Accor with their Sofitel, Mercure, Novotel, Compri, Ibis, Motel 6, Formule 1 and Hotelia brands; Forte plc with several of their brands; Iberotels; Sol Hotels; Ladbroke Hotels; the Wagon-Lits chain; Kentucky Fried Chicken; Chi-Chi's; Bonanza; Dominoes; TGI Fridays; Conrad International; and Radisson Hotels.

While the hospitality industry worldwide is having to cater to an increasingly international and diverse consumer, the majority of research conducted in the area of internationalization of the hospitality industry to date has focused on the supply side of the equation by examining the implications of internationalization for the management of hospitality organizations (see, for instance, Nowlis, 1990; Crawford-Welch, 1991; Beattie, 1991; Olsen, 1991;

Horsburgh, 1991; Teare, 1991; Adams, 1991). With limited exceptions, such as Litteljohn and Slattery (1991), little research has been conducted into the demand side of the equation in terms of investigating the characteristics of the international consumer. The increase in internationalization in the hospitality industry has resulted in, and will continue to result in, significant shifts in demand characteristics which are worthy of investigation.

The purpose of this chapter is to offer some insights into how the international hospitality industry should research and cater to the needs, wants and desires of the international consumer by describing and analyzing major trends occurring on the demand side of the hospitality equation. The first part of the chapter will quantify the growth of the international consumer in Europe, the USA and the Far East – the three major markets for international tourism. The second part of the chapter will identify and discuss major trends that are evolving on the demand side of the international hospitality industry, and suggestions will be offered concerning how hospitality organizations can best adapt and cater to these trends. While the trends identified are not intended to be inclusive of every single trend impacting the demand patterns of the international consumer in the global hospitality industry, they are representative of some of the more significant shifts impacting the industry.

The international consumer: global comparisons

Europe has a major share of world tourism arrivals and revenue with 62 percent of all international arrivals and 52 percent of receipts from international arrivals estimated at $134 017 million for 1990 (see also Table 1.5). Tourism represents 5.5 percent of Europe's gross domestic product and directly employs 7.5 million persons. While a substantial portion of travel to European Community nations arises within Europe, nearly 18 percent of the travelers in 1985 came from other parts of the world, chiefly North America. In 1988 the flow of international tourists to Europe represented a turnover of $103 billion (WTO, 1992), or 7 percent of the world trade in goods and services (Akerhielm *et al.*, 1990). In France 38 percent of all tourism is international, compared to 29 percent in Germany, 29 percent in Italy, 59 percent in Spain, and 42 percent in the United Kingdom (Litteljohn and Slattery, 1991). Table 14.1 shows the diverse profile of international markets which the European hospitality industry is having to cater to.

In comparison, the United States earns more from international tourism than any other nation in the world and has done so for at least a decade, even though for most years there exists a negative balance in its international travel and tourism account since outbound tourism surpasses inbound tourism. Total receipts for international tourism to the USA in 1990 were estimated at $40.5 billion. In 1990 the USA held approximately 10 percent of the world share of international tourist receipts. Hospitality organizations are arguably the most culturally diverse businesses in the United States today.

The Far East too is experiencing a dramatic increase in international consumers. According to the World Tourism Organization, arrivals to East Asia

Table 14.1   Nationality mix of guests to major European cities

	Percentage of guest nights							
City	Europe	USA and Canada	Japan	Middle East	Australasia	South America	Far East	Other
Amsterdam	50.0	23.0	3.0	2.0	0.5	1.0	2.0	7.0
Brussels	70.0	18.0	1.0	0.4	0.7	0.7	1.0	3.0
Frankfurt	52.0	22.0	6.0	1.0	0.5	0.5	1.0	2.0
Geneva	44.0	19.0	4.0	4.0	1.0	2.0	3.8	4.0
Istanbul	58.0	3.5	2.0	3.5	0.3	0.3	0.7	22.0
London	50.0	26.0	2.8	3.0	1.0	0.8	1.0	1.2
Madrid	53.0	22.0	1.0	0.4	0.1	3.0	0.3	7.0
Munich	71.0	7.0	2.5	0.9	0.1	0.1	0.1	5.0
Paris	49.0	24.0	5.0	4.7	0.3	1.4	1.4	1.0
Vienna	53.0	13.0	10.0	2.8	3.0	1.2	2.3	4.0

Source: Pannell Kerr Forster (1989)

and the Pacific increased fourfold over the ten-year period from 1975 to 1985. This area now ranks second among regions in the world receiving international tourists, surpassing North America. Moreover, it is the fastest-growing region in the world in terms of tourist arrivals. Travel to East Asia for the period 1975–85 increased by 7.2 percent and to the Asia-Pacific region as a whole by 4.3 percent, a rate almost double that of world travel. East Asia and the Australia–New Zealand region are the fastest-growing areas within the Asia-Pacific region. Examples of individual countries in the Far East experiencing unprecedented growth rates in the international consumer include Korea, Thailand and Singapore, to name a few.

According to a US Department of Commerce report, Korea received only 6700 foreign travelers in 1958. Slightly more than 75 percent of these travelers were United States citizens and a large portion of these were business travelers. In the next fifteen years there was a rapid growth in visitor volume, and in 1973 arrivals totaled 680 000. Visitor volume increased to 957 000 in 1980 and surged to 2 million in 1988 with receipts of over $3 265 232. The annual average growth rate in visitor arrivals was 11.7 percent in the 1980s (Chon and Shin, 1990).

Thailand exemplifies a modern-day success story for the development of international tourism. The numbers of international tourists to Thailand have increased by a multiple of 177 in the 25 years since tourism data were first collected in 1960. Between 1960 and 1976 foreign visitors to Thailand increased from 81 340 to 1 098 442 or 13.5fold. This increase is slightly below the figure for Singapore but far below the almost 45.6fold increase for Malaysia, where the 1963 base was 26 865 international visitors. Tourism became Thailand's number one source of international revenue in 1982 and has remained in first place through 1985, surpassing agricultural products. Tourism is an activity that involves approximately 80 percent of the population of around 50 million (Gibbons and Fish, 1988).

Singapore in 1984 hosted 355 international and regional conventions – this was more than any other Asian city and sixth worldwide. That same year, almost 3 million tourists visited Singapore by air, sea or land. Total tourism earnings have been consistently above US$1.8 billion since 1982. Recent expansions of the tourism infrastructure in Singapore have substantially increased the visitor breakeven point, and continued increases in the tourism growth rate will be necessary in the near future (Calantone *et al.*, 1989).

One can clearly see that the rise in international tourism is a global phenomenon and one which therefore impacts hospitality organizations irrespective of their geographic location. Given the growth in international travel and tourism, it is projected that the following trends will come into play in the international hospitality industry of the 1990s.

Demassification of the international consumer

Today's international consumer is more than willing to pay for highly customized products and services. In the international hospitality industry there is no such thing as a mass market. Mass marketing is a vestige of the past:

> the mass market has split into ever-multiplying, ever-changing sets of mini-markets that demand a continually expanding range of options, models, types, sizes, colors, and customizations. (Toffler, 1980, p. 248)

> the 1980s – a decade of unprecedented diversity ... advertisers are forced to direct products to perhaps a million clusters of people who are themselves far more individualistic and who have a wide range of choices in today's world. The multi-option society is a new ball game, and advertisers know that they must win consumers market by market. (Naisbitt, 1982, pp. 231–2)

Demassification means that international hospitality corporations are having to become increasingly sophisticated and precise in the simultaneous segmenting and targeting of multiple target markets. Rapp and Collins (1992) suggest that we will see the advent of 'individualized marketing' in the 1990s. By this they mean 'a very personalized form of marketing that recognizes, acknowledges, appreciates, and serves the interests and needs of selected groups of consumers whose individual identities and marketing profiles are or become known to the advertiser'. The future of the international hospitality industry will not be in mass marketing but in micro-marketing through effective and efficient database development and management.

There are five broad elements to micro-marketing. First, hospitality operators will have to become and remain 'close to the customer'. International hospitality corporations will have to know their customer and know their competitor's customer. In the 1990s knowing the competitor's customer will only be achieved through knowing the competitor's database.

Second, international hospitality organizations will have to engage in greater degrees of customization. Product/services will have to be tailored to meet individual needs and tastes, or at a minimum corporations will have to ensure that their provision has enough inherent flexibility to adapt to the needs and wants of very specific target markets which may span across geographic borders.

Third, greater use will be made of targeted and new media. In order to reach micro-markets, international hospitality organizations will have to use the appropriate media such as cable television. Some estimates suggest that network television currently experiences a 30 percent audience loss because of 'physical' zapping (viewers leaving the room during commercials), a 13 percent audience loss from electronic zapping (using a remote control to flick through channels during commercials), and a 4 percent audience loss as a result of video recorders which have the capacity to stop recording during commercial breaks (Rasp and Collins, 1989). This poses serious questions concerning the cost benefits of using network television to attract customers.

Fourth, greater use of nonmedia will be required, the most popular type of which is the sponsoring of sports events. Unfortunately, we have yet to see major involvement by hospitality corporations in such events, despite their proven success with such giants as Procter and Gamble and Kraft.

Fifth, greater emphasis will be required on relationship marketing: that is, marketing to protect the consumer base in an effort to attract, maintain and enhance customer relationships (Lewis and Chambers, 1989).

Profiling the international consumer

Database profiling will become the rule for catering to the needs and wants of the international consumer. Thanks to increases in the sophistication of current technology, detailed profiles of millions of prospects and customers can be developed using not only standard descriptive criteria such as geographic location, age, income and sex, but also more accurate and sophisticated psychographic and benefit profiles.

Because the cost of assessing data has fallen so swiftly, many people in marketing do not fully comprehend what database marketing can mean and what it can do. In 1973 it cost $7.13 to access 1000 bits of information; 1000 bits equals about twenty words of data – about enough to record a consumer's name, address and purchase. Today it costs about a penny to do the same thing (Rapp and Collins, 1989). In the 1990s the databases of hospitality corporations will become their own private marketplace where they can promote additional sales, cross-promote, explore new channels of distribution, test new products, add new revenue streams, start new ventures, and build lifetime customer loyalty. However, it is one thing to gather information about the international consumer through the mechanism of databases. In the 1990s a sustainable competitive advantage will not be achieved through the simple gathering of information in databases; it will be achieved through the timely and accurate interpretation of that information. The competitive edge will not come from having information, rather it will come from how that information is used. Database marketing will become the rule for reaching the international consumer in the 1990s.

There are four kinds of information about the international consumer that hospitality firms should be collating in a marketing database. These are declared information, implied information, overlaid information and appended information.

Declared information is what the guest has directly revealed by filling out some sort of form such as a registration card, a comment card or an in-room marketing survey. Implied information is developed by finding a high correlation between the database information and other obtainable data: for instance, if we know that our guest is upper income and has a large family, this strongly implies that he or she has need for family-oriented vacation packages. Overlaid information comes from comparing individual records with adjusted census data. An excellent example of this kind of information can be seen in the USA. As early as 1974, computer scientist Jonathan Robin developed this capability to a high degree by combining census data with zip codes and consumer surveys. He programmed a computer to sort the nation's 36 000 zip zones into 40 'lifestyle clusters'. The system is called PRIZM (Potential Rating Index for Zip Markets). Hospitality organizations can call upon several public databases in different countries and 'overlay' this public domain information on to their own proprietary database and thereby transfer valuable outside information to each individual customer's file.

The final kind of information is appended information. This involves matching up two or more sources of information about a customer. For example, a hotel may have a file of international customers who have claimed some form of discount as a result of membership in a frequent stay program. The hotel might then obtain a list of international customers who stay in their hotel more than twice a year. By matching the two lists, the computer can find out which customers who frequent the hotel more than twice a year are not members of the frequent stay program and append that information to their files for potential sales presentations on the benefits of being a member of the frequent stay program.

Databases have been used extensively in other industries at an international level, but have not yet made a significant impact in the hospitality industry. For example, in Europe, Systems Marketing Company forged 'Superlink', Europe's largest database of identified car customers and prospects. They reported at that time that its 1.2 million car-buyer profiles were being utilized more comprehensively than any other database in the world. In less than seven years, the program cut the cost of an incremental sale in half. The potential for transferring this database knowledge and technology into the international hospitality industry is enormous and largely untapped.

One area of the international hospitality industry where database marketing has begun to make an impact is in the $7 billion casino segment. For example, Las Vegas alone in 1991 was host to approximately 20 million gamblers from all corners of the globe. Faced with fierce competition in a crowded industry, the smartest casinos are blazing new trails in building a database and using it for niche marketing. In exchange for filling out a detailed questionnaire which gathers such diverse information as age, frequency of gambling, games preferred, gambling budgets, model of car driven, number and type of household pets, favorite sports, and so on, guests are given discounts on services. Many casinos can track players' activity by encouraging them to use magnetic-strip plastic cards that register their plays, and this information is also then fed into a database. The casino is then in a position to devise specific promotions for different customer segments within the database. For example, if you are a slot-machine or blackjack player, you may receive an invitation to a slot or blackjack tournament. If you are a fan of boxing or of Frank Sinatra, you will be notified when there is going to be an event you may wish to attend. The databases also tell the casinos where their customers come from and how they travel. By analyzing which countries and specifically which geographic areas of those countries their international customers come from, casinos can get a more valid and reliable idea of where advertising should be concentrated (Rapp and Collins, 1992).

Some hospitality organizations, in their eagerness to develop statistically sophisticated profiles of their consumers at both a national and an international level, have perhaps been somewhat overzealous in their pursuit of establishing a customer database. Oftentimes, a database has been developed using computer hardware and software which fulfills the short-term requirements of the organization but cannot be expanded to meet long-term goals. When developing a database, hospitality organizations should be sure to assess their long term needs accurately and not be penny wise but dollar foolish. Figure 14.1 provides a list of several questions which organizations should ask themselves before they make the commitment to any one specific database package.

- How might your hotel/restaurant best capture names, addresses and other personal data from the international customer?

- Which computer hardware and software would permit your hotel/restaurant to do marketing to your own in-house database?

- Could your hotel/restaurant analyze its customer data to determine its ideal international customer profile, then test target marketing to 'clones' of your best customers selected from public databases covering your market penetration area?

- Is your hotel/restaurant grading your international customers by recency, frequency and monetary value of purchases scoring system?

- How might your hotel/restaurant test and measure cost efficiency of promotion to each decile of your international customer database from most likely to least likely purchaser?

- How might your hotel/restaurant use computer overlays of outside lists to reveal the demographic and psychographic profiles of the best customers in the database?

- How can you use overlays to identify, extract and mail to your hotel/restaurant's best international prospects out of public domain lists in your trading area(s)?

- How could your hotel/restaurant devise an offer to appeal to a specific promising segment of your international market, and use the responses to build a special database subgroup?

Figure 14.1 Checklist for developing a database of international consumers

Changing demographics and lifestyles
of the international consumer

International consumers are no longer neatly lined up as large, simple, visible target groups. The world's constantly changing demographic mix means that often yesterday's targets are simply not there today. For example, in the USA 53 percent of all households have only one or two members, and of the 10.4 million households formed between 1980 and 1988, half were formed by singles. Moreover, the era of a youth-dominated culture in the USA is ending. Never before in the history of the United States has there been such an old population. The Census Bureau forecasts that by the year 2000 the median age will reach 36.4 years, compared to 31.5 years in 1987. It is the 35–44 and 45–54 age groups (the baby boom generation) that will make up the largest segment of the US population by 2005. For years marketers have been preoccupied with the young baby boomers. But now the size and power of the youth market is shrinking. The 'bulge in the python' has moved further along. The 77 million US baby boomers are reaching middle age. 'This will create a new customer culture and dramatically alter the financial landscape of America, service will be valued above price, quality over quantity', predicts Doris Walsh, publisher of *American Demographics* magazine.

In addition to the changing age structures in the USA there are other demographic trends impacting the demand patterns of consumers, be they domestic or international in nature. For example, one in four US homes now consists of a person living alone, compared to about one out of ten 30 years ago. The Census Bureau estimates that this group will continue to expand, growing to 33.7 million households by 2000. These loners are more prone to impulse buying because there is no other household member around to disagree with or question the purchase. The number of unmarried couples living together has risen in the last two decades from about half a million to 2.5 million. The number of working women in the workforce continues to rise, up to nearly 58 million in 1990, about 10 million more than a decade earlier. Today 56 percent of all US women are working outside of the home.

Many of the changes being experienced in the USA certainly have their parallel in Europe, Australia, Japan and other developed nations. For example, Europe is currently undergoing a demographic metamorphosis which could be termed the 'graying of Europe'. In Britain the 16–19 age group will decrease from 3.7 million in 1983 to 2.7 million in 1993. By the year 2000 every age group over 50 in Europe will have increased by nearly a third, and those 75 and older by nearly a quarter.

People are staying healthier and living longer. In 1776 life expectancy was just 35 years – today it is 70. There are 30 million people in the USA over 65 – more than the entire population of Canada. In Europe, by the year 2000 between one-quarter and one-third of the people will be 50 or older. By the year 2010, about 25 percent of the population of France will be 60 or older, compared to 18 percent a generation earlier. In Japan, life expectancy is now 77 years for men and 83 years for women. In Brazil, in 1980, half of the population was under 20. By the year 2000, the under-20 segment will have shrunk by 20 percent, and the increase in the adult population will be in the over-40 segment.

Throughout the world an era dominated by youth is ending. Adweek's *Marketing Week* notes that what we eat; what we wear; where, how and when we travel; what we buy and why we buy it – all will change as vast numbers of consumers face the opportunities and milestones of their journey beyond youth. Nostalgic for their carefree childhood, baby boomers are seeking comfort in the familiar pursuits and products of their youth. As marketers, we have been looking at the 18–34 and 35–49 age groups, and beyond 49 we have tended to assume that the world ceases to exist, that we simply 'fall off the edge'. To be successful in the 1990s, hospitality operators in the international arena have no choice but to take into account the dynamic and volatile changing demographic structure of international consumers. One method of ensuring that operators keep abreast of changing demographics is through the creation of sophisticated consumer databases to profile their international consumer, as discussed earlier in this chapter.

Catering to the schizophrenic international consumer

The international consumer, experiencing too fast a pace and too little time, is being forced to assume multiple roles and adapt easily. Individuals have different and often conflicting needs, wants and desires dependent upon the role they are playing at any given point in time. Rapp and Collins (1992) state:

> For millions of people, almost every minute of their waking hours is blocked out and booked up for working … commuting … computing … jogging … shopping … entertaining … 'quality time' with the children … movie going and movie viewing at home … and each member of the family 'grazing' separately at the refrigerator or microwave at different times. More and more people are giving up leisurely dining and turning to bolting their food standing up in a fast-food restaurant – or gulping a quick cup of soup zapped in the microwave – everybody seems to feel worn out by the demands of work, family and personal achievement. (p. 15)

Societies in developed nations are becoming time-poor and money-rich. Like all consumers, the international consumer is looking for value in time, not just value in money. Time will be the currency of the 1990s.

In an attempt to cater to the multiple roles adopted by the consumer at different times, corporations competing in the international hospitality industry have engaged in the development of product line extensions and product portfolios: that is, the development of several different brands and/or products offered by one single organization. Examples of multiple brands include Accor and their Novotel, Sofitel, Ibis and Formula 1 chains; Choice Hotels and their Quality Inns, Quality Suites, Clarion Inns, Clarion Suites,

Comfort Inns, Comfort Suites, EconoLodges, Sleep Inns, Rodeway Inns and Friendship Inns; and Forte Hotels with their Travelodge, Viscount, Post Houses and Little Chef.

There exists an abundance of evidence from other industries to suggest that the pursuit of a multibrand strategy can be successful at the international level. For example, the soft drinks industry has been very successful in reaping the benefits of a global multibrand strategy, with organizations like Coca-Cola and Pepsi-Cola offering multiple brands to multiple markets (such as New Coke, Coca-Cola Classic, Diet Coke, Caffeine Free Coke, Caffeine Free Diet Coke, Cherry Coke, Tab and Fresca). Another industry which has been extremely effective in the development and marketing of multiple brands is the beer industry: for example, Anheuser Busch with Budweiser, Budweiser Light, Michelob, Michelob Dry, Michelob Light and so on.

In the international hospitality industry we have been less successful in the pursuit of multibrand strategies. There are two primary reasons for this lack of success. First, the lack of success is due to confusion between the related, but distinctly different, strategies of market segmentation, product segmentation and product differentiation. Second, in their attempts to develop multiple brands, many hospitality organizations neglected the golden rule of marketing and became product oriented as opposed to market oriented.

Market segmentation requires a state of demand heterogeneity such that the total market demand can be disaggregated into segments with distinct demand functions. Product segmentation is a process whereby the product differentiates for the same market, as in the case of the plethora of brands in the lodging industry. The market is sought to fit the needs of the product rather than vice versa. Product differentiation involves offering a product which is perceived by the customer to differ from its competition along certain physical and/or nonphysical attributes. It is suggested that differentiation in the international hospitality industry should pursue a strategy of differentiation in conjunction with a strategy of market segmentation and not product segmentation (as is currently practiced in the lodging industry, which has only led to the creation of customer confusion). The theoretical underpinnings of pursuing a multibrand strategy revolve around the more efficient and effective targeting and meeting of target market needs and wants. To avoid confusing the customer, international operators should adopt a true market orientation combined with sound positioning strategies and the use of inferential variables for purposes of segmenting the market and developing their databases. Differentiation created through the pursuit of a multibrand strategy, if implemented correctly, should clarify any customer confusion which may exist, and create brand awareness and loyalty.

However, one has to question the astuteness of pursuing a multibrand strategy in the international hospitality industry when conventional wisdom suggests that what little brand loyalty may exist is decreasing. This leads to the next demand-side trend projected to impact the international hospitality industry in the 1990s – a decrease in brand loyalty.

The decline of brand loyalty among international hospitality consumers

There is compelling evidence to suggest that there is a decline in brand loyalty across most product categories, not just in the hospitality industry. The belief that once consumers buy a brand they will stay there, is not true. It is suggested that brand loyalty may not exist in the hospitality industry, but rather that brand preference may be the relevant issue. The emphasis on discounting as a means of attempted differentiation is indicative of the lack of success in creating heavy brand-switching costs among consumers in the international hospitality industry. Every time the brand is discounted or promoted, confidence and respect is withdrawn until eventually the brand no longer has any equity in the eyes of the consumer. It is well documented that brand loyalty also varies by demographics. Families have been found to be more brand-loyal than singles. This does not bode well given the rise in single households both in Europe and in the USA.

Brand loyalty is often the core of a brand's equity or worth. As brand loyalty increases, the vulnerability of the customer base to competitive action is reduced. As shown in Figure 14.2, there are several levels of brand loyalty. Brand loyalty is closely tied to the use experience and cannot exist without

Figure 14.2 Levels of brand loyalty

prior purchase and use experience. As the term implies, loyalty is to the brand not to the product. A lack of a true customer orientation among many international hospitality operators has resulted in many international consumers failing to progress past level 5 of the brand loyalty ladder shown in the diagram. In order for operators to develop and maintain brand loyalty among international consumers, they need to court these consumers with attributes other than price. Courting the international consumer with prices and discounts creates price loyalty, not brand loyalty. Since price is an attribute easily copied by the competition, it does not lead to a sustainable competitive advantage in what is a volatile, complex and dynamic international operating environment. In fact, it often dilutes brand equity which in turn reduces brand loyalty.

To create and maintain brand loyalty in the international hospitality industry, operators must follow five steps. They must (a) treat the customer right, e.g. through valid and reliable market research; (b) stay close to the customer, e.g. the case of Disneyland; (c) measure and manage customer satisfaction, e.g. the case of Marriott Hotels and Domino's Pizza; (d) create switching costs, e.g. through the use of frequent stay programs; and (e) provide extras, e.g. exceeding consumer expectations. Selling to old customers and creating loyalty has been proven to be more profitable than selling to new customers. Operators on the international scene need customer retention programs; they need to calculate and/or estimate the relationship between customer retention levels and profitability – for instance, by conducting a customer retention analysis.

The success of a branding strategy at the international level depends upon creating, and more importantly maintaining, a clear differentiation in the minds of the consumer. Each brand must stand for a unique combination or package of goods and services. If branding and positioning strategies have been successfully implemented, there should be no reason to engage in discounting as a means of creating differentiation within a product class. Discounting has been primarily brought about by a lack of comprehensive and market-oriented segmentation and differentiation strategies. It is detrimental to the industry as a whole in the long run and is no long-term solution to declining occupancies.

To cater to the multiple and ever-changing demands of the international consumer, and to create and maintain differentiation, brand equity and competitive advantage, operators at the international level will be forced to adopt a value marketing strategy. Value marketing simply consists of (a) offering products/services that perform; (b) offering more than the customer expects; (c) giving guarantees; (d) avoiding unrealistic pricing; (e) giving the customer the facts; and (f) building relationships. It offers a way out of the discounting trap in which many international operators find themselves. If a brand has value, operators will find that consumers will be more than willing to pay a premium price for it. But operators should be aware of the potential pitfall – brands must have substance to support their promises, or their brand equity will deteriorate and competitive advantage will be lost.

International operators will increasingly have to honor the first command-ment of marketing: listen to the customer. Operators can no longer afford to adopt a selling orientation (finding someone to come through the doors, as opposed to marketing a solution to a designated market's needs); a product orientation ('Build a better mouse trap and the world will beat a pathway to your door'); or an operations orientation ('This is a great business to be in, if only the customers didn't get in the way'), as they have often done in the past (Lewis and Chambers, 1989). The adoption of a true marketing orien-tation (communicating to and giving the target market customers what they want, when they want it, where they want it, at a price they are willing to pay) will no longer be voluntary. It will be a prerequisite for survival in tomorrow's global marketplace.

From 'location, location, location' through 'service, service, service' to 'value, value, value'

Conventional wisdom in the field of hospitality management has long held that the three most important variables that increase the probability of success in the industry are 'location, location and location'. In the late 1980s we saw the transition to placing a greater emphasis on 'service, service, service' as the variable increasing the probability of success. As a result of the increased volume of sophisticated international consumers and the growth in the levels of sophistication among these consumers, the 1990s will see the emphasis being placed on 'value, 'value, value'. The challenge facing international operators is not one of solely having a good location and providing excep-tional service. The challenge is providing both location and service entwined in a price/value relationship which exceeds consumer expectations.

To meet the increasingly customized demands of the international con-sumer, hospitality operators in the 1990s must (a) determine the consumer's elements of value in his or her perception of using the operation's products and services in multiple countries; and (b) discover, if possible, any unex-ploited opportunities to add value to the experience and thereby gain higher customer approval or competitive advantage.

Albrecht (1992), the customer service guru, postulates a four-tier hierarchy of customer value as shown in Figure 14.3. The basic level consists of the absolutely essential attributes of the experience, either tangible or intangible; without them, there is no point in trying to do business. These include the bed, the food, the drink, the polite receptionist, etc. The expected level con-sists of the associated attributes of the experience that the customer has come to take for granted as part of general business practice. For example, the res-taurant will have a reasonable selection of menu items and reasonable prices, or the hotel will have a reliable system for guest messages. The desired level consists of attributes the customer does not necessarily expect, but knows about and appreciates if the experience includes them. These would include waiters suggesting special items that may or may not be on the menu. The final level is the unanticipated level and consists of 'surprise' attributes that

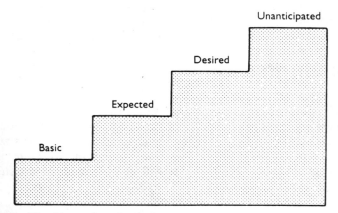

Figure 14.3 The hierarchy of customer value
Source: Albrecht (1992). Reprinted by permission of HarperCollins Publishers Inc.

add value for the customer beyond his or her typical desires or expectations. For example, the hotel clerk might offer the newly arrived a complimentary glass of juice while he or she takes care of registering the guest. Attributes that are basic and expected are not elements of competitive advantage. They are a minimum requirement to compete – they are minimum threshold attributes. Differentiation occurs and competitive advantage is set only when desired and unanticipated attributes are manipulated.

International hospitality organizations should be asking four basic questions to discern customer value, and setting value levels in such a fashion that they are able to develop a sustainable competitive advantage at the international level. These basic questions are shown in Figure 14.4. The international consumer of the 1990s is a sophisticated global citizen who demands value and is unwilling to accept anything less.

Traditionally, international operators have been somewhat negligent in managing the intangible elements of the hospitality experience, the atmospherics, the service and the value elements. The 1990s will require greater emphasis on managing the intangibles and creating a sustainable competitive

---

- What attributes of the customer experience are of particular value?
- How desirable is each attribute relative to the others?
- How well do we score, compared to the relevant competitors, on those factors that are most valued?
- What can we do to add value to the customer experience and thereby provide a differentiated or breakaway experience?

Figure 14.4 Checklist for discerning customer value

advantage through the development and maintenance of a differentiated price/value relationship in the eyes of the consumer.

Conclusion

While by no means offering an exhaustive account of every major trend impacting the international hospitality consumer, an attempt has been made in this chapter to outline and discuss what are believed to be some of the more significant trends impacting the demand side of the hospitality industry equation. International hospitality operations of the future have no option but to take into account the increasingly sophisticated demands of the international consumer when they are formulating and implementing strategies and tactics.

References

Adams, D. J. (1991) 'Do corporate failure prediction models work?', *International Journal of Contemporary Hospitality Management*, vol. 3, no. 4, pp. 25–9.

Akerhielm, P., Dev, C. S., and Noden, M. A. (1990) 'Europe 1992: neglecting the tourism opportunity', *Cornell HRA Quarterly*, May, pp. 104–11.

Albrecht, K. (1992) *The Only Thing That Matters*, New York: Harper Business Books.

Beattie, R. M. (1991) 'Hospitality internationalization: an empirical investigation', *International Journal of Contemporary Hospitality Management*, vol. 3, no. 4, pp. 14–20.

Calantone, R. J., Benedetto, A., Hakam, A., and Bojanic, D. C. (1989) 'Multiple multinational tourism positioning using correspondence analysis', *Journal of Travel Research*, Fall, pp. 25–32.

Chon, K. S., and Shin, H. (1990) 'Korea's hotel and tourism industry', *Cornell HRA Quarterly*, May, pp. 69–73.

Crawford-Welch, S. (1991) 'International marketing and competition in European markets', *International Journal of Contemporary Hospitality Management*, vol. 3, no. 4, pp. 47–54.

Gibbons, J. D., and Fish, M. (1988) 'Thailand s international tourism: successes and current challenges', *International Journal of Hospitality Management*, vol. 7, no. 2, pp. 161–6.

Gross, W. (1989) 'Best Western stakes out global position', *ASTA Agency Management*, February, pp. 65–70.

Horsburgh, S. (1991) 'Resources in the international hotel industry: a framework for analysis', *International Journal of Contemporary Hospitality Management*, vol. 3, no. 4, pp. 30–6.

Lewis, R. C., and Chambers, R. (1989) *Marketing Leadership in Hospitality: Foundations and practices*, New York: Van Nostrand Reinhold.

Litteljohn, D., and Slattery, P. V. O. (1991) 'Macro analysis techniques: an appraisal of Europe's main hotel markets', *International Journal of Contemporary Hospitality Management*, vol. 3, no. 4, pp. 6–13.

Naisbitt, J. (1982) *Megatrends*, New York: Warner Books.

Nowlis, M. (1990) 'Educating hospitality industry managers for the global village', *IMHI Cornell ESSEC Journal*, Spring, pp. 2–7.

Pannell Kerr Forster and Associates (1989) *Statistical Report Outlook in the Hotel and Tourism Industries*, Eurocity Survey, London: Pannell Kerr Forster.

Olsen, M. D. (1991) 'Structural changes: the international hospitality industry and firm', *International Journal of Contemporary Hospitality Management*, vol. 3, no. 4, pp. 21–4.

Rapp, S., and Collins, T. (1989) *Maxi-Marketing: The new direction in advertising, promotion, and marketing strategy*, New York: New American Library.

Rapp, S., and Collins, T. (1992) *The Great Marketing Turnaround*, New York: Penguin.

Teare, R. (1991) 'Developing hotels in Europe: some reflections on progress and prospects', *International Journal of Contemporary Hospitality Management*, vol. 3, no. 4, pp. 55–9.

Toffler, A. (1980) *The Third Wave*, New York: William Morrow and Co.

World Tourism Organization (1992) *Yearbook of Tourism Statistics*, vol. 1, 44th edition.

15

Managing cross-cultural hospitality enterprises

Abraham Pizam

'What is good for General Motors is good for the USA'; 'What is good for the USA is good for the rest of the world'; 'Japanese and American management are 95 percent the same, and differ in all important respects'. These are three famous quotations. The first is by C. E. Wilson, the chairman of General Motors corporation in the 1950s, the second by an anonymous American organizational theorist and the third by T. Fujisawa, the co-founder of Honda Motor Corporation. They express divergent philosophies on the universality of organizational structures and organizational behavior. In different words, these individuals try to answer the question: do organizational structure and organizational behaviour vary across corporate and national cultures?

The objective of this chapter is to answer this and several other questions such as: Do cultures differ from each other, and if they do, what are their effects on cross-cultural management? How can an American hotel manager in France predict whether he or she will encounter difficulties when employing an American managerial technique such as management by objectives (MBO)? Can a Japanese hotel corporation that has purchased a new property in the USA successfully introduce the proven total quality management (TQM) approach that has worked so well in its hotels in Japan? Finally, can the Disney corporate culture which operates successfully in California and Florida be effective in Paris? In other words, is there a hierarchy of cultures, such as that portrayed in Figure 15.1, suggesting that lower-level cultures have to be subordinated to higher-level cultures; that unless managerial practices and organizational structures are congruent with corporate cultures, and in their own turn, corporate cultures are compatible with national cultures, these practices, structures and cultures will not be productive? Before trying to answer these questions and present the reader with the relevant evidence to support one opinion or another, we must first define the concept of culture.

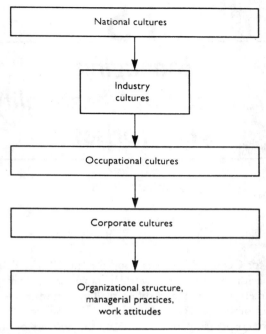

Figure 15.1 A hierarchy of cultures

Culture

Culture exists everywhere, and everyone belongs to at least one. It can be applied to any size of social unit that has had the opportunity to learn and stabilize its views of itself and the environment around it (Schein, 1990, p. 8). Culture exists at various levels of society (see Figure 15.1): At the *national* level – American, French, Japanese; at the *ethnic* level – Chinese and Malay in Malaysia or WASPS, Blacks and Hispanics in the USA. Culture can also be applied to other social units such as: *occupational groups* – lawyers, accountants, physicians; *corporations* – IBM, Shell, Pepsico, Disney; and even *industries* – mining, electronics, restaurants and hotels.

'Culture' is an umbrella word that encompasses a whole set of implicit, widely shared beliefs, traditions, values and expectations that characterize a particular group of people. It identifies the uniqueness of the social unit, its values and beliefs (Leavitt and Bahrami, 1988). Unfortunately, when one tries to define culture concisely and in a precise way difficulties occur. Tylor (1877), in one of the first comprehensive treatises of culture, defined it as 'that complex whole which includes knowledge, belief, art, law, morals, customs, and any capabilities and habits acquired by man as a member of society'. Linton (1945), in what is perhaps one of the most quoted definitions, relates to culture as 'a configuration of learned behaviors and results of behavior whose component parts are shared and transmitted by the members of a particular society'. Kroeber and Kluckhohn (1952) gathered 164 different definitions of culture ranging in scope from narrow and restrictive to wide and comprehensive, and ended up proposing their own definition:

> Culture consists of patterns, explicit and implicit of and for behavior acquired and transmitted by symbols, constituting the distinctive achievement of human groups, including their embodiment in artifacts; the essential core of culture consists of traditional (i.e. historically derived and selected) ideas and especially their attached values; culture systems may, on the one hand, be considered as products of action, on the other as conditioning elements of further action. (p. 181)

More recent definitions of culture were proposed by Barnouw (1963), Hofstede (1980), Terpstra and David (1985) and Schein (1990), to mention just a few. Barnouw defines culture as 'a way of life of a group of people, the configuration of all of the more or less stereotyped patterns of learned behavior, which are handed down from one generation to the next through the means of language and imitation' (1963, p. 4). In Hofstede's work, culture is 'the collective programming of the mind which distinguishes the members of one human group from another ... the interactive aggregate of common characteristics that influence a human group's response to the environment' (1980, p. 25). Terpstra and David offer the following definition: 'Culture is a learned, shared, compelling, interrelated set of symbols whose meaning provide a set of orientations for members of a society' (1985, p. 15). Finally, Schein sees culture as 'a pattern of basic assumption – invented, discovered, or developed by a given group as it learns to cope with its problems of external adaptation and integration – that has worked well enough to be considered valid and, therefore, to be taught to new members as the correct way to perceive, think, and feel in relations to those problems' (1990, p. 9).

The common thread in all these definitions is that culture is a social mechanism that shapes and guides people's thoughts, values and beliefs, and ultimately *controls their behavior*.

Schein distinguishes between three levels of culture: (1) behavior and artifacts (i.e. buildings, art, literature); (2) beliefs and values; and (3) underlying assumptions (i.e. ways of perceiving, thinking and evaluating the world, self and others). These levels are arranged according to their visibility such that behavior and artifacts are the easiest to observe, while the underlying assumptions need to be inferred. Another way of classifying levels of cultures is *explicit* (Schein's level 1) vs *implicit* (Schein's levels 2 and 3). The strength of a culture depends on three things:

> First, the pervasiveness of the norms and behaviors in the explicit culture, and the pervasiveness of the values and beliefs in the implicit culture – i.e. the proportion of members of the social group that firmly hold to the norms and beliefs. Second, the pervasiveness of the beliefs and behaviors themselves – i.e. the range of behaviors and the range of beliefs and values which the culture sets out to control.

Third, the consonance between the explicit and implicit cultures. Fanatical religious organizations provide the best examples of strong cultures. They focus on a wide range of behaviors, and most members of the sect believe deeply in their values (Payne, 1991, p. 27)

Dimensions of national cultural differences

National cultures vary from each other in many respects and in many dimensions. For the last 50 years, various sociologists, anthropologists and social-psychologists have advanced their lists of the major dimensions of national cultural variation. Triandis (1982) in a literature review identified some 30 dimensions suggested by 21 theorists and integrated them in a master list of 20 dimensions divided into three categories: (a) what kind of perceptual differentiations are emphasized in different cultures; (b) how the information extracted from these perceptions is processed and evaluated and (c) what patterns of action result. Table 15.1 lists the above dimensions.

With one or two exceptions, most of the classifications that were summarized in Triandis' review have three main drawbacks. First, they are not

Table 15.1 Triandis' review of dimensions of cultural variation

A. Perceptual differentiations
- (1) What the other does vs who the other is − focus on the family, in-group, age, race, religion, tribe, or status of the other
- (2) Who is in the in-group (professional group, tribe, nation, family, etc.)
- (3) Size of in-group (small vs large)
- (4) Ease of getting into group
- (5) Emphasis on age
- (6) Emphasis on sex
- (7) Emphasis on social class (power distance)
- (8) Self-concept: self-esteem
- (9) Self-concept: high power
- (10) Self-concept: high activity

B. Utilization and evaluation of information
- (11) Ideologism vs pragmastism
- (12) Associative vs abstractive communications
  Field dependent vs field independent
- (13) Human nature is good vs bad (ecosystem distrust)
- (14) Mastery over nature is good vs subjugation to nature is good
- (15) Emphasis on past, present, future
- (16) Emphasis on doing, being, being-in-becoming
- (17) Individualism vs collectivism (n-Ach vs n-Aff, n-Ext) (absolute vs situational ethics)
  Individualism vs conformism
  Familism
- (18) Uncertainty avoidance (tight vs loose society)
- (19) Masculine−feminine goals

C. Patterns of action
- (20) Contact vs no-contact (Dionysian vs Apollonian)

Source: Triandis (1982), pp. 142–3. Reprinted from *International Studies of Management and Organization*, vol. xii, no. 4, 1982–3, by permission of M. E. Sharpe Inc., New York.

empirically supported and have to be taken at face value. Second, these frameworks classify cultures in different categories, but they do not easily distinguish the degree of difference between cultures. Third, they suffer from lack of comprehensiveness (Kale, 1991). One main exception to the above criticism is the work carried out by Hofstede (1980), who conducted a study on 116 000 sales and service IBM employees in 50 countries, for the purpose of uncovering differences in work-related values across countries. From the results of this study Hofstede identified the following four basic dimensions of the differences between national cultures.

1. Power distance – defines the extent to which societies accept inequality in power and consider it as normal. This dimension does not deal with the mere existence of power distance, which is universal, but the magnitude that is tolerated. The Philippines and India were found to be high power-distance cultures, while Austria and Israel were low power-distance cultures.

2. Individualism – is the degree to which cultures encourage individual concerns as opposed to collectivist concerns. In individualist cultures everybody is responsible for himself or herself and his or her immediate family members. The motto is 'take care of numero uno' and 'me first'. Collectivist cultures, on the other hand, have strong ties between their individuals. Everybody is expected to look after the interests of his or her in-groups, such as extended families, clans or organizations. The in-group protects the interest of its members, but in turn expects their permanent loyalty. The USA and Britain scored high on the individualism dimension, while Colombia and Pakistan scored low on individualist and therefore were classified as collectivist cultures.

3. Masculinity – as a characteristic of a culture, opposes femininity. In masculine cultures the social sex roles are clearly differentiated. Men should be assertive and dominating and women should be caring and nurturing. Masculine cultures value money, material standards and ambition. They admire 'macho', 'big' and 'superman' types, and despise the 'weakling' and 'sissy'. In feminine cultures, on the other hand, there are overlapping social roles for the sexes, there is an emphasis on people rather than money, the underdog always gets the sympathy, and ambition or competitiveness are not desirable characteristics. Japan and Austria ranked high on masculinity, while Sweden and Norway ranked high on femininity.

4. Uncertainty avoidance – defines the extent to which people within a culture are encouraged to take risks and can tolerate uncertainty. People weak in uncertainty avoidance tend to accept each day as it comes, take risks easily and do not work too hard. Rules are fewer and can be easily broken or changed. In strong uncertainty-avoidance cultures people feel threatened by uncertain situations, work hard and feel compelled to devise means to beat the future. Rules are adhered to and deviancy is not tolerated (Hofstede, 1984).

Through the use of these scales Hofstede (1980, p. 336) managed to do something which very few researchers and theorists had done before: to distinguish the degree of difference between cultures and to classify countries

Table 15.2 Hofstede's classification of countries according to their cultures

I More developed Latin	II Less developed Latin	
High power distance	High power distance	
High uncertainty avoidance	High uncertainty avoidance	
High individualism	Low individualism	
Medium masculinity	Whole range on masculinity	
BELGIUM	COLOMBIA	
FRANCE	MEXICO	
ARGENTINA	VENEZUELA	
BRAZIL	CHILE	
SPAIN	PERU	
	PORTUGAL	
	YUGOSLAVIA	
III More developed Asian	**IV Less developed Asian**	**V Near Eastern**
Medium power distance	High power distance	High power distance
High uncertainty avoidance	Low uncertainty avoidance	High uncertainty avoidance
Medium individualism	Low individualism	Low individualism
High masculinity	Medium masculinity	Medium masculinity
JAPAN	PAKISTAN	GREECE
	TAIWAN	IRAN
	THAILAND	TURKEY
	HONK KONG	
	INDIA	
	PHILIPPINES	
	SINGAPORE	
VI Germanic	**VII Anglo**	**VIII Nordic**
Low power distance	Low power distance	Low power distance
High uncertainty avoidance	Low–med. uncertainty avoidance	Low–med. uncertainty avoidance
Medium individualism	High individualism	Medium individualism
High masculinity	High masculinity	Low masculinity
AUSTRIA	AUSTRALIA	DENMARK
ISRAEL	CANADA	FINLAND
GERMANY	BRITAIN	NETHERLANDS
SWITZERLAND	IRELAND	NORWAY
SOUTH AFRICA	NEW ZEALAND	SWEDEN
ITALY	USA	

Source: Hofstede (1980) p. 336.

according to their cultures (see Table 15.2). Hofstede used the results of his study not only to classify cultures into eight clusters but to determine which managerial practices and organizational structures will be congruent with which culture, and thus to suggest that Western managerial theories cannot be applied universally.

Organizational cultures

The use of the culture metaphor to describe organizations has captured the imaginations of academics and managers alike in the last decade, as is evidenced by the enormous number of books and articles written on the subject, and the popularity of the *In Search of Excellence* (Peters and Waterman, 1982) best-seller. The emphasis in many of these writings seems to have been on portraying different forms of culture, in some cases implying that it is this factor that determines excellence or mediocrity.

Like any other social unit, organizations are mini-societies that have distinctive cultures. To many people organizational culture represents 'the way things are done here'. To some, it is the *observed behavioral regularities* when people interact at work, the *norms that evolve in working groups*, or the *dominant values espoused by the organization*. To others, it is the *philosophy of management*, the *rules of the game*, or the *feeling* or *climate* that is conveyed by the physical layout. All these meanings reflect the organizational culture, but none of them is the essence of culture. The essence of organizational culture is 'the basic assumptions and beliefs that are shared by members of an organization, that operate unconsciously, and that define in a basic "taken-for-granted" fashion an organization's view of itself and its environment' (Schein, 1990, p. 6). Phrases such as 'Sell it to the sales staff' (Hewlett Packard); 'IBM means service'; 'Never kill a new product idea' (3M); 'No surprise'; (Holiday Inns); 'Quality is job one' (Ford); 'People are products of their environment' (Disney) and 'Quality, Service, Cleanliness, Values [QSCV]' (McDonald's) are all examples of the central values around which different organizations build, and symbolize important aspects of corporate philosophy (Morgan, 1986).

Organizational culture therefore identifies the uniqueness of the organization, its values and beliefs. Because organizational culture, like any other form of culture, is a system that controls the behavior of its members, executives and managers take a strong interest in it. By designing and 'managing' culture, managers can accomplish two important results: '(1) they can establish a base of shared attitudes, beliefs and values throughout the organization, thereby fostering a sense of unity, common purpose, and mutual commitment; and (2) they can also establish a sense of common fate, a feeling shared by workers and manager alike' (Leavitt and Bahrami, 1988, pp. 290–1).

Do organizational cultures make a difference? A review of the literature conducted by Schein (1990, pp. 30–44) shows that organizational (or corporate) cultures have had significant effects on the ability of organizations to enact certain strategies, on the innovativeness and creativity of employees, on the communication patterns, on intergroup conflicts, on productivity, employee satisfaction, leadership styles and so on. By now academics and practitioners alike understand that, when new strategies, policies or practices are incongruent with some of the traditions, values and self-concepts of the organization, these policies will frequently fail. Because strong cultures are powerful mechanisms of control that promote conformity and sameness, managers are interested in 'creating' strong cultures or 'reshaping' existing cultures to produce desired results. To some, this might seem an appropriate and legitimate managerial function, but to others it might seem a form of 'brainwashing' or 'Orwellian manipulation'.

Variations in organizational (corporate) cultures

Corporate cultures, like national cultures, vary in many respects and in many dimensions. However, in contrast to the case of national cultures, social scientists have not been able to develop comprehensive models or lists which enable us to compare corporate cultures along given dimensions. As a result we are left with a literature that is mostly composed of descriptive analyses or case studies.

Such descriptions depict the corporate culture of Hewlett Packard as:

> an informal, caring style ... with open-plan offices ... where people talk about the H-P way ... where MBWA (management by wandering around) is practiced ... an organization that offers generous benefits and has the feeling of a big close family ... where the engineers are kings and consensus and team work are the rules of the game. (Leavitt and Bahrami, 1988, pp. 289–92)

In contrast to this, IBM's Corporate culture has been described as:

> a place where loyalty is so important that no one is ever hired back into the company once they leave to join another company ... where internal competition between groups is encouraged and where sales and marketing reign supreme. (Leavitt and Bahrami, 1988, pp. 289–92)

At Tupperware, one of the strongest manifestations of a peculiar corporate culture that practices positive reinforcement to its utmost level is the famous 'Rally':

> the process of positive reinforcement is ritualized every Monday night, when all the saleswomen attend a 'Rally' for their distributorship. At Rally, everyone marches up on stage in the reverse order of last week's sales, a process known as 'Count Up', while their peers celebrate them by joining in 'All Rise'. Almost anyone who has done anything at all receives a pin or badge, or several pins or badges. The ceremony combines head-on competition with a positive tone that suggests that everyone wins. Applause and hoopla surround the entire event. The whole system, in essence, recreates the pattern for reinforcing desirable behavior evident in so many American parent–child relations. (Morgan, 1986, pp. 119–20)

Once again, contrast this to the corporate culture of ITT (International Telephone and Telegraph) during the leadership of Harold Geneen:

> The 'cut and thrust' corporate culture of ITT under Geneen stands pole apart from the successful team atmosphere of H-P. Geneen motivated people through fear ... he created an atmosphere of 'jungle fighters', power-hungry managers who experience life and work as a jungle where it is eat or be eaten, and where winners destroy losers ... an organization that expected all executives to be company men and women on top of their jobs at all times ... where loyalty to the goals of the organization should take precedence over loyalty to colleagues ... (Morgan, 1986, pp. 125–6)

Closer to home, the culture of the Disney corporation stands apart from any of its competitors. This 'quality', 'guest-driven' culture has been described by its own managers:

> The answer to how Disney does it, is the corporate culture, or 'the way we do things around here'. The organization defines quality service as a series of behaviors exhibited by cast members in the presence of guests. These behaviors include smiling, making eye contact, using pleasant phrases, performing their role functions, and implementing the many other details that add up to the 'personal touch' in the eyes of the guests. At the core of Disney philosophy is the belief that people (both guests and cast members) are products of their environment. To the degree that environments can be controlled, the appropriate reactions of people within that environment can be predicted. Disney, therefore, strives to control within good business sense, as much of the environment at the resort as possible. Both the experience of the guest, as well as the experience of the cast, although adhering to different standards, are orchestrated to be as positive as possible ... The concept of show business is extended throughout the culture and helps in attaining the 'buy in' of the cast. From the beginning, an employee is not hired for a job but, rather, cast for a role in the show, cast members wear costumes, not uniforms. They play before an audience of guests, not a crowd of customers. When they are in a guest environment, they are 'onstage'; when they are in an employee environment, they are 'backstage'. This vernacular communicates to cast members that they are in show business. They are not necessarily to be themselves when on stage, but rather to play a role. The role calls for an 'aggressively friendly' approach, one that incorporates smiles, enthusiasm, sincerity, high energy, and concern for the happiness of the guest. (Johnson, 1991, pp. 39–40)

Another description of Disney's culture as manifested in its hiring and induction process is provided by Van Maanen and Kunda (1989):

> Each successful applicant [for the positions of ride operators during the summer months] must conform to certain highly particularistic standards of appearance; complexion, height and weight, straightness and color of teeth, or disfigurement of any sort are all grounds for flunking the Disneyland body test ... [Ride operators will normally have the following characteristics:] single, white males and females, in their early twenties, of healthy appearance, possibly radiating good testimony of recent history of sports, without facial blemish, of above-average height, with conservative grooming standards ('punk' appearances are taboo) ... There are representative minorities on the payroll, but since ethnicity displays are sternly discouraged by management, minority employees are rather close copies of the standard model, albeit in different colors ... The so-called youth culture is indeed celebrated in and out of the park. Many employees, for example, live together in the large and cheap apartment complexes that surround Disneyland ... Paid employment at Disneyland begins with the much renowned Disney University whose faculty runs a day-long orientation program followed by classes held during a recruit's 40 hours of apprenticeship training on park grounds. Newly hired operators are given a thorough introduction to matters of managerial concern and are repeatedly tested on their absorption of famous Disneyland fact, lore, and procedure. Language is a central feature of university life, and new employees are schooled on its proper use. Customers at Disneyland, for instance, are never referred to as such; they are 'guests'. There are no rides at Disneyland, only 'attractions'. Disneyland itself is a 'park' not an amusement center, and is divided into 'backstage', 'staging' and 'onstage' regions. Law enforcement personnel hired by the park are not policemen but

'security hosts'. Employees do not wear uniforms but check out fresh 'costumes' each working day from 'Wardrobe'. And, of course, there are no accidents at Disneyland, only 'incidents'. ... During orientation, considerable concern is placed on particular values the Disney organization considers central to its operations. These values range from the 'customer is king' verities to the more or less unique kind, of which 'everyone is a child at heart at Disneyland' is a decent example ... Elaborate checks of appearance standards are memorized and recited in the training classroom, and great efforts are spent trying to bring employee emotional response in line with such standards. Employees are told repeatedly that if they are happy and cheerful at work, so too will be the guests at play. Inspirational films, hearty pep-talks, family imagery, and exemplars of corporate performance are all representative of the strong symbolic stuff of these training rituals. (Van Maanen and Kunda, 1989, pp. 58–64)

The above descriptions show the great variance that exists among corporate cultures. As previously indicated, this variance results in a divergence of managerial practices, leadership styles, work attitudes and organizational structures. Here again the question must be posed: to what extent are organizational (corporate) cultures relatively free of national cultures and can they therefore be implemented in any national culture; or are they subjugated to national cultures and required to be congruent with them?

Cultures of industries and occupational groups

Like nations and corporations, industries and occupational groups have cultures too. Although, for the most part, these cultures have neither been extensively documented nor properly classified, the few case studies and short descriptions that have been conducted enable us to draw the conclusion that they do exist. Thus we can speak of the culture of physicians, lawyers, engineers and computer programmers, to name just a few (Kunda, 1991; Couger *et al.*, 1990). For example, Van Maanen and Barley conclude that

Occupational communities were seen to create and sustain relatively unique work cultures consisting of, among other things, tasks, rituals, standards for proper and improper behavior, work codes which surround relatively routine practices and, for the membership at least, compelling accounts attesting to the logic and value of these rituals, standards and codes. (1984, p. 348)

Furthermore we can also distinguish between the cultures of different industries, such as the culture of the mining industry, the electronics industry, the restaurant or the hotel industry.

The restaurant industry

Woods (1989) in a study of five restaurant companies advanced the notion that, although on the surface it seems that the restaurant industry does not have a common culture because the differences between various enterprises are too many, in reality many commonalities do exist. He then proceeds to list some of the elements that in his opinion comprise the culture of this industry:

1. Being a young person's business – a 35-year-old person in this industry is old.
2. The majority of hourly employees are women, while the bulk of managers are men.
3. Most managers rise through the industry ranks.
4. High turnover – the average employee turns over every three months and managers every six months.
5. The industry has a negative image in the public mind.
6. Most stories told by employees to each other revolve around one of the following three categories:
   (a) service
   (b) management–employee relationships
   (c) reaffirming high levels of stress.
7. Most of the rites and rituals and ceremonies are intended to accomplish one of three goals:
   (a) making employees feel a part of the organization
   (b) spreading the culture
   (c) creating specific work environments.
8. Many of the norms describe the relationship between managers and employees – some companies' norms are so employee focused that they detail how managers should react to personal relationships among the employees.
9. The industry is polyglot – it has a jargon of its own full of shorthand terms, acronyms and phrases.
10. A belief that success is determined more by internal actions than by external factors.
11. Agreement that stake-holders could be satisfied through the following three types of action:
    (a) emphasis or re-emphasis on the unit level of operations
    (b) creation of organizations that are more attractive to managers and employees
    (c) controlled expansion.
12. A belief that success depends on the organization's accomplishing the following four things:
    (a) differentiating itself from competitors
    (b) maintaining an attitude of hard work in the organization
    (c) developments in the right markets
    (d) focus on service.
13. A hands-on approach to management.
14. A common belief that managers should act as though they owned the restaurant they managed.
15. A shared belief that successful restaurant people are fun-loving people who have high energy levels and an interest in seeing the results of their work.

16. Recognition that people are the most important asset.
17. Both managers and employees think of their jobs as hard work.
18. High interorganizational mobility – employees and managers move easily from one company to another.

The hotel industry

Following Woods' study, the current author took the above list of eighteen cultural characteristics of the restaurant industry, and asked two groups of managers in two multinational hotel corporations, one in the USA and the other in the UK, to indicate which of the above are appropriate for the hotel industry as a whole. The following factors were selected by a minimum of 66 percent of the participants:

1. Being a young person's business.
2. Most managers rise through the industry ranks (but higher education in hospitality management is slowly replacing experience).
3. High turnover (but lower than in the restaurant industry).
4. Most stories told by employees to each other revolve around one of the following two categories:
   (a) service (but mostly on 'problem guests')
   (b) reaffirming high levels of stress.
5. Most of the rites and rituals and ceremonies are intended to accomplish one of two goals:
   (a) making employees feel a part of the organization
   (b) spreading the culture.
6. The industry is polyglot – it has a jargon of its own full of shorthand terms, acronyms and phrases.
7. Agreement that stake-holders could be satisfied by emphasis or re-emphasis on the unit level of operations.
8. A belief that success depends on the organization's accomplishing the following three things:
   (a) differentiating itself from competitors
   (b) developments in the right markets
   (c) focus on *quality* service (the word 'quality' was added).
9. A hands-on approach to management (management by 'walking around').
10. Recognition that people are the most important asset.
11. Both managers and employees think of their jobs as hard work.
12. High interorganizational mobility – employees and managers move easily from one hotel to another (because 'the fastest way up is out first').

In addition to these factors which were identical in both industries, managers pointed out some additional characteristics that in their opinions were either different from the restaurant industry or not existent there:

13. A belief that success is determined more by *external factors* than by

internal factors (e.g. state of the economy, state of the tourism industry, airline fares, cost of gasoline, value of the currency).
14. Most managers are men (but women have managed to climb out of the housekeeping and front office, which used to be the 'appropriate places' for women).
15. Emphasis on the physical appearance of guest-contact employees.
16. Emphasis on the friendliness of guest-contact employees.

It goes without saying that more research needs to be conducted in this area. However, although both lists are neither comprehensive nor representative of the restaurant and hotel industries as a whole, they nevertheless indicate a certain commonality of features that suggests that these industries might have unique cultures that distinguish them from other industries.

As in the previous two cases, the question must be posed again: to what extent are industries' cultures independent of national cultures and can they therefore be implemented worldwide; or are they subjugated to national cultures and required to be congruent with them? In other words, can we say that the culture of the hotel or restaurant industry is universal, or would it *have to vary* from country to country if it were to be effective?

Now it is time for us to present the cumulative research findings on these questions and discuss the issues of the universality of managerial practices and organizational structures.

The convergence/divergence issue

'Is the diversity of behavior in organizations across cultures increasing, decreasing or remaining the same? Trying to resolve what is commonly labeled the convergence/divergence dichotomy, scholars ask whether organizations worldwide are becoming more similar (convergence) or are maintaining their culturally based dissimilarity (divergence)' (Adler *et al.*, 1986, p. 300). In this section we will discuss the arguments and evidence presented by both sides and try to arrive at certain conclusions.

The convergence (universalistic) process

Arguments that support the convergence process are based on the contention either that some normative systems of organizational design and managerial processes are universally superior or that they are technologically indispensable. Weber (1947) formulated the concept of bureaucracy as the most efficient possible way to organize human effort. The key to bureaucracy was its rationality and impersonality. Weber's intent was to make organizations culture-free, to create a universal system of organization that would be the most efficient system anywhere. Weber's model was further refined by other administrative theorists such as Henri Fayol in France, Gullick and Urwick in England and Frederick Tayor in the USA, all of whom were concerned with the rationality of organizations and therefore developed a series of universal guidelines intended to make organizations more efficient. As a reaction to these implications, theories of human relations were advanced by social-psychologists who devised a whole range of mechanisms and techniques intended to make organizations take into account the needs, feelings and attitudes of their members, and in the process to make them more efficient. Such terms as 'sociotechnical systems', 'organic organizations', 'participative management', 'theory Y', and 'system four' were exported worldwide as universalistic remedies to organizational problems. Those who developed and marketed these techniques truly believed in the superiority of these organizational structures and/or managerial techniques and their universal application (Tannenbaum, 1980, pp. 284–7).

In more modern times other individuals argue that convergence is a process induced by industrialization which is based on science and technology, two supranational processes which are independent of governmental forms and national cultures. Through trade, imitation, economic aid and military channels, there is a worldwide diffusion of industrial technology from developed to developing nations.

> The worldwide diffusion of technology creates a 'logic of industrialism', since it sets up a range of tasks and problems. The pressure towards efficient production will ensure that the most effective ways of tackling these common tasks will be adopted world wide. As this process continues, organizations tackling the same tasks, in whichever culture, will become more and more alike. (Open University, 1985, p. 38)

Researchers such as Child (1981), Child and Tayeb (1983), Cole (1973), Form (1979), Hickson *et al.* (1974), Kerr *et al.* (1952), Levitt (1983), Negandhi (1979, 1985), and Pugh and Hickson (1976) claim that organizational characteristics are similar, if not identical, across nations and for the most part are free from cultural dominance. Researchers supporting the convergence hypothesis argue that 'individuals, irrespective of culture are forced to adopt industrial attitudes such as nationalism, secularism, and mechanical time concerns in order to comply with the imperative of industrialization' (Okechuku and Wai Man, 1991). Typically, such researchers argue that organizational variance depends more on contingencies such as technological development and geographical diversification than on culture:

> Contingencies of technological development, market and geographical diversification, large scale production and close interdependence with other organizations ... impose a logic of rational administration which it becomes functionally imperative to follow in order to achieve levels of performance sufficient to ensure the survival of the organization ... this logic is in all societies irrespective of culture, economic or political system ... (Child and Tayeb, 1983. p. 27)

Levitt fully agrees with the above and states:

> a powerful force drives the world toward a converging commonality, and that force is technology ... the result is a new commercial reality – the emergence of global markets for standardized consumer products ... Gone are accustomed differences in

national or regional preference ... different cultural preferences, national tastes and standards ... are vestiges of the past. (Levitt, 1983, pp. 92–6)

Following a set of studies in Britain, conducted by a team of Aston University researchers headed by Pugh and Hickson, additional studies were undertaken by other collaborators to study the relationship of organizational structure to context in twelve different cultures. Despite the finding that there were many differences between the structures of organizations in different cultures, the researchers concluded that different cultures, by their nature, *did not* produce different organizational structures:

Size and dependence become the bases for an explanation of the broad features of organizations worldwide. It appears to be more important to know how large an organization is, who set it up and what its dependence on the environment is, than the country in which it is located. Certainly, the differences between organizations *within* one country are greater than the average differences *between* countries ... As far as the context/structure relationship goes there would thus appear to be a clear convergence in all countries so far studied. (Open University, 1985, p. 48)

The divergence process

Those scholars who support the divergence process argue that organizations have always been, still are and will always be culture-bound, rather than culture-free. Therefore we should not expect to see any convergence in managerial practices, leadership styles or work attitudes across different cultures, since these are dependent on the implicit model of organizational functioning prevalent in a particular culture. The models in turn are generated by the mental programming occurring within each culture. Change in managerial practices, leadership styles, etc. will develop slowly and will always be induced by a change in culture (Hofstede, 1980). Adler *et al.* reviewed the works of Bass and Eldrige (1973), England (1975), Haire *et al.* (1966), Heller and Wilpert (1979), Hofstede (1980), Laurent (1983), Lincoln *et al.* (1981), Myer and Rowan (1977) and Negandhi (1973). They concluded that 'the principle of equifinality applies to organizations functioning in different cultures and that many equally effective ways to manage exist. The most effective depend, among other contingencies, on the culture(s) involved' (Adler *et al.*, 1986, p. 301).

For example, although the level of industrialization is similar in Japan, the USA and Western Europe, Japanese workers and managers are quite different from American or Western European workers and managers. Several researchers (Dore, 1973; Ouchi, 1981; Ballon, 1983; Kono, 1984; Bartlet and Ghoshal, 1989) have portrayed Japanese employees and managers as possessing the following characteristics which differ significantly from the characteristics of American or Western European employees and managers:

- The organization is viewed as a collectivity to which employees belong, rather than just a work place. They welcome homogeneity and interdependence.

- They identify with their country and organization rather than with their job or occupation (*where* they do it rather than *what* they do).
- They see little conflict between the objectives of the organization and those of the employees (success benefits everyone).
- Managers take a long time to make decisions. They listen a lot, empathize with employees and in most cases prefer decision making by consensus.
- They implement swiftly after a decision has been made.
- They believe in group harmony, cooperation and group achievement.
- They adhere to the practice of paternalism and lifetime employment, which promotes loyalty and long-term commitments.
- They tend to work in small groups and make the best use of the creative skills of all employees, with a commitment to delegation.
- All employees, 'blue collar' and 'white collar', belong to the same unions, and unions are specific to the organization.
- Seniority (which translates into age) and not merit are the basis for pay and promotion.
- They have a single-minded pursuit of product quality.
- They lack distinction between skilled and unskilled operators, which makes it possible for unskilled employees eventually to move into supervisory or managerial positions.
- Demarcation lines between jobs are inconspicuous; there is a significant overlap among jobs.
- Managers are rotated around to different departments.
- Workers learn all the jobs carried in their section to increase flexibility of work.
- Education is highly respected; employees are constantly trained on and off the job, and managers are sent to management development courses.

Morgan (1986, pp. 114–16), quoting Murray Sayle, an Australian expert on Japan, offers an intriguing theory of the historical factors accounting for the collectiveness and solidarity of Japanese organizations:

> He believes that Japanese organizations combine the cultural values of the rice field with the spirit of service of the samurai. While the former is crucial for understanding solidarity in organizations, the latter accounts for many characteristics of management and for the pattern of inter-organizational relations that has played such a crucial role in Japan's economic success.

Like Japanese, Arabs also differ significantly in their work attitudes, leadership styles and managerial practices from Americans and Western Europeans. Muna (1980), Elashmawi (1991), Ali *et al.* (1991) and Atiyyah (1992) summarize a great portion of the English and Arabic language literature on the characteristics of Arab employees and managers as contrasted to their counterparts in the West.

- They place high importance on personal relationships as distinct from role- or task-oriented ones.

- They have no basic separation of business affairs from social or personal life.
- They rate loyalty and trust much more highly than efficiency and performance.
- Because of a strong kinship structure and the obligation to the extended family, they regard nepotism and favoritism as right and proper. Executives use and are used by family and friends as contacts and to put pressure on other organizations and the government.
- They use money to 'oil the wheels of business and government'. Paying money for favors does not have the same negative connotation as in the West.
- They value reputation and 'saving face' highly.
- Because Arab culture is fatalistic, Arab managers allocate very little time and resources to planning, but significantly spend more time on controlling and commanding.
- They rely heavily on intuition and personal judgment in making decisions.
- In most cases, they use an authoritarian style of leadership, but in some countries, such as Saudi Arabia, a consultative style is generally favored.
- Employees' adherence to work norms conducive to high productivity and efficiency is generally weak.
- They have a high aversion to risk taking.
- They have strong loyalty to supervisors and maintain strong friendship ties at work.
- They engage in a ritualistic style of business negotiation, display a high regard for long-term relationships and are affective, appealing to emotions and concession seeking.
- They conduct performance evaluation in an informal style with an absence of systematic controls and established criteria.

The focus on the Japanese and Arabs is intended to be merely illustrative. The point that the divergers are trying to bring across has been put by Morgan as follows:

> culture, whether Japanese, Arabian, British, Canadian, Chinese, French or American, shapes the character of the organization. Thus in Britain, generations of social change and class conflict often perpetuate antagonistic divisions in the work-place that no amount of conciliation and management techniques seem able to overcome. In contrast with the Japanese, the British factory worker often defines himself in opposition to a system he perceives to have exploited his ancestors as it now exploits him. Managerial elites often assume a basic right to rule workers, who they see as having a 'duty to obey'. If we turn to the United States for illustrations of how culture shapes management, the ethic of competitive individualism is probably the one that stands out most clearly. Many American corporations and their employees are preoccupied with the desire to be 'winners' and with the need to reward and punish successful and unsuccessful behavior ... the general orienta- tions in many [American] organizations is to play the game for all it's worth, set objectives, clarify accountability, and 'kick ass' or reward success lavishly and conspicuously ... It is the cultural context that seems decisive. (Morgan, 1986, pp. 117–19)

Implications for hospitality enterprises

By now we have presented some of the evidence produced by the two schools of thought: convergence and divergence. The question, however, still remains. Who is right? Can we say that organizations are becoming more alike regardless of the culture in which they operate? Or can we say that organizational structures and managerial practices are heavily affected by national or ethnic cultures? Do organizational (corporate) cultures determine people's behavior in organizations, or does national or ethnic culture limit the organizational culture influence? Both theories have generated impressive evidence to support their contentions. But could they both be right? Could reputable scholars, using reputable methodologies, form opposite conclusions? Child (1981) analyzing a large number of studies discovered that the majority of those focusing on macro-level variables were finding few differences across cultures, whereas those examining micro-level variables were observing many significant differences. Adler *et al.* (1986), the Open University study (1985), Vertinsky *et al.* (1990), Lansbury and Bamber (1991) and the current author all agree with the above conclusion.

It is therefore possible to conclude that, as far as organizational structure is concerned, culture has little impact. An 800-room hotel in Chicago will be more similar in its organizational structure, division of labor, formalization and specialization of tasks to an 800-room hotel in Tokyo, Bangkok or Athens, than to a 100-room hotel in Chicago. This is despite the fact that the cultures of the USA, Japan, Thailand and Greece are different from each other (see Table 15.2). And indeed if one walks into a McDonald's in New York, London, Singapore or Paris, one will find not only an identical menu but also an identical front-of-the-house and back-of-the-house design and layout with uniform equipment, reporting and control mechanisms.

But when it comes to people's behavior in organizations, culture counts. Therefore when trying to import managerial practices such as leadership styles, communication patterns and motivation techniques, to mention just a few, from one country to another, problems arise. National and ethnic cultures are a major determinant of people's behavior, and when the corporate culture of a hospitality company is incongruent with the national or ethnic culture, the result is failure. Some multinational hospitality corporations (MNHCs) try to apply their Western developed corporate cultures uniformly to all their properties, regardless of their fit to the local culture. Others practice a total 'hands-off' approach and allow each local property to develop a set of practices and philosophies that best matches its local culture. But a small minority of MNHCs engage in the process of bridging culture gaps and sensitizing their headquarters' 'corporate culture keepers' to the effects that national and ethnic culture have on the success of their business. These companies redesign their corporate culture to match the respective requirements of individual national cultures. When, for example, they design human resource management practices such as career management systems, or appraisal and compensation methods, they take into consideration the cultural variations of their enterprises. If they are American companies operating in Germany and France, they may decide to use management by objectives as a performance appraisal technique in Germany, where there is a cultural preference for decentralization and less emphasis on the hierarchy (allowing for two-way communication), but not to use it in France, where there is a high degree of centralization and a large power distance between supervisors and employees. The same will be true for a French MNHC with properties in Arab countries and Austria that considers the design of career management systems. This company might develop formal, long-term individual career plans for its Austrian employees, where there is a culturally compelling need to devise means to 'beat the future', but might avoid this in Arab countries, where man's control over the future is considered minimal.

Last, but not least, what happens to those hospitality companies that cease to be multinational or *polycentric* (see Chapter 11 for a discussion of this term) and become global or *geocentric*? Some would argue that in such cases the corporate culture will override national culture differences and a new supranational entity will result. This entity will have corporate citizens governed by corporate laws and regulations, sharing the same beliefs, traditions and values, moving from country to country and having no loyalty to any individual nation. Companies such as IBM and ITT have been portrayed as 'supranational' or 'global' entities with their passports, flags and the other symbolic paraphernalia associated with nationhood. To others (Hofstede, 1980), this seems to be totally unrealistic. As long as national cultural differences exist, these will influence managerial processes and work attitudes, and a geocentric culture will be neither feasible nor desirable.

To conclude, we started our discussion by posing a few questions on the universality of organizational theories and the impact that national, corporate and industry cultures have on organizational structure and organizational behavior. By now we have partially answered these questions and can conclude that culture counts. So, can an American hotel manager in France predict whether he or she will encounter difficulties when employing an American managerial technique such as management by objectives? As previously discussed, the answer to that is a definite yes. Can a Japanese hotel corporation that purchased a new property in the USA successfully introduce the proven total quality management approach that has worked so well in its hotels in Japan? The answer is: not without major modifications. And can the Disney corporate culture which operates successfully in California and Florida be effective in Paris? Again the answer is: not without major modifications. It is hoped that future researchers will continue to study this fascinating topic and provide some additional answers that will be industry specific and relevant to various national and ethnic cultures.

References

Adler, J. Nancy, Doktor, Robert, and Redding, S. Gordon (1986) 'From the Atlantic to the Pacific century: cross-cultural management reviewed', *Journal of Management*, vol. 12, no. 2, pp. 295–318.

Ali, Abbas, Al-Shakhis, Mohammed, and Nataraj, Somanathan (1991) 'Work centrality and individualism: a cross-national perspective', *International Journal of Manpower*, vol. 12, no. 1, pp. 30–8.

Atiyyah, Hamid S. (1992) 'Research note: research in Arab countries, published in Arabic', *Organization Studies*, vol. 13, no. 1, pp. 105–12.

Ballon, R. J. (1983) 'Non-Western work organization', *Asia Pacific Journal of Management*, vol. 1, no. 1, pp. 1–14.

Barnouw, V. (1963) *Culture and Personality*, Homewood, Ill.: The Dorsey Press.

Bartlett, C. A., and Ghoshal, S. (1989) *Managing Across Borders: The transnational solution*, Boston, Mass.: Harvard Business School Press.

Bass, B., and Eldrige, L. (1973) 'Accelerated managers' objectives in twelve countries', *Industrial Relations*, vol. 12, pp. 158–171.

Child, J. (1981) 'Culture, contingency and capitalism in the cross-cultural study of organization', in L. L. Cummings and B. M. Staw (eds), *Research in Organizational Behavior*, vol. 3, Greenwich, Ct.: Jai Publishers.

Child, J., and Tayeb, M. (1983) 'Theoretical perspectives in cross-national organizational research', *International Studies of Management and Organization*, vol. 7, no. 3–4, pp. 19–32.

Cole, R. E. (1973) 'Functional alternatives and economic development: an empirical example of permanent employment in Japan', *American Sociological Review*, vol. 38, pp. 424–38.

Couger, J. Daniel, Adelsberger, Heimo, Borovits, Israel, Zviran, Moshe, and Motiwalla, Juzar (1990) 'Commonalities in motivating environments for programmer/analysts in Austria, Israel, Singapore and the USA', *Information and Management*, vol. 18, pp. 41–6.

Dore, R. (1973) *British Factory – Japanese Factory*, London: George Allen and Unwin.

Elashmawi, Farid (1991) 'Multicultural management: new skills for global success', *Tokyo Business Today*, vol. 59, no. 2, pp. 54–6.

England, G. W. (1975) *The Manager and His Values: An international perspective from the USA, Japan, Korea, India and Australia*, Cambridge, Mass.: Ballinger.

Form, W. (1979) 'Comparative industrial sociology and the convergence hypothesis', *Annual Review of Sociology*, vol. 5, pp. 1–25.

Haire, M., Ghiselli, E.G., and Porter, L.W. (1966) *Managerial Thinking: An international study*, New York: John Wiley.

Heller, R. A., and Wilpert, B. (1979) 'Managerial decision making: an international comparison', in G. W. England, A. R. Negandhit and B. Wilpert (eds), *Functioning Organizations in Cross-Cultural Perspective*, Kent, Ohio: Kent State University Press.

Hickson, D. J., Hinnings, C. R., MacMillan, C. J. M. and Schwitter, J. P. (1974) 'The culture-free context of organizational structure: a tri-national comparison', *Sociology*, vol. 8, pp. 59–80.

Hofstede, G. (1980) *Culture Consequences: International differences in work-related values*, Beverly Hills, Calif.: Sage.

Hofstede, G. (1984) 'The cultural reality of the quality of life concept', *Academy of Management Review*, vol. 9, no. 3, pp. 389–98.

Johnson, Rick (1991) 'A strategy for service – Disney style', *Journal of Business Strategy*, vol. 12, no. 5, pp. 38–43.

Kale, Sudhir, H. (1991) 'Culture-specific marketing communications: an analytical approach', *International Marketing Review*, vol. 8, no. 2, pp. 18–30.

Kerr, C. J., Dunlop, T., Harbison, F., and Myers, C.A. (1952) *Industrialism and Industrial Man*, Cambridge, Mass : Harvard University Press.

Kono, T. (1984) *Strategy and Structure of Japanese Enterprises*, New York: Macmillan.

Kroeber, A. L. and Kluckhohn, F. R. (1952) *Culture: A critical review of concepts and definitions*, Cambridge, Mass.: Harvard University Press.

Kunda, Gideon (1991) *Engineering Culture: Culture and control in a high-tech corporation*, Philadelphia, PA: Temple University Press.

Lansbury, R. D., and Bamber, G. J. (1991) 'Managers' employment issues: international comparisons between Australia and Britain', *International Journal of Human Resource Management*, vol. 2, no. 3, pp. 285–309.

Laurent, A. (1983) 'The cultural diversity of Western management conceptions', *International Studies of Management and Organization*, vol. 8, no. 1–2, pp. 75–96.

Leavitt, Harold J., and Bahrami, Homa (1988) *Managerial Psychology*, Chicago, Ill.: University of Chicago Press.

Levitt, T. (1983) 'The globalization of markets', *Harvard Business Review*, vol. 83, no. 3, pp. 92–102.

Lincoln, J. R., Hanada, M., and Olson, J. (1981) 'Cultural orientations and individual reactions to organizations: A study of Japanese-owned firms', *Administrative Science Quarterly*, vol. 26, pp. 93–115.

Linton, R. (1945) *The Cultural Background of Personality*, New York: Appleton-Century-Crofts.

Meyer, J. W., and Rowan, B. (1977) 'Institutionalized organizations: formal structure as myth and ceremony, *American Journal of Sociology*, vol. 83, pp. 340–63.

Morgan, Gareth (1986) *Images of Organizations*, Beverly Hills, Calif.: Sage.

Muna, F. A. (1980) *The Arab Executive*, New York: St Martin's Press.

Negandhi, A. R. (1973) *Management and Economic Development: The case of Taiwan*, The Hague: Martinus Nijhoff.

Negandhi, A. R. (1979) 'Convergence in an organizational practice: an empirical study of industrial enterprises in developing countries', in C. J. Lammers and D. J. Hickson (eds), *Organizations Alike and Unlike*, London: Routledge and Kegan Paul.

Negandhi, A. R. (1985) 'Management in the Third World', in P. Joynt and M. Warner (eds), *Managing in Different Cultures*, Oslo: Universitetsforlaget.

Okechuku, Chike, and Wai Man, Viola Yee (1991) 'Comparison of managerial traits in Canada and Hong Kong', *Asia Pacific Journal of Management*, vol. 8, no. 2, pp. 223–35.

Open University (1985) *Technology: A Second Level Course, Managing in Organizations, Block V: Wider Perspectives, Unit 16: International Perspectives*, Milton Keynes: Open University Press.

Ouchi, W. (1981) *Theory Z: How American business can meet the Japanese challenge*, New York: Addison-Wesley.

Payne, Roy (1991) 'Taking stock of corporate culture', *Personnel Management*, vol. 23, no. 7, pp. 26–9.

Peters, Thomas J., and Waterman, Robert H. (1982) *In Search of Excellence: Lessons from America's best run companies*, New York: Harper and Row.

Pugh, D. S., and Hickson, D. J. (1976) *Organizational Structure in its Context: The Aston programme I*, London: Gower.

Schein, Edgar (1990) *Organizational Culture and Leadership*, San Francisco, Calif.: Jossey-Bass.

Tannenbaum, Arnold (1980) 'Organizational psychology', *Handbook of Cross-Cultural Psychology, Social Psychology*, vol. 5, pp. 281–334, Boston, Mass.: Allyn & Bacon.

Terpstra, V., and David, K. (1985) *The Cultural Environment of International Business* (2nd edn.), Cincinnati, Ohio: Southwestern Publishing Co.

Triandis, Harry C. (1982) 'Dimensions of cultural variation as parameters of organizational theories', *International Studies of Management and Organization*, Winter, pp. 134–69.

Tylor, E. B. (1877) *Primitive Cultures: Researches into the development of mythology, philosophy, religion, language, art and custom*, vol. 1, New York: Henry Holt.

Van Maanen, John, and Barley, Stephen R. (1984) 'Occupational communities: culture and control in organizations', in Barry M. Staw and L. L. Cummings (eds), *Research in Organizational Behavior*, vol. 6, Greenwich, Conn.: JAI Press.

Van Maanen, John, and Kunda, Gideon (1989) 'Real feelings: emotional expression and organizational culture', *Research in Organizational Behavior*, vol. 11, pp. 43–103.

Vertinsky, Ilan, Tse, David K., Wehrung, Donald A., and Lee, Kam-hon (1990) 'Organizational Design and management norms: A comparative study of managers' perceptions in the People's Republic of China, Hong Kong and Canada', *Journal of Management*, vol. 16, no. 4, pp. 853–67.

Weber, M. (1947) *The Theory of Social and Economic Organization*, New York: Free Press.

Woods, Robert H. (1989) 'More alike than different: the culture of the restaurant industry', *Cornell HRA Quarterly*, vol. 30, no. 2, pp. 82–97.

16

Technology transfer in the hotel industry

Ray Pine

Technology transfer is a complex process but in simple terms may be regarded as having three main elements: the physical artifacts of transfer (the buildings, equipment, company identity and, in some cases, infrastructure development); any contractual and legal conditions governing the transfer; and human aspects of transfer (the people who are available to ensure that the physical artifacts are available and that the tangible and intangible products associated with those physical artifacts are provided). The physical artifacts of transfer are relatively easy to provide, the only controlling factors being the finances available and the willingness to commit those finances to the specific project. Contractual and legal conditions governing the transfer can be very complicated, involving negotiations and arrangements between several parties, including national and local governments, financiers, owners and management organizations. While the previous two factors are obviously very important, it is my contention that it is the human aspects of transfer which is the most significant factor in successful technology transfer in the hotel industry. My research (Pine, 1991) has looked specifically at this factor, and this chapter will deal specifically with human aspects of transfer.

Technology and technology transfer

In previous work (Pine, 1985, 1987) a definition of technology put forward by Merrill (1968) was adopted in an attempt to make the strong case for appreciating technology as more than just physical artifacts: machines and equipment. Thus, technology is defined as 'a flexible repertoire of skills, knowledge and methods for attaining desired results and avoiding failures under varying circumstances'. Such a broad definition, incorporating methods, processes and organizations, and therefore a strong human element, is necessary for a full appreciation of technology to be achieved. This is especially true in service industries, which are characterized by human interaction as much as by machine- or equipment-supported provision. In searching for an appropriate definition of technology transfer in the hotel industry, consideration has been given to the views of a wide range of authors on many perspectives of technology.

Hawthorne (1971), Stewart (1987) and Seurat (1979) provide basic definitions, all of which identify the transmission of knowledge from the transferor to the transferee. Stewart and Nihei (1987) equate technology transfer with foreign direct investment and the ability of local employees to implement new technology in local organizations. Dahlman and Westphal (1983) identify three levels of technology transfer, which it is possible to align to a hotel industry context.

- Level 1 – 'the capability required to operate a technology, for example, to run and maintain a plant [or hotel]'.
- Level 2 – 'investment capability – that required to create new productive capacity [or new hotels]'.
- Level 3 – 'innovation capability – the ability to modify and improve methods and products [or hotel services and provision]'.

All these levels require different types of skill and different supporting institutions. Levels 1 and 2 are relatively easy to achieve (through learning on the job and through formal training). Level 3 is the most difficult to achieve as it demands not necessarily a highly technical ability, but 'imagination and a mental set always seeking better ways' (Stewart and Nihei, 1987).

The previously listed considerations, plus various others not mentioned here due to lack of space, led to the adoption of the following definition of technology transfer in the hotel industry: 'the ability of local nationals to adopt and adapt existing hotel systems, possibly to the point of creating new systems, to continuously satisfy both international and domestic demand for hotel services' (Pine, 1991). While this definition was developed more specifically to address the problems of transfer from industrialized or economically developed countries to less developed countries, it is equally applicable to technology transfer within a single country. The technology transfer process is more pronounced when considering the development of a US-based internationally branded hotel in, say, a Pacific island. However, it is no less important in the situation where a hotel chain is developing a new property in its home country, or in another economically developed country.

Transfer receivers' knowledge

The reference to 'the ability of local nationals' provides a strong guideline towards effecting successful technology transfer. Those people who will work in the hotel, at all levels, need to be both capable and willing participants in the transfer process. Their ability to benefit from vocational education and training, and their possession of an appropriate attitude and mental set, are linked to the educational provision available in a country. Stewart and Nihei (1987) highlight two factors which are necessary for technology transfer to proceed. The first is general knowledge, disseminated through education to a large enough portion of the population to provide sufficient people who are capable of handling new technology. The second is the propensity to adopt new products and new techniques so that absorptive capacity is fully utilized and technology transfer can actually occur. Stewart and Nihei refer to the work of Niehoff and Anderson (1964) and Novack and Lekachman (1964) to support the argument that these two factors are closely linked, as general knowledge (or information) is an ingredient in willingness to accept change, and that attitudes and values held by the people of the host nation may inhibit change. The technology transfer process must recognize this and allow for accommodation of such attitudes and values, or provide the means through which they can be developed or modified.

Wallender (1979, pp. 26–7) argues that knowledge of the technology being transferred is a prerequisite of the technology receiver, and lists five knowledge categories: general knowledge; industry-specific knowledge; system-specific knowledge; firm-specific knowledge; and ongoing problem-solving capability. Stephenson (1984) summarizes and adds support to this argument in stating: 'Successful recipients of such advanced technology transfer in addition to technical proficiency must be adaptable, have a willingness to accept new ideas, methods and systems, and have or develop the wisdom to know and acknowledge what they do not know' (p. 164). In a developing country context, Shelp et al (1984) proposes that the prevailing conception of technology is to get the 'black box' which contains everything necessary, but that in reality 'the transfer of technology depends more on the capacity of the recipient to absorb it than on any other factor'.

The impact of government policy on technology transfer

There is a political dimension to technology transfer as governments often have a say in technology choice through a wide range of policies. These include economic and industrial policy, education and, with regards to the hospitality industry in particular, their tourism policies.

Industrial policy

Governments in developing countries may not encourage transfer of the latest developments in a particular industry's technology if they do not fulfill a basic job-providing role for as many people as possible. The subject of 'appropriate technology' is widely chronicled and is often linked to the influence that multinational enterprises (MNEs) have in the provision of technology. Extensive reviews of government and multinational enterprise involvement in technology choice are provided by the ILO (1984), Ghosh (1984abcd) and Winston (1979). In many cases of transfer of primary and manufacturing industries it would be necessary to adopt older, more labor-intensive technology, to simplify the available technology or to develop new technology which is specifically targeted at the employment needs of the country, rather than the profit motives of the potential foreign investor.

Such an attitude towards technology choice epitomizes the basic philosophy of the ILO's Tripartite Declaration (Gunter, 1981) which is intended to apply to all industries, including those engaged in the provision of services. Some of the principles recommended are to: 'give due consideration to local practice and respect relevant international standards' (in paras 8–12); 'keep [MNE] activities in harmony with the development priorities and social aims and structure of the country' (in paras 8–12); 'endeavour to increase employment opportunities' (in paras 13–28); 'give priority to the employment and occupational development of nationals of the host country at all levels' (in paras 13–28); 'give consideration to subcontracting to national enterprises, to the use of raw materials and promote their local processing' (in paras 13–28); 'eliminating any discrimination based on race, colour, sex, religion, political opinion, national extraction or social origin' (in paras 13–28; and 'provide relevant training for all levels of [MNE] employees to meet the needs of the enterprise as well as those of the host country' (in paras 29–32).

In the hotel industry, particularly where properties are built in less developed countries, both the developers and the local government would seem to favor the adoption of the most luxurious, highest-standard and therefore most expensive types of hotel. These may be the most appropriate in terms of business projections and status, but are often so alien to the local workforce that personnel problems are inevitable and the tenet of the ILO Tripartite Declaration is ignored, or at best not achieved. An obvious example of this is the way that hotel development in mainland China has concentrated on high-priced, luxury hotels. This has caused many problems in the provision of appropriate staff to maintain the international standard of branded hotels, and has created a narrow and vulnerable market base.

Educational policy

The most important factor in the transfer process is the transfer receiver's ability and willingness to adopt and adapt the particular technology. In service industries, especially hotels, this requires an attitudinal as well as a technical development on the part of the receivers. Often an attitudinal change is the most difficult to achieve, but it is the most important in fulfilling the provision of the many intangible elements of the hotel product. Formal and informal education are keys to the achievement of the necessary attitudinal and technical development of individuals.

Formal education is available through schools, colleges, universities and training centers, located either outside or inside the workplace. Informal education is most obviously gained by work experience. It can also start by entering the workplace as a customer, guest or tourist in a restaurant, hotel or tourism situation, and so there is a workforce-provision benefit in the establishment of a domestic restaurant, hotel and tourism industry. Domestic restaurant industries are common, but hotel and tourism facilities of even basic international standards may not be.

Both forms of education, in addition to normal studies and vocational knowledge, should help to develop an awareness of the norms of other cultures, particularly those of the nationalities which are the most abundant visitors to a particular country, so that some of the potential conflicts which might arise during normal encounters can be resolved, or at least predicted and prepared for.

Education undoubtedly shapes the abilities and motivations of a nation's workforce, but it must be paid for, and governments differ in the priority given to such expenditure. Industrialized countries generally spend a greater proportion of their GNP on education, provide more tertiary-level places for students and have a much lower proportion of adult illiteracy in the population (see Table 16.1). This enables relatively easier technology transfer within and between such countries than is possible with developing countries.

Tourism policy

Planning for international tourism tends to dominate any consideration of domestic tourism in developing countries. International tourism brings in much needed revenue almost immediately and at relatively low monetary cost. However, it is susceptible to international incidents which prevent people traveling or reduce their numbers, through price increases, through fear (of traveling itself or perceived physical danger in the destination) or through political incompatibility between countries.

Domestic tourism is not susceptible to the same level of fluctuations. In addition, it helps to provide a more experienced workforce for later tourism projects, and with proper planning could be gradually upgraded to attract high-volume, low-spend international tourists and eventually to create additional provision for the low-volume, high-spend tourist. Provision for this latter type of international tourist usually happens first in developing countries, creating the type of problems referred to earlier.

Government support for tourism in industrialized countries is usually restricted to the provision of advertising and marketing materials. The private sector funds projects as business propositions, but has the advantage of infrastructure support which is already in place. The situation in developing

Table 16.1 Education provision indicators for 71 countries grouped by economic status

Education provision indicators	Developing countries	Newly industrialized countries	Industrialized countries
Percentage of GNP spent on education	3.8	3.6	5.5
Percentage adult illiteracy	24.5	17.4	3.5
Tertiary students per 100 000 of population	1485	2015	2524

Source: Pine (1991).

countries is quite different, where tourism developments may be the first 'industry' in the locale and so need the parallel development of supporting infrastructure. The cost of this infrastructure development is usually borne by the government.

Obviously careful calculation is needed to ensure the financial viability of any investment, particularly as it may be well beyond the actual needs of the local population. Government policy towards tourism, and hotel, development is crucially important as it affects the developments which are possible now and in the future, and their impact on the local population. Most industrialized and developing countries now recognize the economic and social significance of tourism, and have established some form of national tourism agency. These agencies are in a good position to take an overview of tourism development, provision and utilization, and should be able to recognize common problems.

One such problem, especially in developing countries, is the availability of sufficient suitable labor. However, as shown in Table 16.2, a very small proportion of national tourism agency (NTA) budgets is spent on vocational training, which if available might help to address that problem. In industrialized countries the situation is not so serious because the national education system will provide general education and often the necessary vocationally based education. However, in less developed countries there is unlikely to be such educational provision, and so education and training must be the responsibility of NTAs and other agencies, as well as the hotel companies themselves.

Before 1980 it was the supply of tourism amenities which determined tourist demand. That situation has now changed so that tourism and hotel developers, whether private companies or government-related agencies, must match their planned supply of amenities and facilities to the demand for them. In such a situation it is more difficult to be sure that the foreign exchange hoped for from international visitors will actually materialize. Therefore governments and developers need to study the feasibility of proposed projects very carefully.

To be successful, service technology transfer must be perceived as being beneficial not only to the company, but also to its employees and its

Table 16.2 Percentage budget allocations of NTAs, 1983–85

Budget item	World	Europe	E. Asia and Pacific
Planning and investment	55.2	65.6	29.8
Promotion	29.8	22.8	37.0
General admin. of tourism	11.6	9.4	25.6
Vocational training	2.0	1.2	5.2
Research and statistics	1.4	1.0	2.4

Source: WTO (1986) pp. 27–8.

customers. This is particularly true in developing countries where major goals may not be to improve productivity if that means fewer jobs, or to provide services which staff or customers find unacceptable from a cultural or traditional perspective. There is much scope for expansion of service industries into developing countries, but both the company and the host government should make special efforts to appreciate all of the consequences of such expansion and to devise appropriate national, regional and company policies to ensure that optimum benefits are gained by all parties.

Multinationals and technology transfer

Multinational enterprises are the subject of extensive studies in relation to their influence on economic development and technology choice in countries outside their base location. Various authors (see, for example, Buckley and Casson, 1985; Child, 1982; Germidis, 1977; ILO, 1985; Lall, 1980, 1983; Possas, 1982; and Watanabe, 1980) discuss the way that multinationals develop and transfer technology internationally, and their influence on developing countries. Dunning (1985) provides a definitive treatment of the role of multinationals in the original development of technology and its eventual transfer to other countries where they have an operational base. UNCTC (1982) groups MNE activities with hotels into the following categories:

(a) Those in which it [the MNE] had an equity interest sufficient to ensure that it had some *de facto* if not *de jure* management control;
(b) Those in which it operated some kind of leasing arrangement;
(c) Those in which the main form of association was a management contract; and,
(d) Those in which the main form of arrangement was a franchise or some form of marketing agreement, over and above that which might normally be involved in a referral or reservation system. (p. 27)

Dave' (1984) reviews these types of involvement in more detail and adds a further possibility: the technical services agreement. This type of agreement involves the MNE acting essentially in the role of a consultant, relating to very specific aspects of the establishment or even involving the complete project management of a turnkey operation which is handed over to the hotel owner when fully operational.

The contractual form of such arrangements and the potential effect on technology transfer was the subject of work undertaken for UNIDO by Cieslik (1983). This work does not specify the types of technology available for transfer, but highlights how different arrangements can be used either to minimize or to maximize any transfers. Of serious concern in relation to technology transfer is the lack of contractual reference to the training and development to be provided by the MNE for local staff. In addition, and related to the development of local people, is the normally included clause giving the MNE power to employ expatriate managers and possibly other staff. Both of these factors, if abused, would undermine the host country's longer-term ability to establish its own international standard hotel industry.

As in other industries, technology transfer in hotels is inevitably linked to MNE activity. Such companies cannot avoid playing a role in the transfer process. This role will differ with circumstances and may vary with time. In technology transfer terms, the role of those MNEs involved in the hotel industry may be positive, providing experiential and more formal development opportunities for all categories of staff. These staff can then move into, or initiate, the local hotel industry, injecting and spreading their knowledge to other people and other hotels. There is also an indirect effect on local suppliers of goods and services to the hotel, who are subjected to a level of quality control and management expertise which may trigger them to improve or expand their own business. The MNE role may also be negative, importing all necessary expertise to run the hotel and using local people only for simple operational and supervisory tasks. Although such use benefits the local community immediately in terms of employment, in technology transfer terms it provides nothing more than the example, through its presence, of an international hotel.

My research examined three areas identified in the literature review as technology transfer indicators in service industries: training; the use of company documentation; and contact with corporate personnel (in the form of visits to and from company headquarters). Training will be examined in detail shortly.

For documentation the majority of evidence indicates no difference in the proportion of hotels using company operations manuals, forms and documents, or the proportion which allow such documentation to be changed, or the degree to which change has actually occurred. There is an indication that hotels in developing countries are more likely to use company forms and documents than those in newly industrialized countries. This would be consistent with an increased amount of innovation in the latter countries as technology transfer reaches a more advanced level. There is little evidence to indicate that the frequency of visits is different for different country types or nationality of owner. However, it must be noted that visits for the purpose of receiving or giving training seem to have a very low priority in most hotels and multinational enterprises investigated.

Hotel industry perspective of technology transfer

Multinational hotel enterprises (MNHEs) are very important in the development of hotel industries capable of matching the demands of international travelers. They can help by direct financial investment, but this is not so common in developing countries, where local partners (from the private or the public sector) are involved to provide a large proportion of the financing while the MNHE provides expertise in planning, development and management. The research revealed that MNHEs hold equity in only 6.5 percent of all hotels which responded. This percentage of hotels in which they hold equity, when considered across each type of country group, is 3.5 percent in developing, 10 percent in newly industrialized and 7.7 percent in industrialized countries. Management contracts as a method of MNHE association occurred in 45.5 percent of all hotels, but were more common in developing countries where the figure was 56.1 percent, compared to 50 percent and 36.4 percent for newly industrialized and industrialized countries respectively.

As indicated above, management contracting is the most common form of MNHE involvement in all countries, but especially so in developing countries. Any contracts entered into between local owners and MNHEs need careful scrutiny to ensure not only that the financial conditions are satisfactory but that satisfaction is achieved of the wider technology transfer needs of the owners, as potential hotel industry leaders in that country. Owners, and indeed governments, have a vested interest in assuring that the absolute need for expensive foreign staff is reduced along with parallel preparation of locals to take over from the foreigners.

National or regional governments may themselves have a contract-like involvement in a project, through providing fiscal incentives, granting necessary land-use permissions, allowing the importation of goods and expert personnel, and various other regulatory arrangements. The terms of such agreements, and actual contracts between owners and developers/ management companies, are almost always directly or indirectly financial in nature. As well as attempting to control the worst environmental and social impacts of new projects, governments, and owners, should have a vested interest in ensuring that adequate training, personal development and opportunity for promotion are available to local people. Such a condition is rarely included in a contract or agreement.

In the hotel industry it was found that hotels in industrialized countries have a relatively higher proportion of managers within the total staffing (see Table 16.3). This not only should allow for better control and improved efficiency, but may also provide more regular opportunities for informal training. With regard to the proportion of managers who are foreigners in a hotel, this is highest in developing countries. Furthermore, there appears to be no lessening of the proportion in relation to the age of the hotel, which might have been expected if local staff are competent and allowed to develop into management positions. Of course, this could also occur if these hotels were 'feeding' the rest of the local industry with skilled staff, in which case they would be making a positive contribution to technology transfer. This is an area which deserves a full investigation in its own right.

The view that MNHE hotels are bigger than local hotels is confirmed. The research showed that they are always about double in size, and the size differential does not vary with the economic stage of development of the country. In general, this larger size is necessary to provide the economy of scale advantages available to larger units, which are themselves receiving various pooled services from the parent company. Size advantages are needed

Table 16.3 Mean size and staffing profiles of MNE hotels, grouped by economic status of location country

	Developing countries	Newly industrialized countries	Industrialized countries
Number of rooms	323.30	515.10	316.80
Number of:			
total employees	482.00	816.90	259.40
executive managers	5.70	4.80	5.00
other managers	19.20	42.30	14.20
all managers	24.80	47.00	19.30
supervisors	45.50	98.00	19.70
operative/other staff	403.50	662.60	213.80
Ratios:			
staff: room	1.47	1.86	0.89
employees: manager	21.80	20.00	15.30
employees: foreign manager	197.40	116.90	64.10
rooms: foreign manager	157.60	89.90	86.80
Percentage of foreign:			
executives	52.50	69.80	42.00
managers	50.50	16.30	26.20
all managers	49.80	21.60	32.00
supervisors	38.60	6.10	28.30
operative/other staff	31.50	3.50	28.10

Source: Extract from Pine (1991), p. 178.

more in developing countries: in industrialized countries, hotels are smaller in general but can still exist profitably. Although the size differential is maintained, the absolute size varies between the different types of country. Overall, hotels are biggest in newly industrialized countries, followed by those in developing countries, with the smallest being in industrialized countries. This conclusion is confirmed in both parts of the empirical study undertaken in the research. Although each part of the study differs in the actual magnitude of average size recorded, the pattern is consistent, with the largest mean size occurring in newly industrialized countries, that for developing ones being smaller, and the smallest mean occurring for industrialized countries.

It is assumed that the average size of hotels in a country or location, measured over time, provide a reasonable indicator of the hotel industry's state of development in that country, as well as that of the economy itself. In developing countries MNHEs move in and new, large hotels appear both as resort/leisure accommodation and city-center accommodation for business as well as leisure tourists. But there is probably some itinerant hotel industry which initially keeps the mean size slightly lower than in newly industrialized countries. In these latter countries, the largest hotel mean size reflects the growth of the whole economy and the increased and profitable demand for international standard hotel accommodation from increasing numbers of business travelers, as well as other tourists. This demand is satisfied by increased MNHE activity and, as technology transfer progresses, by local companies developing their own large, high-standard hotel properties. As economic development continues, there is an increased demand from domestic tourism, and the increased efficiency of hotel operation allows smaller, often less luxurious, hotel properties to exist profitably, thereby lowering the mean size of hotels in the industry overall.

The results summarized in Table 16.4(a), indicate that MNHEs in developing and industrialized countries allocate a similar, and quite small, proportion of total operating budgets to training. This happens in developing countries despite the relatively smaller provision of general and vocational education there. However, other training factors, such as the presence of a training manager, a training room and a training department, are less common in hotels in industrialized countries. The proportion of operational budgets dedicated to training was found to be quite small: the mean noted for all MNE hotels was 1.9 percent. In addition to the small level of this percentage, there was no positive evidence to indicate that hotels in developing countries dedicate a greater percentage of operational budgets to training than those in industrialized countries. However, hotels in industrialized countries have the advantage of better provision of general and vocational education, and so it might be expected that the results would show hotels in developing countries to be taking up an obviously greater burden. Table 16.4(b) provides a summary of data gathered relating to training resources available.

Other factors relating to training present some challenge to the insinuations of the last paragraph. For all MNE hotels researched, a greater proportion of hotels in newly industrialized (and then developing) countries had a training manager and a training room than do those hotels in industrialized countries. The latter category had the lowest proportion of hotels with a training department.

Table 16.4(a)   Mean training activity of MNE hotels grouped by economic status of location country

	Developing countries	Newly industrialized countries	Industrialized countries
Number of:			
training staff	3.3	2.9	2.2
certified trainers	12.3	19.7	10.0
Percentage of total staff:			
who are training staff	0.8	0.4	1.1
who are certified trainers	3.7	3.1	4.6
Training as percentage of total operating budget	1.8	1.3	2.2

Source: Extract from Pine (1991), p. 178.

Table 16.4(b) Percentage of MNE hotels, grouped by economic status of location country, which provide specified training facilities

Specified facilities	Developing (57 observations)	Newly industrialized (20 observations)	Industrialized (78 observations)
Training manager	68.4	90.0	58.4
Training department	71.9	85.0	43.4
Training room	68.4	90.0	43.6
Film projector	86.0	90.0	74.4
Slide projector	87.7	100.0	87.2
Overhead projector	91.2	100.0	87.2
TV and video	93.0	95.0	93.6
TV and camera	26.3	50.0	33.3
White/blackboard	96.5	100.0	82.1
Flipchart	93.0	100.0	88.5
Tape/cassette recorder	91.2	95.0	67.9
Books	82.5	95.0	83.3
Magazines/journals	73.7	90.0	71.8
Language laboratory	15.8	50.0	7.7
Training manuals	91.2	85.0	83.3
Job specifications	84.2	85.0	88.5
Operations manuals	82.5	80.0	80.8
Computer-based training	24.6	40.0	50.0

Source: Pine (1991), p. 193.

In addition to the direct aspects of training provision, it is also important to recognize that staff undergoing training are subject to an intense period of personal change and development, and necessary support should be provided. In the workplace this means allowing full resourcing for the whole project and particularly the training element. It is very important to appreciate the receiver's level of knowledge and experience, to realize and accept a possible different tempo and approach to work and learning, and to be sensitive to different cultural and political norms. Attempts to lessen culture shock can be made by early selection and advance preparation of potential staff, and by providing them, and if necessary their family and friends, with full information about the overall project and their specific role and expected duties within it. Language training should be available for staff to allow them to communicate more effectively with managers and guests. Serious consideration should also be given to the provision of language training for foreign managers so that they are in a better position to appreciate difficulties encountered by their own staff and better prepared to integrate with the local culture.

There was no evidence to suggest different proportions of foreign managers in relation to the age of the hotel. This is noteworthy, particularly in relation to MNE hotels in developing countries, as it may indicate their inactivity in developing local people to take over management positions. It may also indicate a continuing unavailability of competent local staff, in which case the general educational provision in that country, as well as the actual development carried out by MNEs, may be at issue.

The view that integration of local managers into MNE subsidiaries is not dependent upon the nationality of the corporate head of the subsidiary was investigated in a hotels context. In this case the majority ownership of each hotel property was used as the dependent variable: that is, whether more than 50 percent of the equity in the hotel was held by foreigners or by nationals of the country in which the hotel was located. Unfortunately, the results for this part of the study were inconclusive as only 55 of the 155 respondents answered the question, and there was no statistically significant difference between national or foreign owners.

Conclusion

One of the key resources needed to operate hotels is people. As a country's hotel industry expands, the employment demand will increase for skilled, competent and suitable people in all categories of hotel staff. The estimated minimum demand for new staff in hotels in the Asia-Pacific part of the world alone totals almost 200 000 in the first part of this decade (Pine, 1990). More than 50 percent of that demand will be in developing countries. Most of these countries have labor availability in quantitative terms, but availability in qualitative terms is open to argument.

International-standard hotels are often outside the cultural and experience backgrounds of potential employees in developing countries. Moreover, it has been established that the ability to understand and communicate with foreigners is an important staff attribute if satisfactory levels of service are to be achieved. Hotels of the future are predicted to become more sophisticated and complex in their service provision and in their use of technologically advanced equipment and operating systems. This will exacerbate the gap which already exists in the basic understanding of the hotel environment by its potential workforce in developing countries, and will place an even greater emphasis on the need for adequate education and training to be available. Governments, hotel developers and managers must appreciate this need and prepare people fully for jobs in such environments.

Technology transfer can only proceed successfully if the technology receivers are capable and willing participants in the transfer process. The provision of a thorough general education plus specific vocational skill development, through vocational education, industry training and work experience, is vital for the continued and successful development of the hotel industry internationally, and particularly in developing countries. In developing countries there is a greater need for the hotel industry itself to provide the necessary education and the opportunity for the personal development of local people.

Successful technology transfer in the hotel industry is dependent upon the availability of employees who are provided with adequate education, training, development and promotional opportunities.

References

Buckley, P., and Casson, M. (1985) *The Economic Theory of the Multinational Enterprise*, New York: St Martin's Press.

Child, S. (1982) 'Multinationals and the transfer of technology to LDCs', *Multinational Business*, pp. 18–20.

Cieslik, J. (1983) *Contractual Arrangements for the Transfer of Technology in the Hotel Industry*, Vienna: UNIDO.

Dahlman, C., and Westphal, L. (1983) 'The transfer of technology: issues in the acquisition of technological capability by developing countries', *Finance and Development*, December, p. 7.

Dave', U. (1984) 'US multinational involvement in the international hotel industry: an analysis', *Service Industries Journal*, vol. 4, no. 1, pp. 48–63.

Dunning, J. H. (ed.) (1985) *Multinational Enterprises, Economic Structure and International Competitiveness*, Chichester: John Wiley.

Germidis, D. (ed.) (1977) *Transfer of Technology by Multinational Corporations*, vols 1 and 2, Paris: OECD.

Gosh, P. K. (ed.) (1984a) *Appropriate Technology in Third World Development*, Westport, Conn.: Greenwood Press.

Gosh, P. K. (ed.) (1984b) *Multinational Corporations and Third World Development*, Westport, Conn.: Greenwood Press.

Gosh, P. K. (ed.) (1984c) *Technology Policy and Development: A Third World Perspective*, Westport, Conn.: Greenwood Press.

Gosh, P. K. (ed.) (1984d) *The New International Economic Order: A Third World Perspective*, Westport, Conn.: Greenwood Press.

Gunter, H. (1981) *The Tripartite Declaration of Principles Concerning Multinational Enterprises and Social Policy*, Geneva: International Labour Organization.

Hawthorne, E. P. (1971) *Technology Transfer*, Paris: OECD, p. 8.

ILO (1984) *Technology Choice and Employment Generation by Multinational Enterprises in Developing Countries*, Geneva: International Labour Organization.

ILO (1985) *Technology Choice and Employment Generated by Multinational Enterprises*, Geneva: International Labour Organization.

Lall, S. (1980) *The Multinational Corporation*, London: Macmillan.

Lall, S. (1983) *The New Multinationals: The spread of Third World enterprises*, Chichester: John Wiley.

Merrill, R. S. (1968) *International Encyclopedia of the Social Sciences*, London and New York: Macmillan and Free Press.

Niehoff, A. H., and Anderson, J. C. (1964) 'The process of cross-cultural innovation', *International Development Review*, 6 June.

Novak, D. E., and Lekachman, R. (eds) (1964) *Development and Society*, New York: St Martin's Press.

Pine, R. J. (1985) 'Catering technology: some issues for effective utilisation', M.Phil. thesis, Huddersfield Polytechnic, UK.

Pine, R. J. (1987) *Management of Technological Change in the Catering Industry*, Aldershot: Avebury.

Pine, R. J. (1990) 'The future demand for manpower in the Asian hotel industry', *Proceedings of the PATA Educators Forum*, Singapore, 11–14 July, pp. 173–89.

Pine, R. J. (1991) 'Technology transfer in the hotel industry', Ph.D. thesis, Bradford University, UK.

Pine, R. J. (1992) 'Technology transfer in the hotel industry', *International Journal of Hospitality Management*, vol. 11, no. 4, (not yet published).

Possas, M. L. (1982) *Multinational Enterprises, Technology and Employment in Brazil*, Geneva: International Labour Organization.

Seurat, S. (1979) *Technology Transfer: A realistic approach*, Houston, Tex.: Gulf Publishing.

Shelp, R. K., Stephenson, J. C., Truitt, N. S., and Waşow, B. (1984) *Service Industries and Economic Development: Case studies in technology transfer*, New York: Praeger.

Stephenson, J. C. (1984) 'Technology transfer by the Bechtel organisation', in Shelp *et al.*, (1984).

Stewart, S. (1987) 'The transfer of high technology to China: problems and options', *International Journal of Technology Management*, vol. 3, no. 1–2, pp. 167–79.

Stewart, T. S., and Nihei, Y. (1987) *Technology Transfer and Human Factors*, Lexington, Mass.: Lexington Books.

UNCTC (1982) *Transnational Corporations in International Tourism*, New York: United Nations Center on Transnational Corporations.

Wallender, H. W. (1979) *Technology Transfer and Management in Developing Countries*, New York: Ballinger.

Watanabe, S. (1980) *Multinational Enterprises and Employment-Oriented 'Appropriate' Technologies in Developing Countries*, Geneva: International Labour Organization.

Winston, G. (1979) 'The appeal of inappropriate technologies', *World Development*, vol. 7, no. 7, pp. 835–45.

World Tourism Organization (1986) *Budgets of National Tourism Administrations 1983–1984–1985*, Madrid: WTO.

Index